NEW MERMAIDS

General editors:
William C. Carroll, Boston University
Brian Gibbons, University of Münster
Tiffany Stern, University of Oxford

General editor for the Bernard Shaw titles:
L.W. Conolly, Trent University

NEW MERMAIDS

CONTENTS

ACKNOWLEDGEMENTS

For their professionalism and courtesy, I am grateful to the staff of the British Library, the Theatre and Performance Archives at the Victoria and Albert Museum, the University of Guelph Archives, the Harry Ransom Center at the University of Texas at Austin, and Inter-Library Loans at Université Laval. Permission to quote from archival materials has been generously granted by the Society of Authors, the British Library, and the Harry Ransom Center. The research for this edition was undertaken in conjunction with projects that were subsidised by a grant from the Fonds québecois de la recherche sur la société et la culture, a Hobby Fellowship awarded by the Harry Ransom Center, and the Dr Robert Anderson Research Trust.

My thanks to Ian Campbell, Jeremy Crow, Charles Del Dotto, Dorothy Hadfield, Guillaume Pinson, Gustavo Rodríguez, Judith Walkowitz, and Matthew Yde for kindly sharing their expertise and extending help in tracking down obscure references. I am fortunate to have been befriended by Robert Anderson and Arlinda Abbott, whose hospitality made my long research stays in London and Austin so pleasant. Thanks also to Margaret Bartley, Anna Brewer, and Claire Cooper at Methuen Drama, to Margaret Berrill, the proofreader, and Simon Trussler for seeing the book through to publication. Leonard Conolly has been the most exemplary general editor I could have hoped for; I am grateful for his keen criticism and helpful suggestions.

My greatest debt is to Anne, Ryan, and Zoé, who have supported me in countless ways over the years. *Je dédie ce livre à vous.*

Brad Kent

BERNARD SHAW: A CHRONOLOGY

For a comprehensive and detailed chronology of Shaw's life, see A.M. Gibbs, *A Bernard Shaw Chronology* (Basingstoke, 2001). Dates of British and foreign productions of Shaw's plays are given in Raymond Mander and Joe Mitchenson, *Theatrical Companion to Shaw* (New York, 1955), and definitive bibliographical information on Shaw can be found in Dan H. Laurence, *Bernard Shaw: A Bibliography*, 2 vols (Oxford, 1983).

1856   Born in Dublin, 26 July, to George Carr Shaw and Lucinda Elizabeth Shaw.

1871   Leaves school and takes an office job with a Dublin property agency.

1876   Moves from Dublin to London.

1879   Completes his first novel, *Immaturity* (first published 1930).

1880   Completes his second novel, *The Irrational Knot* (first published in serial form in *Our Corner*, 1885–7, and in book form 1905).

1881   Completes his third novel, *Love Among the Artists* (first published in serial form in *Our Corner*, 1887–8, and in book form 1900).

1883   Completes his fourth and fifth (his last completed) novels, *Cashel Byron's Profession* (first published in serial form in *To-Day*, 1885–6, and in book form 1886) and *An Unsocial Socialist* (first published in serial form in *To-Day*, 1884, and in book form 1887).

1884   Joins the Fabian Society.

1885   Publishes first music and drama criticism in the *Dramatic Review*. Shaw's criticism (including art and literary criticism) also appeared in periodicals such as the *Pall Mall Gazette*, *The World*, and *The Star* before he began a three-year stint as drama critic for the *Saturday Review* (1895–8).

1891   Publishes *The Quintessence of Ibsenism*.

1892   His first play, *Widowers' Houses* (begun 1884) performed by the Independent Theatre Society, London.

1893   Completes *The Philanderer* and *Mrs Warren's Profession*.

1894   *Arms and the Man* performed at the Avenue Theatre, London, and the Herald Square Theatre, New York. Completes *Candida*.

1896   Meets Charlotte Payne-Townshend, his future wife. Completes *You Never Can Tell* and *The Devil's Disciple*.

1897	*Candida* performed by the Independent Theatre Company, Aberdeen. *The Man of Destiny* performed at the Grand Theatre, Croydon. American actor Richard Mansfield produces *The Devil's Disciple* in Albany and New York.
1898	Marries Charlotte Payne-Townshend. Publishes (in two volumes) *Plays Pleasant and Unpleasant*, containing four 'pleasant' plays (*Arms and the Man, Candida, The Man of Destiny, You Never Can Tell*) and three 'unpleasant' plays (*Widowers' Houses, The Philanderer, Mrs Warren's Profession*). Completes *Caesar and Cleopatra*. *Mrs Warren's Profession* is banned by the Lord Chamberlain from public performance in England. Publishes *The Perfect Wagnerite* (on the *Ring* cycle).
1899	*You Never Can Tell* performed by the Stage Society. Writes *Captain Brassbound's Conversion*.
1901	Publishes *Three Plays for Puritans* (*The Devil's Disciple, Caesar and Cleopatra, Captain Brassbound's Conversion*). Writes *The Admirable Bashville*.
1902	*Mrs Warren's Profession* performed (a private production) by the Stage Society.
1903	Publishes *Man and Superman* (begun in 1901).
1904	Begins his partnership with Harley Granville Barker and J.E. Vedrenne at the Court Theatre (until 1907). Eleven Shaw plays are produced there, including *Major Barbara* (1905).
1905	*Mrs Warren's Profession* performed (then banned) in New Haven and New York. *The Philanderer* performed by the New Stage Club, London.
1906	*Caesar and Cleopatra* performed (in German) in Berlin. Publishes *Dramatic Opinions and Essays*, and writes *The Doctor's Dilemma*.
1908	Writes *Getting Married*.
1909	*The Shewing-up of Blanco Posnet* banned in England, but performed in Dublin. *Press Cuttings* banned in England. Completes *Misalliance*.
1911	*Fanny's First Play* performed at the Little Theatre, London. Runs for 622 performances (a record for a Shaw première).
1912	Completes *Pygmalion*.
1913	*Pygmalion* performed (in German) in Vienna.
1914	*Mrs Warren's Profession* performed by the Dublin Repertory Theatre. *Pygmalion* performed at His Majesty's Theatre, London. Outbreak of World War One. Publishes *Common Sense about the War*.

1917	Visits front line sites in France. Completes *Heartbreak House*.
1918	End of World War One.
1920	*Heartbreak House* performed by the Theatre Guild, New York. Completes *Back to Methuselah*.
1922	*Back to Methuselah* performed by the Theatre Guild, New York.
1923	Completes *Saint Joan*. It is performed in New York by the Theatre Guild.
1924	First British production of *Saint Joan*, New Theatre, London. The Lord Chamberlain's ban on *Mrs Warren's Profession* is removed.
1925	First public performances in England of *Mrs Warren's Profession* (in Birmingham and London).
1926	Awarded the 1925 Nobel Prize for Literature.
1928	Publishes *The Intelligent Woman's Guide to Socialism and Capitalism*.
1929	*The Apple Cart* performed (in Polish) in Warsaw, followed by the British première at the Malvern Festival, where other British premières (*Too True to be Good*, *The Simpleton of the Unexpected Isles*, *Buoyant Billions*) and world premières (*Geneva* and *In Good King Charles's Golden Days*) of Shaw's plays were produced between 1932 and 1949.
1930	Begins publication of *The Works of Bernard Shaw*, completed (in 33 volumes) in 1938.
1931	Visits Russia; meets Gorky and Stalin.
1933	Writes *On the Rocks*.
1936	*The Millionairess* performed (in German) in Vienna.
1938	*Pygmalion* is filmed, starring Leslie Howard and Wendy Hiller.
1939	Outbreak of World War Two. Wins an Oscar for the screenplay of *Pygmalion*.
1940	*Major Barbara* is filmed, starring Rex Harrison and Wendy Hiller.
1943	Charlotte Shaw dies.
1944	Publishes *Everybody's Political What's What?*
1945	*Caesar and Cleopatra* is filmed, starring Claude Rains and Vivien Leigh. End of World War Two.
1950	Dies, 2 November, aged 94, from complications after a fall while pruning a shrub in his garden. Cremated at Golders Green Crematorium on 6 November, his ashes (mixed with his wife's) scattered at his country home in Ayot St Lawrence, Hertfordshire (now a National Trust property), on 23 November.

ABBREVIATIONS

BL   British Library

CL   Bernard Shaw, *Bernard Shaw: Collected Letters*, ed. Dan
            H. Laurence, 4 volumes, Viking, 1965–88

Diaries   Bernard Shaw, *Bernard Shaw: The Diaries, 1885–1897
            with Early Autobiographical Notebooks and Diaries, and
            an Abortive 1917 Diary*, ed. Stanley Weintraub, 2 volumes,
            Pennsylvania State University Press, 1986

DLVF   Dan H. Laurence's Vertical File on *Mrs Warren's Profes-
            sion*, File 10, Box 20, University of Guelph Archives

GR   The first English edition of *Mrs Warren's Profession*, pub-
            lished in *Plays Unpleasant* by Grant Richards, 1898

Holroyd   Michael Holroyd, *Bernard Shaw*, 4 volumes, Penguin,
            1990–3

HRC   Bernard Shaw Collection, Harry Ransom Center, the
            University of Texas at Austin

LC1   Typescript of the play, the licensing copy found in the
            Lord Chamberlain's papers, submitted in 1898: Add. MS
            53654 H, BL

LC2   Second licensing copy of the play, submitted in 1926: Add.
            MS 66402 G, BL

MS   The first manuscript of the play written in three note-
            books: Add. MSS 50598 A, 50598 B, and 50598 C, BL

RN   Rehearsal notes in Shaw's hand from a 1926 production:
            Add. MS 50644, BL

SHAW   *SHAW: The Annual of Bernard Shaw Studies*

s.d.   stage direction(s)

TPA   Theatre and Performance Archives, Victoria and Albert
            Museum, London

INTRODUCTION

The Author

Shaw once reflected of *Mrs Warren's Profession*: 'It's much my best play; but it makes my blood run cold: I can hardly bear the most appalling bits of it. Ah, when I wrote that, I *had* some nerve.'[1] It is not simply among his best and most-performed plays; it also enjoys a reputation as one of theatre's most controversial works. Written in 1893, *Mrs Warren's Profession* was banned from public performance on British stages until 1925. The play's troubles were not, however, confined to Britain: in 1905, the entire cast and management of its New York première were arrested for 'offending public decency'.[2] Yet in the years between its composition and first licensed performance, Bernard Shaw rose from relative obscurity to become the pre-eminent playwright of his generation and second only to Shakespeare in the English language.

George Bernard Shaw – he would later drop the George – was born in Dublin on 26 July 1856, the youngest of three siblings in a middle-class Irish Protestant family. Over the years, his father's alcoholism led to a decline in their financial and social fortunes. His mother took solace in her singing lessons and public performances, eventually leaving her husband to emigrate to England with her music teacher. Shaw himself abandoned school by the time he was sixteen years of age, and eventually found work as a clerk. It was a job that he detested, the young man preferring to spend his time walking the halls of the National Gallery, reading books, and attending the theatre and concerts.

Faced with an increasingly miserable environment, in 1876 Shaw fled Dublin to try his luck in London, where he lived with and was supported by his mother. Although he lacked any formal higher education, he made the most of the opportunities that living in a major metropolis afforded. Attending public lectures ranked as one of his favourite pastimes. One talk in particular that had a lasting effect on him was by the captivating American political economist Henry George, who argued in favour of the nationalisation of land. This was an awakening of sorts for Shaw, who had been studying related subjects in the Reading Room of the British Museum, which he frequented almost daily from 1880 to 1888. Among the books that he consulted was a French-language edition of Karl Marx's *Das Kapital.* He later told Archibald Henderson, one of his many biographers, that upon reading Marx 'I immediately became a Socialist,

---

1 *CL* I, p. 770.
2 *New York Times*, 1 November 1905.

and from that hour I was a man with some business in the world . . . I now set to work to apply my dogged practice to propagating Socialism.'[3]

By this time, Shaw had already begun his literary career with five novels: *Immaturity* (1879), *The Irrational Knot* (1880), *Love Among the Artists* (1881), *Cashel Byron's Profession* (1883), and *An Unsocial Socialist* (1883). While the later four works appeared in magazines, his novels were initially rejected by all publishers he approached. This early lack of success eventually drew Shaw towards the theatre. Yet his origins as a novelist are betrayed in his tendency to write lengthy, psychologically penetrating stage directions. Through some well-placed connections, he eked out a living as a journalist in the mid-1880s, writing book, music, and theatre reviews for the *Pall Mall Gazette*, the *Magazine of Music*, and the *Dramatic Review*.

His political and literary activities brought him into contact with several groups that were frequented by people who would help to shape British culture in the coming years and provide Shaw with a supportive network. One of these organisations was the Fabian Society, whose goal was political reform along Socialist principles, for which Shaw became an active pamphleteer and tireless campaigner. The Fabians became a strong force for change, allowing Shaw and his close friends Beatrice and Sidney Webb, with whom he would co-found the London School of Economics in 1895, to affect the course of politics through their strategy of permeating all spheres of British life with their ideas. Shaw was also involved in the Independent Theatre, a company founded by J.T. Grein in 1891 to provide an outlet for the non-commercial drama of Henrik Ibsen and other modern playwrights. With some encouragement from Grein, Shaw worked on his first play, *Widowers' Houses*, which the Independent Theatre staged in 1892. While it would not lead to him garnering any popularity, the play, which tackled the issue of slum landlordism, in many ways charted the course for his engaged drama.

Arms and the Man (1894) was his next play to be produced, although he had already written *The Philanderer* (1893) and *Mrs Warren's Profession*. Set during the 1885 Serbo-Bulgarian war, *Arms and the Man* deromanticises nineteenth-century ideals of soldiers and armed conflict. Here Shaw developed his strategy of employing comedy to attract audiences to what was generally perceived to be his unpalatable message. Performed during Florence Farr's season at the Avenue Theatre, *Arms and the Man* appeared on 21 April 1894 when it shared the bill with W.B. Yeats' *The Land of Heart's Desire*. After the première, Shaw stood before the applauding audience and, his glorious moment interrupted by a loud

3 *CL* II, pp. 486–7.

boo, exclaimed: 'My dear fellow, I quite agree with you, but what are we two against so many?'[4] Yeats later reminisced that 'from that moment on, Bernard Shaw became the most formidable man in modern letters, and even the most drunken of medical students knew it'.[5]

The reality, however, was that Shaw continued to write good but commercially unsuccessful plays. The one exception was *The Devil's Disciple*, set in the United States during the American Revolution. This found a receptive audience in New York, where it ran for sixty-four performances at the Fifth Avenue Theatre in the autumn of 1897 before embarking upon a successful Mid-West tour the following year. The royalties Shaw earned allowed him to resign as theatre critic of the *Saturday Review*, a position that he had held since 1895 and from which he had criticised the state of drama to shape audiences' tastes to accord with his own plays. By 1898, he considered himself financially independent enough to marry Irish heiress Charlotte Payne-Townsend, with whom he remained until her death in 1943.

In the first decade of the new century, Shaw would go on to secure his reputation as the most important living British dramatist. It was fortuitous that he found in Harley Granville Barker an energetic and talented young actor-writer-director-manager who believed in the New Drama. Barker formed a dynamic partnership with J.E. Vedrenne that lasted the term of the three-year lease they signed on London's Court Theatre in 1904. The two men produced plays by Ibsen, Maurice Maeterlinck, Gerhart Hauptmann, John Galsworthy, Gilbert Murray, John Masefield, Barker, and Yeats. But of the 988 performances at the Court in these years, 701 were of Shaw's plays, causing some to quip that the Court was actually 'the Shaw Repertory Theatre'.[6] Shaw premièred a number of his plays at the Court, including some of his most enduring works: *John Bull's Other Island* (1904, at a command performance of which King Edward VII reputedly laughed so hard that he broke his chair), *Man and Superman* (1903), *Major Barbara* (1905), and *The Doctor's Dilemma* (1907). Barker and Vedrenne also produced the first public performances in London of *Candida* (1894), *How He Lied to Her Husband* (1904), *Captain Brassbound's Conversion* (1899), *The Philanderer*, *The Man of Destiny* (1895), *The Devil's Disciple*, and *Caesar and Cleopatra* (1898), in addition to revivals of such popular favourites as *Arms and the Man* and *You Never Can Tell* (1896).

4 *CL* I, p. 433.
5 W.B. Yeats, *Autobiographies* (London: Macmillan, 1955), p. 282.
6 Dennis Kennedy, *Granville Barker and the Dream of a Theatre* (Cambridge: Cambridge University Press, 1985), pp. 65–6.

Shaw remained on a roll throughout the pre-war period. *Fanny's First Play*, which he had anonymously written to satirise theatre critics, was a smash hit in 1911, running for 622 performances. *Androcles and the Lion*, a tale of the Roman persecution of Christians, likewise found a receptive public when it was staged in 1913. Shaw's star continued to burn brightly with *Pygmalion*, which premièred in Vienna on 16 October 1913 and in London on 11 April 1914. Detailing the transformation of a poor flower-selling girl into a beauty who could pass for a duchess thanks to the linguistic training of her master-creator, *Pygmalion* also earned Shaw an Oscar in 1938 for his screen adaptation and formed the basis for the wildly popular musical *My Fair Lady* (1956). Shaw was the man with the golden touch, adulated by the public for entertaining and challenging them, and for daring to say that which they neither did nor could say themselves. All of that, though, very quickly changed.

With the outbreak of hostilities on the Continent in the summer of 1914 and the entrance of Britain into armed conflict, Shaw published *Common Sense About the War*, a trenchant critique of all of the belligerents. The public perceived this as evidence of his lack of patriotism, which resulted in a rapid decline in his popularity. Throughout these years, Shaw mainly wrote short farces that used the war as a backdrop, among them *O'Flaherty V.C.* (1915), *Augustus Does His Bit* (1916), *The Inca of Perusalem* (1916) and *Annajanska, The Bolshevik Empress* (1917). However, as the fighting dragged on and the number of casualties mounted, public opinion began to turn in his favour again.

The immediate post-war years saw a Shavian renaissance. *Heartbreak House* (1919), which portrays cultured, leisured Europe as heading towards inevitable destruction, was written during the war, but Shaw had held it back from production until he felt enough time had passed. Although it was met with a tepid reaction and much confusion, it has generally come to be recognised as one of Shaw's best plays. His next work was *Back to Methuselah* (1920), a sequence of five plays set in different ages that together form a meditation on Shaw's concept of Creative Evolution. It was with *Saint Joan* (1923), though, that Shaw found his greatest success in years. Drawing upon the archival transcripts of Joan's trial, he used her story to probe the origins of nationalism in European history. The play brought him greater international recognition, most significantly influencing the Swedish Academy to award him the 1925 Nobel Prize for Literature.

The dominant tendency in Shaw's plays following this period was that he now not only analysed highly politicised issues but high politics themselves. From *Saint Joan* this preoccupation weaves through *The Apple*

Cart (1928), *Too True to Be Good* (1931), *On the Rocks* (1933), *The Simpleton of the Unexpected Isles* (1935), *Geneva* (1936), and *In Good King Charles's Golden Days* (1939). By this time, having lost patience with democracy, Shaw turned his support towards the continental dictators, believing that their strength and leadership were exactly what was needed to overcome the economic and political difficulties of the 1930s. In many ways this outlook was in keeping with other giants of modern literature, notably Yeats and Ezra Pound. When one examines Shaw's political views, it is rather tempting to focus exclusively on this later more reactionary period. However, it deserves no more attention – rather less, some would argue – than his long battles that cost him both personally and professionally, such as his desire to eradicate poverty, his support for the suffragette movement, his agitation for nationalised health care, his vocal defence of Oscar Wilde and Sir Roger Casement as they stood trial for homosexuality and treason, and his work on behalf of Irish national interests.

Although he slowed down during World War Two, Shaw continued to write plays into his nineties. His last was *Shakes Versus Shav* (1949), a puppet play in which he gets the upper hand on his predecessor and nemesis. On 10 September 1950, the indefatigable ninety-four-year-old slipped while pruning a tree, landing him in the hospital where he was operated on and had a broken thigh bone set. He was brought to convalesce at his country residence in Ayot St Lawrence, Hertfordshire, where his condition deteriorated until he quietly passed away in the early morning hours of 2 November.

In the weeks leading up to his death, Shaw allowed only a select few visitors to see him. One of his former secretaries reported their final conversation: 'Think of the enjoyment you've given and the stimulus,' she said. 'You might say the same,' he replied, 'of any Mrs Warren.'[7]

The Play's Genesis and Composition

Shaw long credited actress Janet Achurch with giving him the initial idea for *Mrs Warren's Profession*. Achurch had made her stage breakthrough as Nora in the London première of Ibsen's *A Doll's House* (1879) in 1889, which Shaw attended on five occasions; he would later write the title role for her in *Candida*. At one point she mentioned that he should consider writing a dramatic adaptation of Guy de Maupassant's courtesan novella *Yvette* (1884), which features a prostitute mother who reveals her profession to her daughter. He was further inspired when Beatrice Webb suggested that he put on stage a 'modern lady of the governing class – not the sort of thing that theatrical and critical authorities imagine a lady to be'.[8]

---

7 Holroyd III, p. 513.
8 *Daily Chronicle*, 30 April 1898.

Yet the impetus to finally begin writing *Mrs Warren's Profession* on 20 August 1893 came after Shaw borrowed a copy of Arthur Wing Pinero's *The Second Mrs Tanqueray* from his good friend William Archer.[9] He worked on his play while fulfilling a busy schedule, jotting down dialogue on the train as he travelled to Monmouth to visit the Webbs on 26 August. The title came to him on the following day, and by 30 August he had written the first act. On 4 September he wrote to Achurch to announce that the second act was half finished and to indicate that he had broken away from de Maupassant's narrative: 'The play progresses bravely; but it has left the original lines. I have made the daughter the heroine, and the mother a most deplorable old rip (saving your presence). The great scene will be the crushing of the mother by the daughter. I retain the old roué, but keep him restrained by a continual doubt as to whether the heroine may not be his daughter. The young lover's father, an outrageous clergyman, is in the same perplexity, he also being an old flame of the mother's. The lover is an agreeable young spark, wholly good-for-nothing. The girl is a quite original character. The mother, uncertain who the girl's father is, keeps all the old men at bay by telling each one that he is the parent.'[10]

Throughout his stay with the Webbs, which lasted until 18 September, Shaw worked away on his new play while he attended to revisions of their forthcoming book, *The History of Trade Unionism*, and refined *The Philanderer*. Back in London, he completed the second act on 26 September and immediately began reading the play to friends. The third act caused him some frustration, but he finally completed it on 24 October, the delay probably the result of having completely changed the thrust of the play. The original Act III begins where the eventual Act IV does, in Honoria Fraser's Chancery Lane chambers. After writing some fifteen pages of dialogue, Shaw struck it all out and embarked on the third act as we know it today, opening in the rectory garden.[11] He finished the play on 2 November and went to Achurch's home the next day to share it with her.

In what must be seen as fit of professional competitiveness, if not pure jealousy, Shaw offered *Mrs Warren's Profession* to J.T. Grein on 12 December, the day after he saw Pinero's play performed. He suggested Achurch as Vivie, Bernard Gould as Frank, Charles Charrington (Achurch's husband) as Crofts, Rutland Barrington as the Reverend Gardner, and 'anybody who can play Cayley in *The Second Mrs Tanqueray*' as Praed. Mrs Warren, he emphasised, 'must be an actress of considerable power,

9 *Diaries*, p. 962.
10 *CL* I, p. 404.
11 Add. MSS. 50598 B, BL.

and of some humour'. Although Archer suggested Alexis Leighton for the role, Shaw preferred Mrs Patrick Campbell, who was currently starring as Paula Tanqueray. As he noted, 'The part is a vulgar one; but unless the vulgarity is the artistic vulgarity of a refined actress, just as the immorality must be the artistic immorality of a woman whom the audience respects, the part will be unendurable ... There is a reputation to be got out of the part.'[12] However, as Grein did not think much of the play and knowing that no commercial manager would risk touching it, Shaw put it aside for a few years.

Influences, Sources, and Analogues

The three most evident sources for *Mrs Warren's Profession* are de Maupassant's *Yvette*, Pinero's *The Second Mrs Tanqueray*, and Shelley's *The Cenci*. Shaw claimed not to have actually read *Yvette* and that Achurch merely summarised the plot details for him. In de Maupassant's tale, Madame Obardi, an experienced courtesan, hosts men at her brothel soirées. Her daughter Yvette is a young woman who, despite living in her mother's house, has remained amazingly clueless as to her mother's profession, but this cultivated naivety has in part been fed by a steady diet of sentimental novels and a lack of education. In keeping with his tendency when adapting storylines, Shaw's depiction of Vivie, whose name anglicises Yvette's, is an inversion of de Maupassant's daughter: Vivie is raised well away from the mother and she is given a lengthy and strenuous education. In some ways, Yvette represents what would have happened if Mrs Warren, as she rues at the end of the play, had kept Vivie by her side on the Continent instead of sending her to live in England. Shaw, though, was initially drawn to the story of the courtesan, saying to Achurch that he wished to 'work out the real truth of that mother some day'.[13] Like Mrs Warren, Madame Obardi justifies her prostitution through economics: she could not have provided their lavish lifestyle had she observed decorum; a woman of her class would have been good for a scullery maid with no hope for a better station in life. The daughter is incapable of accepting this revelation after witnessing one of her mother's liaisons, attempting suicide to avoid the nasty reality and to escape following the same course as her mother. When she is thwarted, she finally reconciles herself to the profession and takes up with a rake whose advances she had until then ignorantly mistaken as a romantic courtship. Unlike Yvette, Vivie's strong personality and ability to make a living

12 *CL* I, p. 412.
13 *Daily Chronicle*, 30 April 1898.

independent of further parental support allow her to reject her mother and her mother's profession.[14]

Pinero's play differs significantly from Shaw's in that the protagonist is what has been termed a 'fallen woman' or a 'woman-with-a-past', and not a prostitute. Instead of directly exchanging sex for money, Paula Tanqueray was seduced as a young woman and married a wealthy widower some years later. When her past comes to light, it causes the dissolution of her step-daughter's engagement, but the resulting tensions in the relationships are lessened through her not being the birth mother. She comes to regret the damage and pain that she has caused and kills herself to make amends. Shaw considered this ending a cop-out, and took Pinero to task in a review of the published text. Of Paula's flight from her husband when he is judgemental of her, Shaw wrote: 'One can imagine how, in a play by a master-hand, Paula's reply would have opened Tanqueray's foolish eyes to the fact that a woman of that sort is already the same at three as she is at thirty-three, and that however she may have found by experience that her nature is in conflict with the ideals of differently constituted people, she remains perfectly valid to herself, and despises herself, if she sincerely does so at all, for the hypocrisy that the world forces on her instead of for being what she is.'[15] *Mrs Warren's Profession* was thus modestly offered as being crafted by just such 'a master-hand'.

In the earliest days of the composition of his play, Shaw admitted that he had 'skilfully blended' the plot of *The Second Mrs Tanqueray* with that of *The Cenci*.[16] Shelley's gothic horror play had been published in 1819 but it was not performed in England until a private staging by the Shelley Society in May 1886. For this production, Shaw orchestrated the press campaign to stir up public interest and to combat attacks on the perceived immorality of the play. This experience taught him the value and methods of promoting controversy that he would so adroitly adopt in future years. The play's contentious issue was not its historical veracity, but the portrayal of Beatrice's rape at the hands of her villainous father. While incest is important in creating uncertainty throughout *Mrs Warren's Profession*, the stronger links between the two plays are instead the intergenerational struggles between two dynamic personalities and the curse of the elders upon their children.[17] The same might be said of

---

14 For a longer consideration of the comparative aspects of *Yvette* and *Mrs Warren's Profession*, see Geoffrey Bullough, 'Literary Relations of Shaw's Mrs Warren', *Philological Quarterly* 41.1 (1962), 339–58.

15 *The Saturday Review*, 23 February 1895.

16 *CL* I, p. 403.

17 For a comparative reading of these two plays, see Betty Freeman Johnson, 'Shelley's *Cenci* and *Mrs Warren's Profession*', *The Shaw Review* 15.1 (1972), 26–34.

Ibsen's *Ghosts* (1881), which also has incest and similar generational conflicts at its centre; like *The Cenci*, the London production of *Ghosts* was the focus of an organised effort, in which Shaw participated, to circumvent the authorities of the day.[18]

The broader genre of prostitute literature to which *Mrs Warren's Profession* and *Yvette* belong traces its British origins back to royalist pamphlets in the seventeenth century. As opposed to acting as a force for change, these forerunner texts employed the figure of the prostitute to symbolise democracy and the ungovernable classes in order to consolidate power in the aristocracy.[19] Within a century, the topic had become so popular that many of the day's best-known authors wrote prostitute narratives, including Aphra Behn, Eliza Haywood, and Daniel Defoe. Indeed, Shaw had read Defoe's *Moll Flanders* in January 1893, some seven months before he began writing *Mrs Warren's Profession*.[20] One of the eighteenth century's most scandalous successes was John Cleland's *Memoirs of a Woman of Pleasure* and it is possible that it might have influenced Shaw: the old brute who pays so he can attempt to rape and deflower Fanny Hill is, like Vivie's lecherous and violent pursuer, named Crofts.[21]

The tone of prostitute literature has an enormous range, with the genre developing into two distinct trends: reformist and libertine. Reformist tales depict prostitution as a harrowing occupation and a necessary evil for women to endure in order to survive in an exploitative society, while libertine stories tell of a woman who reaches the heights of luxury and relishes the riches and amoral lifestyle of the heroine, generally delighting in the accumulation of sexual conquests, money, and material goods.[22] The one aspect that both of these types share, and which would have appealed to Shaw, is their fixation on economics. Writers throughout the eighteenth century used prostitutes to explore the changing relationships between people in an increasingly mercantile and

---

18 For more on the links between *Ghosts* and *Mrs Warren's Profession*, see Bernard F. Dukore, *Money and Politics in Ibsen, Shaw, and Brecht* (Columbia, MO: University of Missouri Press, 1980), pp. 27–49.

19 Melissa M. Mowry, *The Body Politic in Stuart England, 1660–1714: Political Pornography and Prostitution* (Aldershot: Ashgate, 2004).

20 *Diaries*, p. 893.

21 For more on the links between Shaw's play and prostitute literature of the eighteenth century, see Brad Kent, 'Eighteenth-Century Literary Precursors of *Mrs. Warren's Profession*', *University of Toronto Quarterly* 81.2 (2012), 187–207.

22 Laura T. Rosenthal, *Infamous Commerce: Prostitution in Eighteenth-Century British Literature and Culture* (Ithaca, NY: Cornell University Press, 2006), pp. 97–128. See also Bradford K. Mudge, *The Whore's Story: Women, Pornography, and the British Novel, 1684–1830* (Oxford: Oxford University Press, 2000).

urban culture and to understand the concomitant seismic social shifts that were occurring in Britain.[23]

By the nineteenth century, prostitute literature had lost much of its sociological appeal and instead became infused with a puritanical streak led by reformers and evangelicals who sought to save women from damnation. This was accompanied by a relative move away from the topic as a focus for major writers; prostitutes now found themselves pushed to the margins of both society and literature.[24] Yet while fallen women, such as Little Emily in Charles Dickens' *David Copperfield* (1850) and the title character of Elizabeth Gaskell's *Ruth* (1853), dot the landscape of early Victorian literature, they are absolutely at the fore in the century's final decade, indicating a millennial hysteria for changing sexual mores in the wider society and a desire to question and push those boundaries in more advanced circles.[25] To take just a few of the better-known examples, Thomas Hardy's *Tess of the D'Urbervilles* (1891) and *Jude the Obscure* (1895) were the targets of censorship campaigns and venomous press. The attacks were in part instigated by the depictions of Tess, Arabella, and Sue Bridehead, many critics believing that the uproar led Hardy to abandon the novel and instead turn to poetry. And Oscar Wilde, whose own sexuality would notoriously be put on trial, had success with his woman-with-a-past play, *Lady Windermere's Fan* (1892), in which Mrs Erlynne saves her daughter from committing adultery through her own caution-ary experience.[26] But all these antecedents, despite the provocative and

23 In addition to Rosenthal, see Sophie Carter, *Purchasing Power: Representing Prostitution in Eighteenth-Century English Popular Print Culture* (Aldershot: Ashgate, 2004).

24 This is borne out by the fact that there are no monographs on prostitutes in Victorian literature. Instead, they are included in studies on the larger category of the fallen woman. See, for example, Amanda Anderson, *Tainted Souls and Painted Faces: The Rhetoric of Fallenness in Victorian Culture* (Ithaca, NY: Cornell University Press, 1993); and Tom Winnifrith, *Fallen Women in the Nineteenth-Century Novel* (New York: St Martin's Press, 1994).

25 There are a number of excellent studies of the subject of fallen women in the *fin-de-siècle* period of British literature. For studies that place Shaw in the vanguard of this genre, see Sos Eltis, 'The Fallen Woman on Stage: Maidens, Magdalens, and the Emancipated Female', in *The Cambridge Companion to Victorian and Edwardian Theatre*, ed. Kerry Powell (Cambridge: Cambridge University Press, 2004), pp. 222–36; and Martin Meisel, *Shaw and the Nineteenth-Century Theater* (Princeton, NJ: Princeton University Press, 1963), pp. 141–59.

26 For comparisons of *Lady Windermere's Fan* and *Mrs Warren's Profession*, see Wendell Stacy Johnson, 'Fallen Women, Lost Children: Wilde and the Theatre of the Nineties', in *Sexuality and Victorian Literature*, ed. Don Richard Cox (Knoxville, TN: The University of Tennessee Press, 1984), pp. 196–211; and Bernice Schrank, 'Mrs Erlynne, Mrs Warren and the Nineteenth-Century Stage Stereotype of the Fallen Woman', in *The Internationalism of Irish Literature and Drama* (Gerrards Cross: Colin Smythe, 1992), pp. 134–45.

reformist impulses of most of their writers, finish just as conservatively as Pinero's play: Moll Flanders repents at the end for the wicked life she has led; Fanny Hill, like Kitty's sister Liz, retires in wealth to the countryside; Gaskell's Ruth dies, having selflessly devoted herself to mothering her illegitimate child and attending to the terminally ill; Tess is executed for murdering her seducer; Sue leaves Jude believing that their unmarried status has led to their suffering, which is only compounded with the return of Arabella and Jude's eventual death; and Emily and Mrs Erlynne conveniently leave England to avoid contaminating it, the one heading to Australia, the other the Continent, fittingly the sites of criminal transport and excessive vice.

Indeed, by the *fin-de-siècle* the decadence and immorality evident in English letters' fascination with fallen women were traced directly to France. England's old rival, it was opined, was guilty of infecting its body politic with these ideas, French literature being utterly consumed with courtesans and loose-living thrill-seekers such as those who chase after Madame Obardi and Yvette.[27] Shaw winks at this in *The Philanderer*, when, in referring to Grace, Julia says to Charteris: 'Look at what the creature reads – filthy, vile French stuff that no decent woman would touch.'[28]

Shaw, though, quite enjoyed French literature. Among others, he was a big fan of Alexandre Dumas, *père*, having read *The Three Musketeers* (1844) and *The Count of Monte Cristo* (1846). Dumas had also written a courtesan novella, *Fernande* (1844), which is believed to have inspired his son, Alexandre Dumas, *fils*, to fictionalise his own experiences with the courtesan Marie Duplessis, renamed Marguerite Gautier, in *La Dame aux Camélias* (1848). Marguerite's story is the young Dumas' best-known work, and he turned it almost immediately into a play that took all of Europe by storm – save in England, where it was banned.[29] The Italian composer Giuseppe Verdi, who attended the opening night performance in Paris in 1852, was so inspired by it that he composed an adaptation, the opera *La Traviata* (1853).[30] A fervent music lover, Shaw attended the

27 For more on the ubiquity of prostitutes in French literature and paintings of the nineteenth century, see Charles Bernheimer, *Figures of Ill-Repute: Representing Prostitution in Nineteenth-Century France* (Cambridge, MA: Harvard University Press, 1989).

28 Bernard Shaw, *The Philanderer*, in *Plays Unpleasant*, ed. Dan H. Laurence (London: Penguin, 2000), p. 111.

29 John Russell Stephens, *The Censorship of English Drama, 1824–1901* (Cambridge: Cambridge University Press, 2010), pp. 82–4. Shaw subsequently reviewed competing London productions of the play, featuring two of the greatest actresses of the era, Eleonora Duse and Sarah Bernhardt, in *The Saturday Review* on 15 June 1895. See Bernard Shaw, *Our Theatre in the Nineties*, Volume I (London: Constable, 1932), pp. 148–54.

30 *La Traviata*, translated, means the corrupted, or fallen, woman.

opening night of a revival of *La Traviata* at the Covent Garden Theatre on 12 March 1887.[31]

The prevalence and importance of the fallen woman to continental literature in the period is evident in some of its landmark works. The married heroines of Gustave Flaubert's *Madame Bovary* (1857) and Leo Tolstoy's *Anna Karenina* (1877) have affairs to escape the dissatisfaction of their unhappy marriages. Émile Zola, another favourite of Shaw, began his exploration of the theme in the *L'Assommoir* (1877), which painfully details the tormenting downfall of the washerwoman Gervaise, and used it as his main subject in *Nana* (1880), the tale of Gervaise's daughter who rises from the slums of Paris to become the *demi-monde*'s most celebrated courtesan. Yet despite the scandal that each of these works provoked, they remain just as conformist as their British counterparts in ensuring that their sinful women meet fitting ends: the fallen Emma Bovary and Anna Karenina commit suicide; and the prostitutes Fernande, Marguerite, and Nana all conveniently die of various illnesses. While Dumas *père* and *fils* exploited their prostitutes to heighten sentimentality, Zola used Nana to criticise the decadence and hypocrisy of mid-century France, her diseased death and the ruin of her aristocratic lovers coinciding with the downfall of the Second Empire. However, by ending the book in this manner, Zola avoided extending the critique to potentially implicate contemporary society. In marked contrast, Kitty exits *Mrs Warren's Profession* completely unrepentant; she curses Vivie and regrets that she has not raised her in her brothels. Although she probably departs the Chancery Lane office to return to her continental houses of ill-repute, which would possibly leave England safe from her influence, she threatens: 'From this time forth, so help me Heaven in my last hour, I'll do wrong and nothing but wrong. And I'll prosper on it' (IV.755–7). In doing so, Shaw decidedly broke from convention. Kitty's threat is a challenge to audiences that seeks to propel them towards reform.

In addition to literary models, Shaw drew inspiration from the world around him and named his characters accordingly. Although he had happily left Ireland long before writing his play, he remained interested in Irish matters. In the late nineteenth century, Irish politics were dominated by the movement for Home Rule, spearheaded by the Irish Parliamentary Party and its charismatic leader, Charles Stewart Parnell. In 1880, Parnell met Katherine O'Shea, a separated wife who is better known to history as Kitty, and they soon embarked on an affair that lasted for more than a decade. The relationship was known to many in political circles, but when William O'Shea openly named Parnell as co-respondent in his

---

31 He reviewed this production in the *Pall Mall Gazette*, 14 March 1887.

divorce case in 1890, the public furore brought about Parnell's downfall and his premature death. This led to the division of the Irish nationalist cause in Parliament, which hindered the Home Rule campaign for years to come. In typical fashion, Kitty O'Shea, the fallen woman, shouldered some of the blame for the political fallout, just as Kitty Warren would bear being labelled immoral by those who refused to probe the issue of prostitution more deeply.

Prostitution

In 1885, eight years before Shaw began writing *Mrs Warren's Profession*, William T. Stead, the editor of the *Pall Mall Gazette*, turned his investigative crusading journalism to uncovering the sordid world of prostitution. In July of that year, he ran a series of articles under the title 'The Maiden Tribute of Modern Babylon'. The public was enthralled by the paper, in particular by a harrowing and dramatic account of the purchase of a thirteen-year-old girl for £5. Shaw, who was working at the *Pall Mall Gazette* at the time, was so horrified by the story that he personally offered Stead 'to take as many quires of the paper as I can carry and sell them (for a penny) in any thoroughfare in London'.[32] Readers were similarly moved to outrage, which some in government circles feared would boil over into protests and riots. To quell the growing anger, Parliament quickly passed the Criminal Law Amendment Act which raised the age of consent from thirteen to sixteen and increased penalties for streetwalkers and brothel-keepers.[33]

Stead was a part of a long line of reformers and sociologists who had taken to writing on the evils of prostitution. The earliest of the more scientific publications was *De la prostitution dans la ville de Paris* (1836). Written by Alexandre Parent-Duchâtelet, a young doctor who had also reported on Paris' sewage system out of concern for public hygiene, the study was influential for the way it systematically analysed the subject using data that had been collected through medical and police reports, in many ways setting the template for future work. Parent-Duchâtelet detailed such diverse aspects as the careers of prostitutes' fathers, the regions from which the women had come to the capital, their levels of education, the different

32 Holroyd I, p. 290.
33 For an account of the importance of Stead's journalism on British modernism's engagement with prostitution, including a compelling examination of its effects on Shaw's plays, see Celia Marshik, *British Modernism and Censorship* (Cambridge: Cambridge University Press, 2006). In an ironic twist, Stead was later convicted under the terms of the Act his story had helped to create. Even though he had safely placed her in the care of the Salvation Army in France, the thirteen-year-old girl's father had not granted permission for her to leave the country; Stead was found guilty of abduction.

classes of prostitutes and their own slang vocabulary to provide the most accurate portrait of the profession to have been produced at that time.

The 1850s saw sociological interest in prostitution peak with the appearance of similar studies. The first of these was the comprehensive *London Labour and the London Poor* (1851), written by Henry Mayhew, a prominent journalist. Others written by doctors who had experience with treating prostitutes and were concerned with public health followed. Among these are William Acton's *Prostitution Considered in its Moral, Social, and Sanitary Aspects* (1857), William W. Sanger's *The History of Prostitution* (1859), and James Miller's *Prostitution Considered in Relation to its Cause and Cure* (1859). All four of these authors, like Parent-Duchâtelet, argued that economics was a principal factor in perpetuating the profession: women were forced into it because they had no other way to make a living or were in need of augmenting a pitiable wage to earn their bread. This conclusion struck against the grain of much popular belief, which pointed to individual immorality and lasciviousness as leading women to become and remain prostitutes.

The reaction to these reports from politicians was a deafening silence followed by gross injustice. No meaningful legislation regarding prostitution was proposed until the mid-1860s. However, the stated concern was not for the women but the health of the armed forces, as large numbers of troops had become infected with venereal diseases. In response, the government passed a series of Contagious Diseases Acts from 1864 to 1869. Under these laws, the police could take any woman into custody and force her to undergo medical examination and treatment until such time as the authorities saw fit. Were she to refuse, she could be imprisoned. Nothing, then, was done to provide a poor woman with other career choices or to increase her chances to succeed, but much was done to harass her once she had become a prostitute or was even suspected of being one. The double standard of criminalising the woman while leaving her male clients and procurers untouched provided further evidence of the oppression that women suffered in Victorian Britain. Shaw remarks in his preface to *Mrs Warren's Profession* that he found it scurrilous to leave the issue to 'the medical gentlemen who would compulsorily examine and register Mrs Warren, whilst leaving Mrs Warren's patrons, especially her military patrons, free to destroy her health and anybody else's without fear of reprisals' (see Appendix IV, p. 123). The Acts were eventually repealed in 1886, in no small part because of Stead's work.[34]

---

34 For more on the political context surrounding the play, see John Allett, '*Mrs Warren's Profession* and the Politics of Prostitution', *SHAW* 19 (1999), 23–39.

By the time that Shaw wrote *Mrs Warren's Profession*, very little had changed in the official regard and treatment of prostitutes. For this reason, the play's perspective aligns closely with those reformist scientific studies of prostitution published over thirty years earlier.[35] Shaw's purpose, he said, was 'to draw attention to the truth that prostitution is caused, not by female depravity and male licentiousness, but simply by underpaying, undervaluing, and overworking women so shamefully that the poorest of them are forced to resort to prostitution to keep body and soul together' (see Appendix IV, p. 120). For the socialist Shaw, writing on prostitution allowed him to attack the most exploitive and horrific aspects of capitalism in a much more charged manner than he had previously done.[36] He considered that the trade, like all capitalist ventures, preyed upon the poor. This predatory nature is evident in his portrayal of Crofts, who is animalised in his various descriptions as possessing '*bulldog jaws*' (I.341–2), the 'Sort of chap that would take a prize at a dog show' (I.607), 'excellent company for the bull-pup' (II.464–5), '*prowling*' on repeated occasions (II.361 and 412), having '*a carnal gleam in his eye*' (II.414), watching '*with a crafty air*' (III.332), and '*panting with fury*' (III.575). The other two characters who are directly linked with prostitution are likewise animalised: Mrs Warren is described as panting and whimpering (II.567–9) and is compared to a sparrow (IV.472–3) and the Reverend Samuel Gardner is said to have 'the irresoluteness of a sheep and the pompousness and aggressiveness of a jackass' (III.123–4). When Crofts threatens Vivie after her refusal of his marriage proposal, Frank has to defend her with a hunting rifle, '*stalking him cautiously*' until he leaves the garden (III.592), although he believes that it would be 'Much more sportsmanlike to catch him in a trap' (III.599–600). While the rifle is a dramatic device, as seen with Vivie's grabbing the barrel and pointing it towards her breast, it is also relevant for its symbolic violence. In this scenario, Shaw appears to suggest that prostitution, and by extension capitalism, can only be tamed with extreme measures. Capitalism's worst aspects must be turned away, or it must be defanged and declawed, which could only be done by ameliorating the living and working conditions of the poorest sections of society.

35 For a similar study published closer to the period in which Shaw wrote his play, see August Bebel, *Woman in the Past, Present, and Future* (London: The Modern Press, 1885).

36 There has been some debate whether the play is more of a propagandistic tract or a work of high artistic achievement. See, for example, Charles A. Carpenter, *Bernard Shaw and the Art of Destroying Ideals: The Early Plays* (Madison, WI: University of Wisconsin Press, 1969); and Charles A. Berst, *Bernard Shaw and the Art of Drama* (Urbana, IL: University of Illinois Press, 1973).

Among the early sociologists, Sanger considered not simply poverty but more specifically the ills of British factories and low pay as significant contributors to prostitution.[37] Miller similarly suggested: 'Look to the female operatives in large towns – the sewing girls, milliners, factory workers, etc. It is generally understood, so as to be quite proverbial, that out of these the ranks of the fallen are mainly recruited.'[38] These conclusions have been borne out by more recent historians of the period.[39] Kitty herself became a prostitute because she feared the hazardous conditions of the whitelead factory that poisoned her half-sister and she was unable to scrape together any savings or live decently as a working girl. Crofts, too, recognises how these factors help to swell prostitution's ranks, acknowledging the role that his brother plays by underpaying the hundreds of girls in his employ. Shaw thus presents his audience with a harsh social cause for prostitution as opposed to presenting more salacious and sentimental grounds, such as being led astray, seduced, and eventually abandoned by a lover. In so doing, he refuses to blame the young woman who makes an error in judgement and instead holds the system responsible for starving considerable numbers of its population into such degrading work.

Renowned anarchist Emma Goldman, a great admirer of Shaw, considered that *Mrs Warren's Profession* tends to infuriate 'because it goes to the bottom of our evils; because it places the accusing finger upon the sorest and most damnable spot in our social fabric – SEX as woman's only commodity in the competitive market of life'.[40] Kitty emphasises this in her description of the limited choices young women of her class faced: either drudgery, in which they wore out their health and appearance for other people's profits, or as public performers, if they were talented enough. Otherwise, if they were attractive and had the ability to please men, they could trade on their good looks, instead of letting the shopkeepers and restaurant owners do so, and have 'all the profits' to themselves (II.762–3). This, she suggests, was no worse than marriage, the only other viable option for women. Indeed, Kitty considers prostitution and

37 William W. Sanger, *The History of Prostitution* (New York: Arno Press, 1972), pp. 332–4.

38 James Miller, *Prostitution Considered in Relation to its Cause and Cure* (Edinburgh: Sutherland and Knox, 1859), pp. 6–7.

39 See, for example, Frances Finnegan, *Poverty and Prostitution: A Study of Victorian Prostitutes in York* (Cambridge: Cambridge University Press, 1979); and Judith R. Walkowitz, *Prostitution and Victorian Society: Women, Class, and the State* (Cambridge: Cambridge University Press, 1980). For a study of the efforts to reform these fallen women, see Linda Mahood, *The Magdalenes: Prostitution in the Nineteenth Century* (London: Routledge, 1990).

40 Emma Goldman, *The Social Significance of Modern Drama* (Boston: Gorham Press, 1914), p. 186.

marriage to be much the same thing: 'What is any respectable girl brought up to do but to catch some rich man's fancy and get the benefit of his money by marrying him?' she says. 'As if a marriage ceremony could make any difference in the right or wrong of the thing!' (II.768–72).

Crofts' proposal to Vivie furthers this link. Rather than opting for romance, charm or compatibility, Crofts woos Vivie with financial and social incentives in a manner that lays bare the bartering of marriage contracts as a capitalist venture.[41] Even the Reverend Samuel Gardner, who pretends to uphold morality, advises his son Frank that because he lacks both brains and money, he had better turn his 'good looks to account by marrying somebody with both' (I.657–8). The young man, in the only instance he appears to pay heed to his father, dutifully sets his calculating eyes on Vivie.

If the attack on the sacrosanct institution of marriage was not enough to render the play questionable in the eyes of many people in Victorian Britain, the inclusion of incest consigned it to the realm of the unperformable. Shaw recognised this during the composition of the play. In the early manuscripts, Crofts' eventual line 'Why, for all I know, I might be her father' (I. 485) originally read 'All I ask you to tell me – and I consider it a right to know it, mind – is, am I her father?' This was a far more explicit admission of his sexual relationship with Kitty, which would put his proposal to Vivie in jeopardy. Likewise, Crofts, in discussing the potential marriage (II.383), asks, 'Maynt a man take an interest in a girl – a fatherly interest?' Shaw, though, struck out the phrase following the dash and made further cuts to their conversation, in particular to the lines in which Kitty asks Crofts whether he can be sure if Vivie is not his own daughter, and Crofts lowers his voice to respond: 'How do *you* know that that maynt be one of the fascinations of the thing? What harm if she is?'[42]

In the final version of the play Shaw does allow Crofts to say that in marrying him, Vivie will keep the secret of the origins of their money 'in the family, so to speak' (III.427–8). And Crofts reveals the possibility, which is left unresolved at the play's end, that Vivie and Frank are half-siblings, conjecturing that Vivie is the Reverend Samuel Gardner's

---

41 For Shaw's intellectual debts to writers in his portrayal of the subjugation of women in British society, see Norbert Greiner, 'Mill, Marx and Bebel: Early Influences on Shaw's Characterization of Women', in *Fabian Feminist*, ed. Rodelle Weintraub (University Park, PA: Penn State University Press, 1977), pp. 90–8. It is notable that these are all male writers. Shaw was also influenced by Mary Wollstonecraft, whom he even refers to in his stage directions of *The Devil's Disciple*. Wollstonecraft explicitly calls marriage 'legal prostitution' in *A Vindication of the Rights of Men* and describes traditional marriage as little more than an exchange of a woman's duty towards her husband in return for a life of relative material comfort in *A Vindication of the Rights of Woman*.

42 Add. MSS. 50598 A, BL. See note to II.410–16.

daughter. The subject of incest abounds in the play, with only Praed not implicated, for incest was not understood to be merely the sexual coupling of people of close blood relations; it was also defined as the sexual coupling of one person with two or more members of the same family. Therefore, Frank's overtures to Mrs Warren would be incestuous as his father was her former client and he has already 'made love' to Vivie (II.59–62).[43] Kitty hints at this aspect of their relationship in comically dismissing her passionate embrace as 'only a motherly kiss' (II.59). Shaw claimed that incest, along with venereal disease and abortion, were the stage's great taboos, but he felt that he had to include it as a topic because he considered it to be 'one of the inevitable dilemmas' of prostitution.[44] He incorporated incest to make vice unattractive and impel people towards political and social reform through the eradication of poverty.[45]

The New Woman

Gender politics were intimately linked with Shaw's economic interest in prostitution. For Shaw, society needed to revise the way in which it viewed women as either domesticated angels or unholy whores. The 'Woman Question', as it became known, dominated public discussion and was the subject of a great many plays in the *fin-de-siècle* period. This was in part brought to the fore through Nora's revolutionary closing of the door on hearth and home at the end of *A Doll's House*. Following the play's London première, newspaper columns grappled with trying to understand how a wife and mother could possibly abandon her family.

43 Although making love indicates a sexual relationship in the twenty-first century, in the *fin-de-siècle* period the expression generally implied only active wooing.

44 Shaw, 'Dramatic Censorship', *The Nation*, 16 November 1907.

45 For a longer account of incest in the play, see Petra Dierkes-Thrun, 'Incest and the Trafficking of Women in *Mrs Warren's Profession*: "It Runs in the Family"', *English Literature in Transition, 1880–1920* 49.3 (2006), 293–310. Germaine Greer, who consistently misreads Shaw and his context, has claimed that incest in the play has 'a great deal to do with the plot and not much to do with the theme' of prostitution. She takes further exception to the fact that Shaw did not detail the daily horrors a prostitute undergoes without understanding the censorious society for which he wrote and the impossibility of mounting such a play at that time. But here Greer ignores Kitty's description of a prostitute's life: 'Ive often pitied a poor girl, tired out and in low spirits, having to try to please some man that she doesnt care two straws for – some half-drunken fool that thinks he's making himself agreeable when he's teasing and worrying and disgusting a woman so that hardly any money could pay her for putting up with it. But she has to bear with disagreeables and take the rough with the smooth, just like a nurse in a hospital or anyone else. It's not work that any woman would do for pleasure, goodness knows; though to hear the pious people talk you would suppose it was a bed of roses' (II.784–94). See Germaine Greer, 'A Whore in Every Home', in *Fabian Feminist*, ed. Rodelle Weintraub (University Park, PA: Pennsylvania State University Press, 1977), pp. 163–6.

Her independence and devotion to her self were seized upon as being alternately admirable and courageous, and detestable and cowardly. In response, a more assertive, intellectual, and independent woman, a free spirit who earned her own way and chose her own relationships, arose in the 1890s: the New Woman.[46]

The New Woman comes to life in Vivie.[47] She is foreshadowed at the opening of the play through her surroundings, which include a bicycle (a revolutionary mode of transport at the time that facilitated individual independence, was mounted in a decidedly unladylike fashion, and obliged one to sweat and exert oneself in public) and a pile of '*serious-looking books*', not sentimental and romantic novels (I.8–14). When Vivie does read for pleasure, it is detective stories, which she enjoys with a cigar and whisky (I.215–16). The stereotype of the New Woman is further embodied in Vivie's physical appearance: '*She is an attractive specimen of the sensible, able, highly-educated young middle-class Englishwoman. Age 22. Prompt, strong, confident, self-possessed. Plain business-like dress, but not dowdy. She wears a chatelaine at her belt, with a fountain pen and a paper knife among its pendants*' (I.39–44). This athleticism, autonomy, will, and education set her decidedly apart from the Victorian ideals of womanhood and gave theatre audiences a new character with which to reckon.

Shaw had already established the ground for the New Woman in *The Quintessence of Ibsenism* (1891), his political and social analysis of the Norwegian playwright's oeuvre. In a section entitled 'The Womanly Woman', he argued against traditional marriages, asserting that women had to be free in their decisions in order to give their love any value. To

---

46 For more on the rise of the archetype of the New Woman in the 1890s and its effects on literature and society, see Ann L. Ardis, *New Women, New Novels: Feminism and Early Modernism* (New Brunswick, NJ: Rutgers University Press, 1990); Ann Heilman, ed., *Feminist Forerunners: New Womanism and Feminism in the Early Twentieth Century* (London: Pandora, 2003); Elaine Showalter, *Sexual Anarchy: Gender and Culture at the Fin de Siècle* (Harmondsworth: Penguin, 1990); and Catherine Wiley, 'The Matter with Manners: The New Woman and the Problem Play', in *Woman in Theatre*, ed. James Redmond (Cambridge: Cambridge University Press, 1989), pp. 109–28. For Shaw's own relationship with the New Woman, see Sonja Lorichs, 'The "Unwomanly Woman" in Shaw's Drama', in *Fabian Feminist*, ed. Rodelle Weintraub (University Park, PA: Pennsylvania State University Press, 1977), pp. 99–111; and Kerry Powell, 'New Woman, New Plays, and Shaw in the 1890s', in *The Cambridge Companion to Bernard Shaw*, ed. Christopher Innes (Cambridge: Cambridge University Press, 1999), pp. 76–100. For a survey of the limited existence and expectations of girls in this period, see Carol Dyhouse, *Girls Growing up in Late Victorian and Edwardian England* (London: Routledge, 1981).

47 For other plays featuring New Woman protagonists, see Jean Chothia, ed., *The New Woman and Other Emancipated Woman Plays* (Oxford: Oxford University Press, 1998).

those who claimed that a woman's place was in the home, he countered: 'The domestic career is no more natural to all women than the military career is natural to all men.'[48] Women had become slaves to the home because that is where society had cast them, not because they were especially fit for the role: 'If we have come to think that the nursery and the kitchen are the natural sphere of a woman, we have done so exactly as English children come to think that a cage is the natural sphere of a parrot: because they have never seen one anywhere else.' And so, Shaw concluded, women must follow the path of Nora Helmer: 'The sum of the matter is that unless Woman repudiates her womanliness, her duty to her husband, to her children, to society, to the law, and to everyone but herself, she cannot emancipate herself.'[49] According to Shaw, the solution was for the womanly woman to become the unwomanly woman.

Vivie's education is key in this move towards a more modern self. Her mother's money allowed her entry into one of the world's leading institutions. Cambridge's Newnham College was founded in 1871, just two years after Girton, the first women's college at the university. Although women were permitted to attend most lectures, they were not granted degrees. Despite finishing tied for third overall in the mathematical tripos, a gruelling series of exams, Vivie therefore left the university without a BA, unlike the scores of men who would have finished well behind her.[50] Frank notes this gendered distinction in saying that she has '*what amounts to* a high Cambridge degree' (I.672–3, emphasis added). Her performance is all the more impressive because it is in a subject that has traditionally been dominated by males. In the end, it will allow her to embark upon a well-paying career which will in turn permit her to live comfortably and remain free from the tyrannies of parental control and marital demands.

While Crofts, Kitty, and the Reverend Samuel Gardner emphasise society's expectations in repeatedly demanding that Frank and Vivie unquestionably respect them, Praed is the one character of the older generation who claims to value a break from the past. Praed's denigration of convention, his allegiance to the Gospel of Art, his work as an architect, his devotion to a life of romance and beauty, and his trips to the Continent, all mark him as a dandy, one who wilfully eschews masculine

---

48 Bernard Shaw, *Shaw and Ibsen: Bernard Shaw's The Quintessence of Ibsenism and Related Writings*, ed. J.L. Wisenthal (Toronto: University of Toronto Press, 1979), p. 129.

49 Ibid., p. 130.

50 For more on Vivie's education in its context, see L.W. Conolly, 'Who Was Phillipa Summers? Reflections on Vivie Warren's Cambridge', *SHAW* 25 (2005), 89–95; and William A. Dolid, 'Vivie Warren and the Tripos', *The Shaw Review* 23.2 (1980), 52–6.

orthodoxies.[51] Indeed, Praed embraces the feminine. While he has a standing friendship of sorts with Frank, the young man troubles him. His real sympathies lie with the women, with Kitty and Vivie. Praed functions, then, as more than just a simple dramatic device to further the story and help fill the audience in on the characters' pasts and intentions through private discussions. His challenge to traditional masculinity works in conjunction with Vivie's challenge to traditional femininity to demonstrate that both sides of the gender divide are equally constructed, based not on biology but rather on convention.

Kitty's single motherhood is further signalled as a sign of such unconventionality. Were it not for her brashness, and if she would only be repentant, Frank suggests that his mother would take to her as she has in the past to other such women. But she refuses to supplicate herself before society. She is right to charge at the play's end that she and Vivie are cut of the same cloth: they both feel most at ease in the public pursuits of business than in retiring to the private world of the domesticated. The prostitute becomes similar to the New Woman in that both threaten society in sexual, social, and economic terms.[52] Yet some critics have questioned just how radical this alignment is.[53] After all, Kitty does nothing to upset the status quo in continuing the trade in women's bodies for money and Vivie takes up actuarial work for those who will pay her well. The young woman, the one who might have held out some hope for a better future, believes that we all have a free will and rejects the notion that circumstances have much bearing on who people turn out to be.

This is not someone who suggests that she will have any truck with women who blame society for their predicaments. When Frank pointedly asks her why she has hired a male staff instead of giving one of her own sex a chance, Vivie sidesteps the question in asking him why he has come to see her. Her only concern is the numbers with which she works. The last line of the play signals that '*she goes at her work with a plunge, and soon becomes absorbed in its figures*' (IV.789–90). But the figures before

---

51 For more on the dandy, see Jessica R. Feldman, *Gender on the Divide: The Dandy in Modernist Literature* (Ithaca, NY: Cornell University Press, 1993); James Eli Adams, *Dandies and Desert Saints: Styles of Victorian Masculinity Literature* (Ithaca, NY: Cornell University Press, 1995); Susan Fillin-Yeh, ed., *Dandies: Fashion and Finesse in Art and Culture* (New York: New York University Press, 2001); and Ellen Moers, *The Dandy: Brummell to Beerbohm* (Lincoln, NE: University of Nebraska Press, 1978).

52 For a study of how New Women were depicted as criminals and menacing threats to society, see Elizabeth Carolyn Miller, *Framed: The New Woman Criminal in British Culture at the Fin de Siècle* (Ann Arbor, MI: University of Michigan Press, 2008).

53 See, for example, Kerry Powell, 'New Woman, New Plays, and Shaw in the 1890s'; and J. Ellen Gainor, *Shaw's Daughters: Dramatic Narrative Constructions of Gender* (Ann Arbor, MI: University of Michigan Press, 1991).

her are not merely numbers: they are also representative of humans, of the figures that pass through her mother's hands and into the clutches of her male clients. Despite her pretences to be the play's moral compass and as one who represents radical rebellion, the daughter will be just as tainted by dirty money as her mother. She claims, after all, to have met in the course of her work with 'one or two women *very* like' her mother (I.324–5, original emphasis). The New Woman thus fails to act as an agent of reform. Shaw appears to steer us towards the conclusion that she must align her potential with positive political and social engagement in order to induce any meaningful change.

Censorship and Early Production History

It is difficult to think of a play with a more troubled production history in British theatre than *Mrs Warren's Profession*. Although it was composed in 1893, it only received its first unexpurgated licensed performance in Britain over thirty years later. At the time, playscripts had to be submitted with a nominal fee to the Office of the Lord Chamberlain. The Lord Chamberlain, who acted on the advice of his Examiner of Plays, could then license the play, demand revisions, or ban it altogether.[54]

Shaw knew early on that *Mrs Warren's Profession* would not be licensed, believing that it would find a likely home with the Independent Theatre. Because the Independent Theatre's productions were private affairs, with costs covered through membership fees as opposed to general ticket sales, they were safe from prosecution and relatively protected from larger market forces. J.T. Grein had asked about the play just after it was completed, but Shaw was rather vague on the plot, only admitting that Mrs Warren was 'a woman of bad character, proprietress of two *maisons tolérées* in Brussels, and of similar establishments in other continental cities'.[55] Shaw took until 13 February 1895 before he read the play to Grein, whose response was not favourable.[56] By June 1896, Shaw recognised that there was 'no question of its immediate or remote production'.[57]

---

54 For excellent studies of the British censorship of plays, see L.W. Conolly, *The Censorship of English Drama, 1737–1824* (San Marino, CA: The Huntington Library, 1976); John Russell Stephens, *The Censorship of English Drama, 1824–1901* (Cambridge: Cambridge University Press, 2010); Steve Nicholson, *The Censorship of British Drama, 1900–1968, Volume One: 1900–1932* (Exeter: University of Exeter Press, 2003); Steve Nicholson, *The Censorship of British Drama, 1900–1968, Volume Two: 1933–1952* (Exeter: University of Exeter Press, 2005); Steve Nicholson, *The Censorship of British Drama, 1900–1968, Volume Three: The Fifties* (Exeter: University of Exeter Press, 2011); and Dominic Shellard and Steve Nicholson with Miriam Handley, *The Lord Chamberlain Regrets: A History of British Theatre Censorship* (London: The British Library, 2005).

55 *CL* I, p. 412.

56 *Diaries*, p. 1065.   57 *CL* I, p. 632.

As Shaw turned his attention to publishing his plays, he became concerned with first securing their rights of representation, or performance copyright, which would ensure that he as the author would receive all royalties stemming from productions. Yet these rights could only be obtained if the play were performed before it was published. Aware that even a private London production of *Mrs Warren's Profession* was unlikely, Shaw looked to Ireland, which was beyond the Lord Chamberlain's jurisdiction. In May 1897, he contacted Edward McNulty, a childhood friend, and suggested that they 'engage one of the obscure little theatres in Dublin' to stage a simple reading of the play with the smallest amount of advertising possible.[58] A confederate would then pay a one guinea fee which would constitute it as a legitimate public performance. For whatever reason, though, the venture fell through.

With the impending publication of *Mrs Warren's Profession* as the third of his *Plays Unpleasant*, Shaw's attempt to have the play licensed became more pressing. When it was submitted on 11 March 1898, George Redford, the Examiner of Plays, wrote to say that he was unable to recommend it to be licensed. Shaw responded the next day. He had anticipated the rejection in recognising 'the impossibility of anyone dividing with me the responsibility for such a play', and requested that Redford note the offending passages.[59] Shaw went so far as to suggest that he license 'the first act, with the exception of the duologue between Praed and Crofts; the third act down to the beginning of the scene between Crofts and Vivie; and the last act from the entry of Praed onward, wholly omitting the 2nd act & leaving Mrs W's profession unspecified'. Redford, though, refused to play the part of Shaw's editor, stating that 'it is not for me to attempt any "dramatic expurgation" with the blue pencil'. The onus was instead on the author 'to submit, or cause to be submitted, a licensable play'.[60]

Over a year earlier, Shaw had raised the possibility that if the play were rejected by the Examiner, he would make Mrs Warren 'a washerwoman or a pickpocket or whatever will enable him to license enough of the text to protect me'.[61] Recalling this strategy and keeping to the cuts he proposed to Redford, he hurriedly rewrote the script. In the new garden scene, Crofts says to Frank and Vivie before leaving: 'It may interest you, since youre so fond of one another. This young lady's mother was convicted five times of shoplifting before she took to her present trade of training

58 *CL* I, pp. 757–8.
59 *CL* II, p. 13.
60 *CL* II, p. 14.
61 *CL* I, pp. 796–7.

young girls to the profession of larceny'.[62] In doing so, Shaw simultaneously made the profession more palatable and effaced any hint of incest. Appeased by these amendments, the Lord Chamberlain licensed the play for performance at the Victoria Hall on 30 March 1898, where it received its copyright reading with Annie Horniman, the future financial backer of Ireland's Abbey Theatre and Manchester's Gaiety Theatre, as Vivie. The performance was just in time: two weeks later, the play was published on both sides of the Atlantic.

The fortunes of *Mrs Warren's Profession* took a decided turn for the better in the new century. The Stage Society, formed in 1899 to replace the defunct Independent Theatre, opened its first season with Shaw's *You Never Can Tell* and closed it with *Candida*; it would also mount a production of *Captain Brassbound's Conversion* the following year, and later *Man and Superman* and *The Admirable Bashville*.[63] In the summer of 1901, the Stage Society opted to perform *Mrs Warren's Profession*, but it needed to rent a space for its performances as it did not have its own theatre. Because Shaw's play had yet to be licensed and managers feared crossing the Lord Chamberlain's Office knowing that the unexpurgated version had been banned, thirteen theatres, three hotels, two music halls, and the Royal Society of British Artists refused to hire out their premises.[64] Shaw feared as much, believing that the 'sole obstacle to the performance is the intimidation of the Censor, and his absolutely autocratic power – to ruin any West End manager who offends him, without reason given or remedy available'.[65] The Stage Society's efforts were hindered by newspaper articles that heaped scorn on the play before it had even been performed. The *Pall Mall Gazette*, for which Shaw had once worked, warned playgoers that they would be subjected to 'the moral miasma' of the play and wondered whether they would be 'fascinated by Mr Shaw's genius in proving that black is whiter than white, provided that an economic standard can be established'.[66] The *Daily Telegraph* seconded this opinion, fearing 'an hysterical outcry such as greeted the staging of *Ghosts*'.[67] The actors themselves wavered on whether or not they should perform in it, perhaps most understandably those who were approached to star as Kitty Warren.[68] Despite such widely

62 Add. MSS. 53654 H, BL. See note to III.611–14.

63 Holroyd II, p. 92.

64 Holroyd II, p. 95.

65 *CL* II, p. 243.

66 *Pall Mall Gazette*, 28 October 1901. All newspaper reports of the 1902 production have been taken from clippings in Box 1 of the Stage Society's files, TPA.

67 *Daily Telegraph*, 12 November 1901.

68 *CL* I, p. 566; *CL* II, p. 242. Both Mrs Theodore Wright, who was originally offered the role

known concerns, the management of the Lyric Theatre courageously agreed to allow a production on 5 and 6 January 1902.

The play starred Fanny Brough as Kitty Warren, Madge McIntosh as Vivie, Julius Knight as Praed, Charles Goodhart as Sir George Crofts, Cosmo Stuart as the Reverend Samuel Gardner, and Harley Granville Barker as Frank. The audience was estimated to be about 500 people, most of whom, reviewers noted with shock, were women. Critical opinion was rather split on the play, though it leaned towards favouring the position of the Lord Chamberlain to uphold the ban. Yet even those who came out against the play had to admit that the cast gave an outstanding performance. The *St James's Gazette*, for example, remained convinced that 'the tendency of the play is wholly evil' but that the 'excellent acting secured toleration for the performance' and hoped that in the future the Stage Society would 'eschew dramatic garbage'.[69] The *Globe* reviewer was 'unable to define the nature of the piece lest he should outrage the susceptibilities' of his readers.[70] The *Daily Graphic* similarly argued that the subject 'is, frankly, unmentionable in the columns of a newspaper, and is, we hold, unsuitable to stage exposition', while conceding that Shaw and Scandinavian dramatists 'furnish good opportunities to actors and that yesterday's presentation was admirable'.[71] The subject was so horrifying to the *Daily Telegraph* that it simply stated that Shaw 'rightly described the piece as "unpleasant." No further comment is called for.'[72] Less prudishly, the reviewer for the *World* argued that the play's 'radical defect . . . is the terrible, consistent didacticism that permeates every scene and conditions every character'. But he qualified that it 'is not the theme of the play that makes it impossible for the general public: it is the manner of presentment, together with one or two individual details wholly extrinsic to the theme', a likely nod to the subject of incest.[73]

Perhaps the most revealing review was penned by J.T. Grein in *The Sunday Special*.[74] It is rather difficult to reconcile his comments with the man who over ten years earlier had dared to thumb his nose at the establishment in staging Ibsen's *Ghosts*, given that play's notoriously dark depiction of illegitimate birth, alcoholism, madness, incest, social and religious hypocrisy, and venereal disease. Yet Grein wondered how Shaw's

had the Independent Theatre produced it in 1895, and Fanny Brough, when she was approached by Shaw to star in it for the Stage Society, were at first shocked by the play.

69 *St James's Gazette*, 7 January 1902.
70 *Globe*, 7 January 1902.
71 *Daily Graphic*, 7 January 1902.
72 *Daily Telegraph*, 7 January 1902.
73 *World*, 15 January 1902.
74 *The Sunday Special*, 12 January 1902.

play could be performed before an audience, worrying that 'too much knowledge of the seamy side is poisonous, for it leads to pessimism, that pioneer of insanity and suicide' and that the representation of prostitution 'was unnecessary and painful'. It was for these reasons, he claimed, that the Independent Theatre never performed the play.

Mrs Warren's Profession lost much of its public interest once it had played for the London cultural and intellectual elite. However, audiences and critics would come to take note of it again following its production in America by Arnold Daly. In the two years before he took on *Mrs Warren's Profession*, Daly had managed Broadway productions of *Candida*, *The Man of Destiny*, *How He Lied to Her Husband*, and *You Never Can Tell*. Despite these successes, Shaw believed that his courtesan play would create 'a frightful scandal'.[75] He advised Daly to 'frame a warning that will not attract the wrong people and keep away the right people', fearing that it would otherwise cause serious theatregoers and people who could affect reform to refrain from attending and instead draw only 'those who like licentious entertainments'.[76] Daly, though, failed to proceed with caution. In the autumn of 1905, on the heels of a disastrous run of *John Bull's Other Island*, Shaw's first failure in America, an anxious Daly pushed *Mrs Warren's Profession* into production.

Without a pre-performance system of censorship, American theatres were free to produce anything they wished but they were open to prosecution for whatever appeared on stage. These relative freedoms therefore came with attendant risks and they could potentially spark controversy and theatre of their own making in the form of public protests and courtroom trials. Just such a spectacle occurred in the lead up to the opening night on 30 October when Anthony Comstock and the New York Society for the Suppression of Vice campaigned against the play. In an attempt to create a media event, newspapers published correspondence between Comstock and Daly. Comstock had written Daly to remind him of the laws as they would be applied to 'one of Bernard Shaw's filthy products'; Daly responded by inviting Comstock to attend a performance, but Comstock refused.[77] The show was to have two previews in New Haven, Connecticut, but it was closed down by the local Chief of Police after only one night, a decision that was supported by the city's Mayor.[78] William McAdoo, New York City's Police Commissioner,

---

75 *CL* II, p. 432.

76 *CL* II, p. 464.

77 *New York Times*, 25 and 26 October 1905.

78 George E. Wellwarth, '"Mrs Warren" Comes to America, or the Blue-Noses, the Politicians and the Procurers', *The Shaw Review* 2.8 (1959), 9–11.

obtained a copy of the play which he diligently read, pencilling in excisions.[79] In the meantime, Daly had undertaken his own pre-performance censorship in editing the text to avoid further trouble.[80] However, his efforts would save neither him nor the play.

On opening night, crowds had formed outside of the Garrick Theatre, with an estimated 2,000 to 3,000 people turned away at the door. Extra police arrived to maintain order.[81] This evident popularity stirred the New York critics. The *New York Herald* called the play 'morally rotten' and noted that while some lines had been omitted and others toned down, 'there was superabundance of foulness left. The whole story of the play, the atmosphere surrounding it, the incidents, the personalities of the characters are wholly immoral and degenerate. The only way successfully to expurgate *Mrs Warren's Profession* is to cut the whole play out. You cannot have a clean pig stye.'[82] *The New York Times* was likewise unimpressed, claiming that 'it is not only of vicious tendency in its exposition, but it is also depressingly stupid'.[83] The audience was more divided. *The New York World* polled the 963 audience members as to the fitness of the play with 576 responding; of these, 304 thought that the play was suitable to be presented on the American stage, 272 people disagreeing. Business had been brisk at the box office with more than $10,000 in receipts collected; tickets were scalped for well above their face value.[84]

The next day, on 31 October, the authorities came down in favour of the minority of spectators and the majority of critics. McAdoo, who had watched the première from a box seat, arrested the theatre owner, the manager, and the play's cast to prevent a second performance. The accused appeared before the courts on 14 November on the charge of offending public decency. After some bickering between the attorneys for both sides, the judge adjourned the case. Meanwhile, Daly was released on $500 bail. The playscript was submitted as evidence. As he left the bench, the judge was heard uttering: 'I wish I could delegate to somebody else the reading of this prompt book.'[85] Shaw opened up to journalists in a bid to take his case to the court of public opinion. Claiming that he simply sought to reform a misguided society, he argued: 'The old notions of morality have had their day; they are now obsolete and must make way for a new morality – a morality more humane and more in accordance

---

79 *New York Times*, 28 October 1905.
80 *New York Times*, 30 October 1905.
81 *New York Times*, 31 October 1905.
82 *New York Herald*, 31 October 1905.
83 *New York Times*, 31 October 1905.
84 *New York Times*, 1 November 1905.
85 *New York Times*, 15 November 1905.

with the new conditions of things, with the necessities and wants of the modern world.'[86]

When the Special Sessions met to determine a verdict on the play, the justices declared 'it fraught with "shock producers" and "repellent things"'. However, they concluded, '"it appears that instead of exciting impure imagination in the mind of the spectator, that which is really excited is disgust; that the unlovely, the repellent, the disgusting in the play are merely accessories to the main purpose of the drama, which is an attack on certain social conditions relating to the employment of women which the dramatist believes, as do many others with him, should be reformed"'.[87] The defendants were thus acquitted. When Shaw was contacted by the *World* for his comments, he cabled: 'STRANGE COUNTRY WHERE THE PRESS IS BLIND AND THE EYES OF JUSTICE OPEN I AM PROFOUNDLY GRATEFUL.'[88] To *The New York American*, Shaw emphasised how important it was that his case had been heard and his character – as well as the characters of Daly and his company – had been vindicated in the United States, whereas in Britain the play had been kept from the stage by an institution that functioned *in camera* and had no mechanism of appeal.[89] As though to accentuate this divide, Mary Shaw, the lead actress in Daly's production though no relation of the playwright's, would successfully reprise her role as Kitty Warren in 1907.[90] Over the next year, productions of the play were mounted throughout Europe, notably in Moscow, Berlin, Stockholm, Budapest, Madrid, and Munich.[91] Yet, another request to stage the play in Manchester was refused by the Lord Chamberlain.[92]

Meanwhile, the cultural and political classes were engaged in debates on the future of stage censorship in Britain that had been provoked by the banning of Barker's *Waste* and Edward Garnett's *The Breaking Point*. Refused licences in 1907, these two plays had become a rallying point for playwrights and their supporters, including the Committee for the

86 '"My Plays Advocate Moral Reform!" Says Shaw', *The Theatre Magazine*, December 1905.

87 *New York Times*, 7 July 1906.

88 *CL* II, 632.

89 *CL* II, 633.

90 Mary Shaw was a revered actress closely aligned with the New Drama, especially Ibsen's plays. For her account of the New York production and her later tour of *Mrs Warren's Profession* throughout the United States, see Mary Shaw, 'My Immoral Play: The Story of the First American Production of *Mrs Warren's Profession*', *McClure's Magazine* 38 (April 1921), 684–94.

91 L.W. Conolly, '"Mrs Warren's Profession" and the Lord Chamberlain', *SHAW* 24 (2004), 58; and essays in L.W. Conolly and Ellen M. Pearson, eds, *Bernard Shaw on Stage: Papers from the 1989 International Shaw Conference* (Guelph, ON: University of Guelph, 1991).

92 *CL* II, pp. 707–8.

Abolition of the Office of Dramatic Censor, which counted Max Beerbohm, Walter Raleigh, Beatrice and Sidney Webb, and Winston Churchill among its membership.[93] Shaw had also been vocal, writing articles and letters to the press to maintain wide interest and stir sympathy for his fellow professionals.[94] As a result of these protests, a delegation of playwrights, led by J.M. Barrie, Arthur Wing Pinero, Gilbert Murray, and Sir William Gilbert, was invited to meet with government officials on 25 February 1908. Sensitive to the situation, the government convened the Joint Select Parliamentary Committee on the Censorship of Plays in July and August 1909. Despite persuasive testimony from many people, including Shaw, on the need for institutional reform, the outcome was largely the maintenance of the status quo, the only significant change being that the Lord Chamberlain could now call upon a council of advisors and not simply one Examiner in questionable cases.[95] However, there was now a broader acceptance of the modern drama that was part and parcel of shifting social norms and mores.

By 1912, there was enough interest to revive *Mrs Warren's Profession* in London that Edy Craig and the Pioneer Players undertook another private performance. Craig had a good theatre pedigree: her mother was the famous actress Ellen Terry; she had apprenticed under Henry Irving at the Lyceum Theatre and later acted in two Shaw plays, as Proserpine Garnett in *Candida* and Mrs Bridgeworth in *Getting Married*; and she had been on the managing board of the Stage Society when *Mrs Warren's Profession* was selected for its 1902 performances. The Pioneer Players was founded as 'a theatrical organisation run by women and dedicated to presenting plays by and about women'.[96] As *Mrs Warren's Profession* was still controversial, only two performances were scheduled, for 16 and 18 June at the King's Hall, Covent Garden. Even so, the selection led to several members resigning from the board, but the play went ahead despite such difficulties.

Gertrude Kingston and Ellen O'Malley, the latter the inspiration for Ellie Dunn in *Heartbreak House*, starred as Kitty and Vivie Warren. As a sign of the changes in public morality, critics were more receptive of the play. The reviewer for the *Manchester Guardian*, for example, claimed: 'Most sensible people now recognise it as a reasoned and eloquent plea

---

93 David Thomas, David Carlton, and Anne Etienne, *Theatre Censorship: From Walpole to Wilson* (Oxford: Oxford University Press, 2007), pp. 77–82.

94 See, for example, 'Waste and the Censor', *The Nation*, 8 February 1908.

95 Nicholson, *The Censorship of British Drama, 1900–1968, Volume One: 1900–1932*, pp. 46–70.

96 James Fisher, 'Edy Craig and the Pioneer Players' Production of "Mrs Warren's Profession"', *SHAW* 15 (1995), 39.

for looking at things as they are. The play is clear-sighted, it is logically convincing, it is witty, and the author's view which it expresses rings true with a broad humanity and sympathy.'[97] The more balanced and less hysterical reception suggested that perhaps the censorship was erring in still refusing it a licence.[98] Two further productions, a private one in Glasgow in 1913 and a public one in Dublin in 1914, showed that by this time very little scandal would come of its performance.[99] Nevertheless, the Lord Chamberlain's Office would not back down for over a decade.

The first instance of this continued intransigence came in 1916 with George S. King's application to stage the play at the Repertory Theatre, Plymouth. Ernest Bendall and George Street, the two Examiners of Plays at the time, believed that there was no reason to reverse the ban.[100] Not even a year had passed when another manager, Edwin T. Heys, expressed interest in producing it. Shaw attempted to diminish Heys' expectations and warn him off, claiming that the play 'is frightfully out of date by this time'.[101] Heys, however, ignored Shaw's advice and applied for a licence on 9 June 1917.[102] When he was turned down, Heys drew up a petition, believing that *Mrs Warren's Profession* was, like Ibsen's *Ghosts*, and Eugène Brieux's *The Three Daughters of M. Dupont* and *Damaged Goods*, a moral play.[103] He sent the petition to the Lord Chamberlain on 9 October with five pages of signatories that comprised a who's who of British society, among them a number of Right Honourables, 35 Members of Parliament, several knights, Annie Horniman, Ellen Terry, Mrs Patrick Campbell, William Archer, J.M. Barrie, Eugène Brieux, John Galsworthy, Lady Augusta Gregory, Henry Arthur Jones, Arthur Conan Doyle, G.K. Chesterton, Arthur Pinero, and H.G. Wells. Lord Sandhurst, the sitting Lord Chamberlain, could not be persuaded, judging that the play 'presents nothing to ameliorate affairs'.[104] This was also the case when Bache Matthews, manager of the Birmingham Repertory Theatre, submitted it on 30 June 1921. Although Street advised that the play should now be licensed, the Lord Chamberlain remained obstinate in his refusal, as he would when Matthews applied for a second time in 1922.

97 *Manchester Guardian*, 17 June 1912.

98 For a survey of the critical reception in 1912, see Fisher, *op. cit.*, pp. 49–53.

99 Conolly, *op. cit.*, pp. 61–5.

100 Memoranda by Bendall and Street, 5 October 1916, LCP Corr 1924/5632 *Mrs Warren's Profession*, BL.

101 Letter from Shaw to Heys, 1 May 1917, File 6, Box 38, HRC.

102 Letter from Heys, 9 June 1917, LCP Corr 1924/5632 *Mrs Warren's Profession*, BL.

103 Petition, LCP Corr 1924/5632 *Mrs Warren's Profession*, BL.

104 Memorandum by Lord Sandhurst, October 1917, LCP Corr 1924/5632 *Mrs Warren's Profession*, BL.

Matters changed for the better when Charles Macdona, the manager of a provincial touring company, submitted the play on 16 August 1924. Street reiterated his belief that the play should be licensed and Lord Cromer, the new Lord Chamberlain, concurred. While Cromer stated his respect for his predecessors, he differed in his conclusion, believing that it would 'be absurd to go on refusing a Licence to this Play, ignoring the march of time and the change it brings about in public opinion'.[105] Shaw hinted that the licence might have come about because of the 'odor of sanctity' about him following the production of *Saint Joan*.[106] But he scuttled the production for some time in refusing every actress that Macdona proposed and as a result it did not open until 27 July 1925 at the Prince of Wales Theatre in Birmingham. The reviewer for the *Birmingham Gazette*, who celebrated the actors' performances, called *Mrs Warren's Profession* 'one of the finest plays in the Shavian catalogue' and 'the most truly moral play ever produced on the English stage'.[107] Public opinion had indeed changed since Shaw wrote the play.

Later Productions

As one might expect, there was significant interest in the play following its licensing. Macdona brought his production to London, staging it at the Regent Theatre throughout the autumn of 1925 and again at the Strand Theatre from 26 March to 1 May 1926. It was then produced at the Little Theatre in February 1928 and the Court Theatre in March and April 1931. The reviews now bore out Shaw's fears that the play had become dated. One critic labelled it a 'museum piece'. Another lamented that what had once been 'daring' social commentary had become 'so ordinary (and so old-fashioned)'. Miriam Lewes, who starred as Kitty, was lauded for playing 'with an air of dilapidated splendour that is quite irresistible' and for being 'realistic, vigorous, and far more moving than one might be likely to think Mrs Warren in print'.[108] This was a far cry from the outraged response the play provoked a couple of decades earlier: the woman many people could not tolerate was now viewed as possessing a certain humanity and eliciting admiration.

Now that the public's curiosity had been sated again, the play saw an extended absence from London stages until January 1947, when it was produced at the Theatre Royal. It was revived again three years later at the

---

105 Report by Lord Cromer, 17 August 1924, LCP Corr 1924/5632 *Mrs Warren's Profession*, BL.

106 *CL* III, p. 883.

107 *Birmingham Gazette*, 28 July 1925.

108 See the articles dated 30 and 31 March and 5 April 1931 in the file on the 1931 production, TPA.

Arts Theatre and in November 1951 at the Richmond Theatre, followed by a run beginning in July 1953 at the Grand Theatre in Croydon. This increase in popularity probably had as much to do with the play's continued topicality as with a sentimental appreciation and re-evaluation of Shaw following his death in 1950. The Royal Court Theatre even celebrated his centenary with three matinee performances of the play on 24, 26, and 27 July 1956. *Mrs Warren's Profession* had come a long way: instead of being feared as propaganda that would provoke social reform or trashed as smut, it was a means of recognising Shaw's vitality and his legacy to British and world theatre.

Yet even in surprising quarters it was still regarded as an agent of immorality. The Comédie Française, which in the nineteenth century had brought courtesan plays to Britain, banned *Mrs Warren's Profession* in February 1955. While it was in rehearsals, board members reviewed the script and decided against it, calling it 'amoral', 'boring' and 'unsuitable for presentation at the French national theatre'.[109] The cast was unequivocally displeased at this 'unprecedented turn of events'.[110] The play had already had productions in Paris, in 1912 and 1921,[111] which further attests to the bizarre nature of the decision. One is tempted to think that Shaw was chuckling somewhere.

When not banned, productions of *Mrs Warren's Profession* have been formative in the development of new theatrical modes abroad. The play's performance at the New Shanghai Theatre in October 1920, for example, is viewed by scholars as the first meaningful staging of a Western realist play in China.[112] At this time, Shaw and Ibsen were considered important figures for Chinese reformers who sought to overturn firmly entrenched traditions. However, the conservative society was not ready for such change and the production was considered a failure. Ticket sales were abysmal, the show drawing in only a bit more than 20 per cent of what the theatre had made for a recent run of *Live Buddha Ji Gong*, a popular comedy. Most of the people who ventured to attend wished that they had not: several women walked out of the theatre as Mrs Warren revealed her past to Vivie in the second act, and by the end of the performance three-

---

109 *The Times*, 23 February 1955.
110 *Daily Telegraph*, 23 February 1955.
111 Jean-Claude Amalric, 'The Production of Shaw's Plays in France', in Conolly and Pearson, *op. cit.*, pp. 82–3.
112 For more on this production, see Wendy Chen, 'The First Shaw Play on the Chinese Stage: The Production of *Mrs Warren's Profession* in 1921', *SHAW* 19 (1999), 99–118; and Kay Li, '*Mrs Warren's Profession* in China: Factors in Cross-Cultural Adaptations', *SHAW* 25 (2005), 201–20. Drawing upon newspaper advertisements, Li corrects the confusion over the actual dates of the performance which had been expressed in several earlier studies.

quarters of the audience had left. The poor reception was thought to be influenced not simply by the script but a variety of factors: the audience was ill-prepared for the realist style in a culture that prized more ritualistic acting; the actors themselves were not sufficiently trained to respond to the different methods the play demanded; and the media was unsupportive. The lesson learned was that Western plays could not simply be adopted but had to be adapted, revising the plot, characters, language, and customs for Chinese audiences.

From the latter half of the twentieth century, the play has appeared on stages in the London area about twice a decade: 1961 at the Richmond Theatre, 1965 at the Hampstead Theatre, 1970 at the Old Vic, 1977 at the Peacock Theatre, 1985 at the Lyttelton Theatre, 1989 at the Orange Tree Theatre, 1997 at the Richmond Theatre, 2002 at the Strand Theatre, and 2010 at the Comedy Theatre. There were also productions further afield, in 1980 at the Nottingham Playhouse, 1990 at Glasgow's Citizens Theatre, 1995 at Theatr Clwyd in North Wales, 2004 at the Cork Opera House, and 2007 at the Royal Lyceum in Edinburgh. Most of these were fairly run-of-the-mill productions. By 1970, reviewers could reflect in amazement 'that such an immensely righteous sermon, so witty and light-handedly cogent would ever possibly have been considered an offence against public decency and unworthy of public showing'.[113] Theatre programmes around this time had ceased to be simple paper flyers listing cast members, and instead included glossy features running to several pages with lengthy histories of prostitution and gendered politics. In many ways, these in-house essays have guided critical reception, most reviewers now situating audiences in the play's socio-political context before they consider the productions for the acting, directing, costumes, and set design. *Mrs Warren's Profession* has become for many people a play that is important for better understanding both the society of *fin-de-siècle* England and the more radical efforts of artists and playwrights. Yet the constant revivals also suggest that there is something more immediate about the play.

A number of these recent productions have created some fuss, though rather tame by the turbulent historical standards of the play's early performance history. The National Theatre's production at the Lyttelton Theatre in 1985, for one, was perhaps more notable for how it came about as opposed to anything inherent in the show itself. Originally, Shaw's play was not scheduled as a part of the season. Joan Plowright was to star as Phoebe Rice in John Osborne's *The Entertainer*, but Osborne publicly came out against her and sabotaged the production. This was

113 *Globe*, 31 December 1970.

rather curious as Plowright had acted alongside her future husband Laurence Olivier as Jean Rice (Phoebe's step-daughter) in the original London run in 1957 and the film version of the play in 1960. Sir Peter Hall, the director of the National Theatre, reacted by casting Plowright as the title character in *Mrs Warren's Profession*.[114] Given Osborne's stated dislike of Shaw, the choice must have also been a way of getting a measure of revenge. The critics, though, were divided over Plowright's acting, some of them perhaps anticipating a more powerful performance considering that the play was selected expressly for her. Instead, Jessica Turner, a relative ingénue, garnered many of the accolades for her portrayal of Vivie.

The 2002 production at the Strand Theatre similarly attempted to capitalise on star power. This time Hall directed Brenda Blethyn as Kitty and his daughter Rebecca Hall, who had appropriately just left Cambridge University without taking a degree, as Vivie. Critical reception of the acting was largely mixed, again perhaps stemming from high expectations unmet, although for her role Hall received the Ian Charleson Award for the best classical stage performance in Britain by an actor under thirty. In 2010, Felicity Kendall drew much of the attention for her portrayal of Kitty Warren, a casting decision which ran against type for an actress who is better known for lighter material. These recent London productions bear out Shaw's belief that *Mrs Warren's Profession* is a star-making, if not also a star-attracting, vehicle. Yet now that performing as an unrepentant prostitute no longer bears the same stigma that it once did, the choice for an actress to accept the part might appear more daring than it actually is, especially given the play's acceptance in the canon of modern literature.

The 2004 production at the Cork Opera House took matters in another direction by setting the play in the 1950s. However, in doing so its thrust was completely changed. Vivie's stance is not so rebellious in the wake of the New Woman, the suffragettes, and the Bright Young Things as it is when it is laying the ground for such movements. More worryingly, as one reviewer noted, it sheds a different light on Kitty, as her brothel proprietorship on the Continent, particularly in Vienna but also in Ostend, Brussels, and Budapest, would have meant that she would have had to negotiate with Hitler's Nazis.[115] Too many disturbing questions are thus raised as for whom exactly she was catering and, if she drew her girls from the poorest and most degraded quarters of society, what sort of women would have been in her employ. One would also have to

114 *London Standard*, 29 July 1985.
115 *Irish Times*, 12 August 2004.

imagine that her days in Budapest as an arch-capitalist would have been rather improbable in Communist Hungary.

As might be expected, the play has been a fairly regular part of the repertoire of the Shaw Festival in Niagara-on-the-Lake, Canada. Although the festival was begun in 1962, it was not until its fifteenth season, in 1976, that a production of Mrs Warren's Profession was mounted, an oversight that does not appear so incredible when one considers that it only first tackled Saint Joan in 1981. Further productions followed in 1990, 1997, and most recently in 2008. All were generally well received by the press. Polish director Tadeusz Bradecki's 1997 production was particularly acclaimed for its inclusion of music-hall numbers opening the show and between acts. This staging provocatively juxta- posed Shaw's drama with the popular entertainment that dominated British theatre when he wrote it, effectively allowing the audience to grasp the revolutionary aspect of his craft.

Mrs Warren's Profession has also remained popular on the world's stages. As it played at the Comedy Theatre in London's West End, there were several North American revivals running more or less concurrently: in 2010 there were productions at the Shakespeare Theatre Company in Washington, DC, at the California Shakespeare Theater, and on Broad- way at the American Airlines Theatre, where the renowned Cherry Jones turned in a riveting performance as Kitty. And a year earlier, the play had a well-received run at Houston's Alley Theatre. A part of this con- temporary interest might very well be linked to what is referred to as 'museum theatre': shows that remain locked in their particular context allowing the audience to undertake a night of historical tourism. However, one of the most common refrains from critics in recent years has been the depressing contemporaneity of the piece. Since 1980 there has been much mention, for example, of the play's condemnation of neo-conservative values. Writing of the 1989 production at the Orange Tree Theatre, Michael Billington argued that the play 'emerges as the most devastating indictment of the Thatcherite ethos to be seen on the London stage', a compliment he extended to include David Hare's The Secret Rapture (1988).[116] In 2002, Benedict Nightingale likewise sug- gested to readers that 'the play raises questions that are still current today, not just about economic morality, but about the impact of environment and the boundaries of personal responsibility. There's a moment when Vivie seems to be putting the Thatcherite case against her mother's Marxist fatalism.'[117]

116 Guardian, 11 September 1989.
117 The Times, 12 October 2002.

Critics have broadened their concern to render predatory capitalism as culpable despite its being sexed up with the gloss of international finance and globalisation. In 1985, one reviewer warned audiences that 'if you dismiss as outdated Shaw's indictment of society for having financial stakes in various moral cesspools, you need only think of how many high street banks, pension funds, etc. have investments in South Africa, the Soviet Union, or the armaments trade'.[118] 'How relevant to our own day is *Mrs Warren's Profession*?' another reviewer asked in 2010. 'Well, the women in the audience may not have purchased their clothing with brothel rents, but how much of it was made in China, where women are treated worse than the prostitutes from which the title character makes her money?'[119] Indeed, we are all still as implicated in and responsible for prostitution today as audiences were at the time that Shaw wrote his play.

Note on Money

It is notoriously difficult to convert money from one period of time into another. Doing so even as I write this might not be wise, as inflation, deflation, economic crises, and fluctuations in the market values of commercial goods and services can render the most precise calculations obsolete tomorrow. However, we can compare the various salaries and yearly stipends the characters receive to have some idea of the difference in lifestyles each would have.

In tying for third place in the mathematical examinations, Vivie receives £50 (I.153), though she complains that she would not do it again unless she were paid £200 (I.170–1). £50 is also the amount that the young Samuel Gardner offered Kitty Warren to get his letters back, but the earlier manuscript has him offer her £500 (I.687). Some years earlier, Mrs Warren made only four shillings per week, or £10.40 per year, plus her board, working fourteen-hour days as a barmaid, which, she says, 'was considered a great promotion' from her former employment as a scullery maid (II.718–21). Mrs Warren's one sister was paid nine shillings per week, or £23.40 a year, working twelve-hour days in an environment so toxic that it killed her (II.696–9). Her other sister was married to a man who had a decent position as a government labourer. The sole breadwinner in the family, he was responsible for keeping his wife and three children on 18 shillings per week (II. 699–703), or £46.60 per year. Frank's lament that even if his father were to cut his sisters off he would have *only* £400 per year on which to live sheds as much light on his expensive habits as it does on the expectations that society has on individuals to spend

118 *Sunday Times*, 13 October 1985.
119 *Independent*, 30 March 2010.

money as a putative sign of their self-worth (IV.422–4). Given these figures, the £40,000 that Crofts has invested in the chain of brothels is a staggering sum (III.421–2). Considering that he garners 35 per cent in the worst of times (III.434–5), he takes in at least £14,000 per year, or enough for 300 workers in the Deptford dockyards.

Note on the Text

The copy-text for the play is Constable's *Plays Unpleasant* (1931), the standard edition and the last authoritative version that Shaw published in his lifetime. Three other sources were consulted in the production of the definitive text: *The Bodley Head Bernard Shaw: Collected Plays with their Prefaces*, Volume I (1970), and *Plays Unpleasant* (Penguin, 2000), both of which were edited by Dan H. Laurence; and L.W. Conolly's *Mrs Warren's Profession* (Broadview, 2005). These later editions were helpful in confirming the few errors that I found in Shaw's work, which I have silently corrected.

In the annotations, I have indicated revisions that Shaw made to *Mrs Warren's Profession* over the years. A facsimile of the first script of the play was published by Garland in 1981. This is a copy of manuscripts 50598 A, 50598 B, and 50598 C in the British Library. I have found it helpful to consult the originals to clarify some parts where the reproduction is not entirely legible (especially the case in instances where Shaw crossed out material). I have also noted the ways in which Shaw expurgated and amended his text in the version that was licensed by the Lord Chamberlain in 1898. This material is taken from manuscript 53654 H, again located in the British Library. After the full text was finally licensed for the 1925 production in Birmingham, Shaw submitted a slightly altered script to the Lord Chamberlain. This version, the British Library's manuscript 66402 G, has a few interesting revisions that I have noted. The first published text of *Plays Unpleasant* (Grant Richards, 1898) was refined in some ways for the 1931 Constable edition; most of these changes are written in Shaw's hand in manuscript 50599, also of the British Library. I have further indicated Shaw's directions to the actors as they rehearsed the play in 1926 at the Strand Theatre. These insights are kept in his notebook, manuscript 50644 in the British Library. I have only shown variations where I feel that they add something to our understanding of *Mrs Warren's Profession*, the context in which it was written or submitted, and Shaw's changing vision of the play.

Shaw had idiosyncrasies in terms of punctuation and spelling that I have maintained, so some explanation is warranted in the event that readers believe typographical errors have crept into the text. He considered the apostrophe unsightly and thus refrained from using it in contractions except for in cases where it would cause some confusion, such as *he'll*, *it's*, *we're*. However, he more regularly employed apostrophes in the earliest manuscripts; when these documents are cited, apostrophes are kept as they appear in the original. Although an Irishman living in London, Shaw preferred the American form of dropping the 'u' in words ending in -*our*, such as *honor*. Despite these apparent modernisations, he also held fast to some archaic spellings, notably preferring *shew* to *show*.

Shaw signified emphasis in dialogue by spacing his words and, at times, using a slightly larger font, so that *has* appeared as h a s. However, this manner of emphasising words is particularly difficult to detect in some of the editions. To facilitate reading and to minimise the risk of missing these directions, I have changed all emphases to italics. I have also italicised all titles where they are mentioned by other writers in my intro-duction and the appendices to remain consistent throughout the edition. These modifications are in keeping with the other editions of Shaw's plays that have appeared in the New Mermaids series.

FURTHER READING

Unless otherwise noted, the place of publication is London.

Editions
Bernard Shaw, *The Bodley Head Bernard Shaw: Collected Plays with their Prefaces*, 7 vols. (1970–4)

——————, *Mrs Warren's Profession*, ed. L.W. Conolly (Peterborough, ON, 2005)

——————, *Mrs Warren's Profession: A Facsimile of the Holograph Manuscript*, ed. Margot Peters (New York, 1981)

——————, *Plays Unpleasant* (1898)

——————, *Plays Unpleasant* (1931)

——————, *Plays Unpleasant*, ed. Dan H. Laurence (2000)

Correspondence, Diaries, and Writings
Bernard Shaw, *Collected Letters*, ed. Dan H. Laurence, 4 vols. (1965–88)

——————, *The Diaries, 1885–1897*, ed. Stanley Weintraub, 2 vols. (University Park, PA, 1986)

——————, *The Drama Observed*, ed. Bernard F. Dukore, 4 vols. (University Park, PA, 1993)

——————, *Shaw and Ibsen: Bernard Shaw's The Quintessence of Ibsenism and Related Writings*, ed. J.L. Wisenthal (Toronto, 1979)

Biography
A.M. Gibbs, *Bernard Shaw: A Life* (Gainesville, FL, 2005)

Michael Holroyd, *Bernard Shaw*, 4 vols. (1990–3)

Criticism and Stage History
John Allett, '*Mrs Warren's Profession* and the Politics of Prostitution', *SHAW* 19 (1999), 23–39

Charles A. Berst, *Bernard Shaw and the Art of Drama* (Urbana, IL, 1973)

Geoffrey Bullough, 'Literary Relations of Shaw's Mrs Warren', *Philological Quarterly* 41.1 (1962), 339–58

Charles A. Carpenter, *Bernard Shaw and the Art of Destroying Ideals: The Early Plays* (Madison, WI, 1969)

Wendy Chen, 'The First Shaw Play on the Chinese Stage: The Production of *Mrs Warren's Profession* in 1921', *SHAW* 19 (1999), 99–118

L.W. Conolly, '"Mrs Warren's Profession" and the Lord Chamberlain', *SHAW* 24 (2004), 46–95

————— , 'Who Was Phillipa Summers? Reflections on Vivie Warren's Cambridge', *SHAW* 25 (2005), 89–95

Petra Dierkes-Thrun, 'Incest and the Trafficking of Women in *Mrs Warren's Profession*: "It Runs in the Family"', *English Literature in Transition, 1880–1920* 49.3 (2006), 293–310

William A. Dolid, 'Vivie Warren and the Tripos', *The Shaw Review* 23.2 (1980), 52–6

Bernard F. Dukore, *Money and Politics in Ibsen, Shaw, and Brecht* (Columbia, MO, 1980)

Sos Eltis, 'The Fallen Woman on Stage: Maidens, Magdalens, and the Emancipated Female', in *The Cambridge Companion to Victorian and Edwardian Theatre*, ed. Kerry Powell (Cambridge, 2004), 222–36

T.F. Evans, ed., *Shaw: The Critical Heritage* (1976)

James Fisher, 'Edy Craig and the Pioneer Players' Production of "Mrs Warren's Profession"', *SHAW* 15 (1995), 37–56

J. Ellen Gainor, *Shaw's Daughters: Dramatic and Narrative Constructions of Gender* (Ann Arbor, MI, 1991)

Emma Goldman, *The Social Significance of Modern Drama* (Boston, 1914)

Nicholas Grene, *Bernard Shaw: A Critical View* (Basingstoke, 1984)

Christopher Innes, ed., *The Cambridge Companion to Bernard Shaw* (Cambridge, 1998)

Betty Freeman Johnson, 'Shelley's *Cenci* and *Mrs Warren's Profession*', *The Shaw Review* 15.1 (1972), 26–34

Brad Kent, 'Eighteenth-Century Literary Precursors of *Mrs. Warren's Profession*', *University of Toronto Quarterly* 81.2 (2012), 187–207

Kay Li, '*Mrs Warren's Profession* in China: Factors in Cross-Cultural Adaptations', *SHAW* 25 (2005), 201–20

Celia Marshik, *British Modernism and Censorship* (Cambridge, 2006)

Martin Meisel, *Shaw and the Nineteenth-Century Theater* (Princeton, NJ, 1963)

Steve Nicholson, *The Censorship of British Drama, 1900–1968, Volume One: 1900–1932* (Exeter, 2003)

Bernice Schrank, 'Mrs Erlynne, Mrs Warren and the Nineteenth-Century Stage Stereotype of the Fallen Woman', in *The Internationalism of Irish Literature and Drama* (Gerrards Cross, 1992), 134–45

Dominic Shellard and Steve Nicholson with Miriam Handley, *The Lord Chamberlain Regrets: A History of British Theatre Censorship* (2005).

Tony Jason Stafford, '*Mrs Warren's Profession*: In the Garden of Respectability', *SHAW* 2 (1982), 3–11

Rodelle Weintraub, ed., *Fabian Feminist: Bernard Shaw and Woman* (University Park, PA, 1977)

BERNARD SHAW

MRS WARREN'S PROFESSION

A Play

Shaw's original subtitle read: 'A tragic variation on the theme of *Cashel Byron's Profession In Four Acts*' (MS). *Cashel Byron's Profession* (1883), about a boxer, is one of Shaw's novels. The 1902 Grant Richards edition of *Mrs Warren's Profession* included the subtitle 'A Play in Four Acts', and an epigram taken from a passage of William Blake's poem 'Auguries of Innocence': 'The harlot's cry from street to street / Shall weave Old England's winding sheet.'

THE PERSONS OF THE PLAY

[New Lyric Club, London, 5 January 1902]

VIVIE WARREN .... *Madge McIntosh*
PRAED .... *Julius Knight*
MRS KITTY WARREN .... *Fanny Brough*
SIR GEORGE CROFTS .... *Charles Goodheart*
FRANK GARDNER .... *Harley Granville Barker*
THE REVEREND SAMUEL GARDNER .... *Cosmo Stuart*

The Scenes of the Play

Act I   *The Garden of Vivie Warren's Holiday Cottage at Haslemere*
Act II   *Inside the Cottage*
Act III *The Rectory Garden*
Act IV   *Honoria Fraser's Chambers in Chancery Lane*

ACT I

Summer afternoon in a cottage garden on the eastern slope of a hill a
little south of Haslemere in Surrey. Looking up the hill, the cottage is
seen in the left hand corner of the garden, with its thatched roof and
porch, and a large latticed window to the left of the porch. A paling
completely shuts in the garden, except for a gate on the right. The   5
common rises uphill beyond the paling to the sky line. Some folded
canvas garden chairs are leaning against the side bench in the porch.
A lady's bicycle is propped against the wall, under the window. A little
to the right of the porch a hammock is slung from two posts. A big
canvas umbrella, stuck in the ground, keeps the sun off the hammock,   10
in which a young lady lies reading and making notes, her head
towards the cottage and her feet towards the gate. In front of the ham-
mock, and within reach of her hand, is a common kitchen chair, with
a pile of serious-looking books and a supply of writing paper on it.

A gentleman walking on the common comes into sight from behind   15
the cottage. He is hardly past middle age, with something of the artist
about him, unconventionally but carefully dressed, and clean-shaven
except for a moustache, with an eager susceptible face and very
amiable and considerate manners. He has silky black hair, with
waves of grey and white in it. His eyebrows are white, his moustache   20
black. He seems not certain of his way. He looks over the paling; takes
stock of the place; and sees the young lady.

THE GENTLEMAN [*taking off his hat*]
  I beg your pardon. Can you direct me to Hindhead View – Mrs
  Alison's?   25

2 *Haslemere in Surrey* Haslemere is a small town located in the southwest corner of
   Surrey, a county that borders London to the southwest. Shaw later honeymooned in
   the area with Charlotte in the summer of 1898 (Holroyd II, pp. 3–8). Shaw begins
   his reversal of *The Second Mrs Tanqueray* in the play's setting: while Pinero's first act
   is set in London and the following three acts in Surrey, Shaw sets the first three acts
   of his play in Surrey and the last act in London.
4 *of the porch* Shaw originally added: 'Farther back a little wing is built out, making an
   angle with the right side wall' (GR). The cottage became more modest in the revisions.
15–21 'Junius Praed: A man hardly past middle age, architect by profession. Very amiable
   and considerate manners. Pleasant face, silky black hair with waves of grey – almost
   white – in it. White eyebrows, black moustache. A little touchy in temper' (MS).
   Shaw does not include his given name in further versions of the play. All characters
   are described in MS before the text.
24 *Hindhead View* Mrs Alison's cottage is probably named for its perspective of
   Hindhead, a local hill, which also lends its name to the nearby village.

3

THE YOUNG LADY [*glancing up from her book*]

This is Mrs Alison's. [*She resumes her work*]

THE GENTLEMAN

Indeed! Perhaps – may I ask are you Miss Vivie Warren?

THE YOUNG LADY [*sharply, as she turns on her elbow to get a good*   30
look at him]

Yes.

THE GENTLEMAN [*daunted and conciliatory*]

I'm afraid I appear intrusive. My name is Praed. [VIVIE *at once*
throws her books upon the chair, and gets out of the hammock]   35
Oh, pray dont let me disturb you.

VIVIE [*striding to the gate and opening it for him*]

Come in, Mr Praed. [*He comes in*] Glad to see you. [*She proffers*
her hand and takes his with a resolute and hearty grip. She is an
attractive specimen of the sensible, able, highly-educated young   40
middle-class Englishwoman. Age 22. Prompt, strong, confident,
self-possessed. Plain business-like dress, but not dowdy. She wears
a chatelaine at her belt, with a fountain pen and a paper knife
among its pendants]

PRAED   45

Very kind of you indeed, Miss Warren. [*She shuts the gate with*
a vigorous slam. He passes in to the middle of the garden, exer-
cising his fingers, which are slightly numbed by her greeting] Has
your mother arrived?

VIVIE [*quickly, evidently scenting aggression*]   50

Is she coming?

PRAED [*surprised*]

Didnt you expect us?

VIVIE

No.   55

---

34   *Praed* The relevance of Praed's name has a few explanations. It has been viewed as
an anagram of 'padre', thereby suggesting that Shaw was improbably alluding to him
as Vivie's father, and as a reference to Praed Street, a thoroughfare to the north of
Hyde Park, London. 'Praedial', from the Latin *praedialis*, refers to something that is
agrarian or rural. For an analysis of characters' names and their links to the earth,
see Tony Jason Stafford, '*Mrs Warren's Profession*: In the Garden of Respectability',
SHAW 2 (1982), 3–11. L.W. Conolly also suggests that it might have been an allusion
to Winthrop Mackworth Praed (1802–39), a Cambridge-educated politician and
poet. L.W. Conolly, 'Introduction', in *Mrs Warren's Profession* by Bernard Shaw
(Peterborough: Broadview Press, 2005), p. 88.

43   *chatelaine* decorative ornament normally fastened on a belt. It has hooks from which
one can hang a variety of practical articles.

46–8   s.d.: 'glancing dubiously at his hand as he follows her' (MS)

PRAED

Now, goodness me, I hope Ive not mistaken the day. That would
be just like me, you know. Your mother arranged that she was
to come down from London and that I was to come over from
Horsham to be introduced to you.   60

VIVIE [*not at all pleased*]

Did she? Hm! My mother has rather a trick of taking me by
surprise – to see how I behave myself when she's away, I
suppose. I fancy I shall take my mother very much by surprise
one of these days, if she makes arrangements that concern me   65
without consulting me beforehand. She hasnt come.

PRAED [*embarrassed*]

I'm really very sorry.

VIVIE [*throwing off her displeasure*]

It's not your fault, Mr Praed, is it? And I'm very glad youve   70
come. You are the only one of my mother's friends I have ever
asked her to bring to see me.

PRAED [*relieved and delighted*]

Oh, now this is really very good of you, Miss Warren!

VIVIE   75

Will you come indoors; or would you rather sit out here and
talk?

PRAED

It will be nicer out here, dont you think?

VIVIE   80

Then I'll go and get you a chair. [*She goes to the porch for a
garden chair*]

PRAED [*following her*]

Oh, pray, pray! Allow me. [*He lays hands on the chair*]

VIVIE [*letting him take it*]   85

Take care of your fingers: theyre rather dodgy things, those
chairs. [*She goes across to the chair with the books on it; pitches
them into the hammock; and brings the chair forward with one
swing*]

---

60   *Horsham* a market town in West Sussex, just to the south of Surrey

62   *of taking* 'of purposely taking' (MS)

64   Shaw directs: 'I fancy I shall take my mother by surprise – not my <u>mother</u>' (RN).

70–1   *youve come* GR adds: 'believe me'.

79   'Indoors! – on a day like this!' (MS)

86   *dodgy* tricky. The *Oxford English Dictionary* offers this phrase from the play to
      illustrate the term.

PRAED [*who has just unfolded his chair*]   90

Oh, now do let me take that hard chair. I like hard chairs.

VIVIE

So do I. Sit down, Mr Praed. [*This invitation she gives with genial peremptoriness, his anxiety to please her clearly striking her as a sign of weakness of character on his part. But he does not immediately*   95
obey]

PRAED

By the way, though, hadnt we better go to the station to meet your mother?

VIVIE [*coolly*]   100

Why? She knows the way.

PRAED [*disconcerted*]

Er – I suppose she does. [*He sits down*]

VIVIE

Do you know, you are just like what I expected. I hope you are   105
disposed to be friends with me.

PRAED [*again beaming*]

Thank you, my *dear* Miss Warren: thank you. Dear me! I'm so
glad your mother hasnt spoilt you!

VIVIE   110

How?

PRAED

Well, in making you too conventional. You know, my dear Miss
Warren, I am a born anarchist. I hate authority. It spoils the
relations between parent and child: even between mother and   115
daughter. Now I was always afraid that your mother would
strain her authority to make you very conventional. It's such a
relief to find that she hasnt.

VIVIE

Oh! have I been behaving unconventionally?   120

---

94   *peremptoriness* decisiveness
95–6 *But he does not immediately obey* This line does not appear in GR.
101–5 *knows the way . . . Do you know* Praed does not respond in GR. Instead, Shaw
      includes the s.d.: '*Praed hesitates, and then sits down in the garden chair, rather*
      disconcerted.'
104   MS reads:
          VIVIE
          You dont seem comfortable. Shall I let the chair down another notch?
          PRAED
          Not at all – perfectly comfortable, I assure you. Ahem!
111   'How? Spoiled in what way?' (MS)

PRAED

Oh no: oh dear no. At least not conventionally unconventionally, you understand. [*She nods and sits down. He goes on, with a cordial outburst*] But it was so charming of you to say that you were disposed to be friends with me! You modern   125
young ladies are splendid: perfectly splendid!

VIVIE [*dubiously*]

Eh? [*watching him with dawning disappointment as to the quality of his brains and character*]

PRAED   130

When I was your age, young men and women were afraid of each other: there was no good fellowship. Nothing real. Only gallantry copied out of novels, and as vulgar and affected as it could be. Maidenly reserve! gentlemanly chivalry! always saying no when you meant yes! simple purgatory for shy and sincere   135
souls.

VIVIE

Yes, I imagine there must have been a frightful waste of time. Especially women's time.

PRAED   140

Oh, waste of life, waste of everything. But things are improving. Do you know, I have been in a positive state of excitement about meeting you ever since your magnificent achievements at Cambridge: a thing unheard of in my day. It was perfectly splendid, your tieing with the third wrangler. Just the right   145
place, you know. The first wrangler is always a dreamy, morbid fellow, in whom the thing is pushed to the length of a disease.

VIVIE

It doesnt pay. I wouldnt do it again for the same money.

---

128   'I said it with an object Mr Praed. I want to talk to you confidentially – to ask you some questions about my mother. I want to break the ice between us thoroughly before my mother comes' (MS). Shaw struck this out and replaced it with the published line.

144   *Cambridge* Cambridge University was founded circa 1209 by scholars fleeing riots at Oxford University. It is located in the city of Cambridge, 80 kilometres north of London.

144–90   *It was perfectly splendid . . . the tripos.* The Tripos is a sequence of examinations at Cambridge, so named after the three-legged stool upon which the examiner sat in medieval times. A wrangler was one who had finished in the first class. The first, or senior, wrangler was therefore the top performer in the examinations. See William A. Dolid, 'Vivie Warren and the Tripos', *The Shaw Review* 23.2 (1980), 52–6.

PRAED [*aghast*]   150

The same money!

VIVIE

I did it for £50.

PRAED

Fifty pounds!   155

VIVIE

Yes. Fifty pounds. Perhaps you dont know how it was. Mrs
Latham, my tutor at Newnham, told my mother that I could
distinguish myself in the mathematical tripos if I went in for it
in earnest. The papers were full just then of Phillipa Summers   160
beating the senior wrangler. You remember about it, of course.

PRAED [*shakes his head energetically*]

!!!

VIVIE

Well anyhow she did; and nothing would please my mother but   165
that I should do the same thing. I said flatly it was not worth
my while to face the grind since I was not going in for teaching;
but I offered to try for fourth wrangler or thereabouts for £50.
She closed with me at that, after a little grumbling; and I was
better than my bargain. But I wouldnt do it again for that. £200   170
would have been nearer the mark.

PRAED [*much damped*]

Lord bless me! Thats a very practical way of looking at it.

---

150   *aghast* s.d.: 'taken aback' (MS)
155–7   *Fifty pounds! . . . Yes. Fifty pounds* This exchange repeating the amount Vivie is paid
       to excel in her studies does not appear in GR.
158   *Newnham* Newnham College was founded in 1871 to provide university-level
       education for women. It was the second college for women to be established at
       Cambridge.
160   *Phillipa Summers* This is most probably a reference to Philippa Fawcett, who in 1890
       was placed higher than the senior wrangler in the mathematical Tripos. See L.W.
       Conolly, 'Who Was Phillippa Summers? Reflections on Vivie Warren's Cambridge',
       SHAW 25 (2005), 89–95. Philippa Fawcett's mother, Millicent Fawcett (1847–1929),
       was the co-founder of Newnham College and a prominent suffragette.
161–5   *of course . . . she did* These lines do not appear in GR.
173   Before Shaw struck it out, this line reads in MS as:

    PRAED

       Well, I suppose thats right. Its modern. (*brightening up*) At all events, I'm glad
       you didnt take to mathematics because you liked them. One instinctively turns
       away from them to Art – to the beauty and <u>romance</u> of life. After all, a third
       wranglership must imply a great deal of culture of –'

    VIVIE (*shaking her head*)

       No, thanks. I've no turn that way.

VIVIE

Did you expect to find me an unpractical person?   175

PRAED

But surely it's practical to consider not only the work these honors cost, but also the culture they bring.

VIVIE

Culture! My dear Mr Praed: do you know what the mathem-   180
atical tripos means? It means grind, grind, grind for six to eight hours a day at mathematics, and nothing but mathematics. I'm supposed to know something about science; but I know noth-ing except the mathematics it involves. I can make calculations for engineers, electricians, insurance companies, and so on; but   185
I know next to nothing about engineering or electricity or insurance. I dont even know arithmetic well. Outside mathem-atics, lawn-tennis, eating, sleeping, cycling, and walking, I'm a more ignorant barbarian than any woman could possibly be who hadnt gone in for the tripos.   190

PRAED [revolted]

What a monstrous, wicked, rascally system! I knew it! I felt at once that it meant destroying all that makes womanhood beautiful.

VIVIE   195

I dont object to it on that score in the least. I shall turn it to very good account, I assure you.

PRAED

Pooh! In what way?

VIVIE   200

I shall set up chambers in the City, and work at actuarial calculations and conveyancing. Under cover of that I shall do some law, with one eye on the Stock Exchange all the time. Ive come down here by myself to read law: not for a holiday, as my mother imagines. I hate holidays.   205

177   Shaw has Praed begin by reassuring Vivie 'No, no' in GR.
180–90 Shaw directs: 'must move around in the maths speech' (RN).
201   Shaw suggests that the actress begin to smoke here (RN).
201–2 *actuarial calculations and conveyancing* An actuary has come to mean one who
       assesses risks by analysing statistical data, but historically an actuary has also referred
       to the senior official in a savings bank who handles the deposits and the accountant
       of a company. Conveyancing is the drawing up of deeds for the transference of
       property.
205   *I hate holidays* Shaw directs: 'pick it out more' (RN).

PRAED

You make my blood run cold. Are you to have no romance, no beauty in your life?

VIVIE

I dont care for either, I assure you.   210

PRAED

You cant mean that.

VIVIE

Oh yes I do. I like working and getting paid for it. When I'm tired of working, I like a comfortable chair, a cigar, a little   215 whisky, and a novel with a good detective story in it.

PRAED [*rising in a frenzy of repudiation*]

I dont believe it. I am an artist; and I cant believe it: I refuse to believe it. It's only that you havnt discovered yet what a wonderful world art can open up to you.   220

VIVIE

Yes I have. Last May I spent six weeks in London with Honoria Fraser. Mamma thought we were doing a round of sightseeing together; but I was really at Honoria's chambers in Chancery Lane every day, working away at actuarial calculations for her,   225 and helping her as well as a greenhorn could. In the evenings we smoked and talked, and never dreamt of going out except for exercise. And I never enjoyed myself more in my life. I cleared all my expenses, and got initiated into the business without a fee into the bargain.   230

PRAED

But bless my heart and soul, Miss Warren, do you call that discovering art?

VIVIE

Wait a bit. That wasnt the beginning. I went up to town on   235 an invitation from some artistic people in Fitzjohn's Avenue: one of the girls was a Newnham chum. They took me to the National Gallery –

---

219   *It's only that* 'Ah, my dear Miss Warren' (GR)

224–5   *Chancery Lane* runs north from Fleet Street, close to the law courts and legal district of central London. Chancery is a division of the High Court of Justice.

226   *greenhorn* novice in a trade

236   *Fitzjohn's Avenue* A major thoroughfare to the north of central London, south of Hampstead Heath. It has long been a fashionable and expensive place to live, though it is often associated with a paradoxical liberalism in its politics.

238   *National Gallery* Founded in 1824, at its present location in Trafalgar Square since 1838. The National Gallery houses Great Britain's national collection of European paintings.

PRAED [*approving*]

    Ah!! [*He sits down, much relieved*]   240

VIVIE [*continuing*]

    – to the Opera –

PRAED [*still more pleased*]

    Good!

VIVIE   245

    – and to a concert where the band played all the evening:
Beethoven and Wagner and so on. I wouldnt go through that
experience again for anything you could offer me. I held out for
civility's sake until the third day; and then I said, plump out,
that I couldnt stand any more of it, and went off to Chancery   250
Lane. Now you know the sort of perfectly splendid modern
young lady I am. How do you think I shall get on with my
mother?

PRAED [*startled*]

    Well, I hope – er –   255

VIVIE

    It's not so much what you hope as what you believe, that I want
to know.

PRAED

    Well, frankly, I am afraid your mother will be a little   260
disappointed. Not from any shortcoming on your part, you
know: I dont mean that. But you are so different from her ideal.

239–44   Praed's reactions do not appear in GR; instead, Vivie's speech is uninterrupted by either his dialogue or s.d.

   242   *Opera* The Royal Opera House, located in Covent Garden, London. The original theatre was built in 1732. Twice burnt down, the current structure dates from 1858.

   247   *Beethoven and Wagner* Ludwig van Beethoven (1770–1827) and Wilhelm Richard Wagner (1813–83) were German composers. Shaw's characters in *Heartbreak House* believe they hear Beethoven as the zeppelins fly overhead on a bombing mission. He published *The Perfect Wagnerite*, a study of Wagner's *Ring* cycle, in 1898.

247–8   *I wouldnt go through that experience* Shaw directs: 'pick it out' (RN).

   251   *Lane* MS adds s.d.: 'she settles herself comfortably in her chair & takes out a cigar case.' Praed's response is struck out: 'No, no, Miss Warren, please. Excuse me for interrupting you, but if you must shatter my illusions, shatter them a little more gradually. It's a positive shock to the system of a man like me, you know. (She laughs heartily at him) Ah! Thats better so long as you can laugh with real enjoyment. I forgive you everything. I hope theres nothing else about Chancery Lane.' Shaw originally wrote 'Dont laugh at me' following Vivie's laughter.

251–2   *perfectly . . . lady* 'person' (MS)

   259   s.d.: 'gravely' (MS)

VIVIE

Her what?!

PRAED   265

Her ideal.

VIVIE

Do you mean her ideal of ME?

PRAED

Yes.   270

VIVIE

What on earth is it like?

PRAED

Well, you must have observed, Miss Warren, that people who
are dissatisfied with their own bringing-up generally think that   275
the world would be all right if everybody were to be brought up
quite differently. Now your mother's life has been – er – I
suppose you know –

VIVIE

Dont suppose anything, Mr Praed. I hardly know my mother.   280
Since I was a child I have lived in England, at school or college,
or with people paid to take charge of me. I have been boarded
out all my life. My mother has lived in Brussels or Vienna and
never let me go to her. I only see her when she visits England
for a few days. I dont complain: it's been very pleasant; for   285
people have been very good to me; and there has always been
plenty of money to make things smooth. But dont imagine I
know anything about my mother. I know far less than you do.

PRAED [*very ill at ease*]

In that case – [*He stops, quite at a loss. Then, with a forced*   290
attempt at gaiety] But what nonsense we are talking! Of course
you and your mother will get on capitally. [*He rises, and looks*
abroad at the view] What a charming little place you have here!

263–70 This exchange does not appear in GR.
   272 'What is her ideal like?' (GR)
   279 s.d.: 'very firm and businesslike' (MS)
   280 'I know nothing. [*Praed is appalled. His consternation grows as she continues*]. Thats
        exactly my difficulty. You forget, Mr Praed, that I hardly know my mother' (GR).
   289 'much embarassed [*sic*]' (MS)
   291 *attempt at gaiety* 'burst of bonhomie' (MS)

VIVIE [*unmoved*]

Rather a violent change of subject, Mr Praed. Why wont my   295
mother's life bear being talked about?

PRAED

Oh, you really mustnt say that. Isnt it natural that I should have
a certain delicacy in talking to my old friend's daughter about
her behind her back? You and she will have plenty of oppor-   300
tunity of talking about it when she comes.

VIVIE

No: *she* wont talk about it either. [*Rising*] However, I daresay
you have good reasons for telling me nothing. Only, mind this,
Mr Praed. I expect there will be a battle royal when my mother   305
hears of my Chancery Lane project.

PRAED [*ruefully*]

I'm afraid there will.

VIVIE

Well, I shall win, because I want nothing but my fare to London   310
to start there to-morrow earning my own living by devilling for
Honoria. Besides, I have no mysteries to keep up; and it seems
she has. I shall use that advantage over her if necessary.

PRAED [*greatly shocked*]

Oh no! No, pray. Youd not do such a thing.   315

VIVIE

Then tell me why not.

PRAED

I really cannot. I appeal to your good feeling. [*She smiles at his
sentimentality*] Besides, you may be too bold. Your mother is   320
not to be trifled with when she's angry.

VIVIE

You cant frighten me, Mr Praed. In that month at Chancery
Lane I had opportunities of taking the measure of one or two

---

295   *Rather . . . Praed* 'If you think you are doing anything but confirming my worst
suspicions by changing the subject like that, you must take me for a much greater
fool than I hope I am' (MS). GR includes this earlier line, but Praed also adds: 'Your
worst suspicions! Oh, pray dont say that. Now dont.'

303–4   *However . . . nothing* 'However, I wont press you' (GR)

305   *expect* 'strongly suspect' (GR)

311   *devilling* doing work for another without remuneration or recognition

women *very* like my mother. You may back me to win. But if I   325
hit harder in my ignorance than I need, remember that it is you
who refuse to enlighten me. Now, let us drop the subject. [*She
takes her chair and replaces it near the hammock with the same
vigorous swing as before*]

PRAED [*taking a desperate resolution*]   330

One word, Miss Warren. I had better tell you. It's very difficult;
but –

MRS WARREN *and* SIR GEORGE CROFTS *arrive at the gate.*
MRS WARREN *is between 40 and 50, formerly pretty, showily
dressed in a brilliant hat and a gay blouse fitting tightly over her*   335
*bust and flanked by fashionable sleeves. Rather spoilt and
domineering, and decidedly vulgar, but, on the whole, a genial
and fairly presentable old blackguard of a woman.*

CROFTS *is a tall powerfully-built man of about 50, fashion-
ably dressed in the style of a young man. Nasal voice, reedier than*   340
*might be expected from his strong frame. Clean-shaven bulldog
jaws, large flat ears, and thick neck: gentlemanly combination of
the most brutal types of city man, sporting man, and man about
town.*

325   *like my mother* The sentence continues 'who came to consult Honoria' (GR).
330   'after a moment's perplexity' (MS)
333   *Mrs Warren* There is no evidence that Mrs Warren has in fact been married. Her
         name most prosaically recalls the earthen home of rabbits, rather fitting for the
         manager of brothels. The Warren is also the name of Mrs Cortelyon's estate in *The
         Second Mrs Tanqueray*. On 22 July 1950, Shaw received a letter asking him if he took
         the name from a case in 1868 in which a Mrs Warren was fined £20 for 'harbouring
         prostitutes knowingly'. Shaw responded: 'In 1868 I was only twelve years old. The
         name Warren was suggested by a famous case (Virginia Crawford v. Sir Charles
         Dilke) the most scandalous incident in which took place in Warren Street, close to
         my door in Fitzroy Square' (DLVF). Dilke was a promising politician in Gladstone's
         cabinet when in 1885 he was cited as co-respondent in Crawford's divorce as her
         lover, a fact that he strenuously denied. The evidence in the case showed that the
         charge was a fabrication, but the scandal irreparably tarnished his reputation.
333   *Sir George Crofts* The first part of his name might be drawn from the drunken Sir
         George Orreyed of *The Second Mrs Tanqueray*, who is also a baronet and has married
         beneath his station. Its potential link to St George, the patron saint of England,
         would further implicate all of England with responsibility for prostitution. The
         surname Crofts might have been lifted from the name of the lecherous and elderly
         Crofts, who pays for the opportunity to deflower and rape the young Fanny Hill in
         John Cleland's infamous prostitute narrative *Memoirs of a Woman of Pleasure*
         (1748–9). A croft is an enclosed field used for tillage.
334   *formerly pretty* GR has 'good-looking'.
338   *blackguard* one who acts in a dishonourable or contemptible way

VIVIE   345

> Here they are. [*Coming to them as they enter the garden*] How
> do, mater? Mr Praed's been here this half hour waiting for you.

MRS WARREN

> Well, if youve been waiting, Praddy, it's your own fault: I
> thought youd have had the gumption to know I was coming by   350
> the 3.10 train. Vivie: put your hat on, dear: youll get sunburnt.
> Oh, I forgot to introduce you. Sir George Crofts: my little Vivie.
>   CROFTS *advances to* VIVIE *with his most courtly manner. She*
> *nods, but makes no motion to shake hands.*

CROFTS   355

> May I shake hands with a young lady whom I have known by
> reputation very long as the daughter of one of my oldest
> friends?

VIVIE [*who has been looking him up and down sharply*]

> If you like. [*She takes his tenderly proffered hand and gives it a*   360
> *squeeze that makes him open his eyes; then turns away, and says*
> *to her mother*] Will you come in, or shall I get a couple more
> chairs? [*She goes into the porch for the chairs*]

MRS WARREN

> Well, George, what do you think of her?   365

CROFTS [*ruefully*]

> She has a powerful fist. Did you shake hands with her, Praed?

PRAED

> Yes: it will pass off presently.

CROFTS   370

> I hope so. [VIVIE *reappears with two more chairs. He hurries to*
> *her assistance*] Allow me.

MRS WARREN [*patronizingly*]

> Let Sir George help you with the chairs, dear.

VIVIE [*pitching them into his arms*]   375

> Here you are. [*She dusts her hands and turns to* MRS WARREN]
> Youd like some tea, wouldnt you?

---

347   *mater* Latin for 'mother'. Vivie flaunts her education here. The formality of the term
       also serves to distance her from Mrs Warren.
350   *gumption* a colloquial term meaning 'common sense'
353–4 'after a moment's perplexity' (MS)
373   no s.d. in MS
375   '*almost pitching them into his arms*' (GR)

MRS WARREN [*sitting in* PRAED*'s chair and fanning herself*]
  I'm dying for a drop to drink.

VIVIE   380
  I'll see about it. [*She goes into the cottage*]
      SIR GEORGE *has by this time managed to unfold a chair and
  plant it beside* MRS WARREN, *on her left. He throws the other on
  the grass and sits down, looking dejected and rather foolish, with
  the handle of his stick in his mouth.* PRAED, *still very uneasy,*   385
  fidgets about the garden on their right.

MRS WARREN [*to* PRAED, *looking at* CROFTS]
  Just look at him, Praddy: he looks cheerful, dont he? He's been
  worrying my life out these three years to have that little girl of
  mine shewn to him; and now that Ive done it, he's quite out of   390
  countenance. [*Briskly*] Come! sit up, George; and take your
  stick out of your mouth. [CROFTS *sulkily obeys*]

PRAED
  I think, you know – if you dont mind my saying so – that we
  had better get out of the habit of thinking of her as a little girl. 395
  You see she has really distinguished herself; and I'm not sure,
  from what I have seen of her, that she is not older than any of
  us.

MRS WARREN [*greatly amused*]
  Only listen to him, George! Older than any of us! Well, she *has*   400
  been stuffing you nicely with her importance.

PRAED
  But young people are particularly sensitive about being treated
  in that way.

MRS WARREN   405
  Yes; and young people have to get all that nonsense taken out of
  them, and a good deal more besides. Dont you interfere,
  Praddy: I know how to treat my own child as well as you do.
  [PRAED, *with a grave shake of his head, walks up the garden with
  his hands behind his back.* MRS WARREN *pretends to laugh, but*   410
  looks after him with perceptible concern. Then she whispers to
  CROFTS] Whats the matter with him? What does he take it like
  that for?

CROFTS [*morosely*]
  Youre afraid of Praed.   415

385–6   no s.d. for Praed (MS)
  390   *shewn* an archaic spelling of 'shown'. See the Introduction, p. xlviii.
  410   *pretends to laugh* 'laughs' (MS)

MRS WARREN

What! Me! Afraid of dear old Praddy! Why, a fly wouldnt be afraid of him.

CROFTS

Youre afraid of him.   420

MRS WARREN [*angry*]

I'll trouble you to mind your own business, and not try any of your sulks on me. I'm not afraid of *you,* anyhow. If you cant make yourself agreeable, youd better go home. [*She gets up, and, turning her back on him, finds herself face to face with* PRAED]   425 Come, Praddy, I know it was only your tender-heartedness. Youre afraid I'll bully her.

PRAED

My dear Kitty: you think I'm offended. Dont imagine that: pray dont. But you know I often notice things that escape you; and   430 though you never take my advice, you sometimes admit afterwards that you ought to have taken it.

MRS WARREN

Well, what do you notice now?

PRAED   435

Only that Vivie is a grown woman. Pray, Kitty, treat her with every respect.

MRS WARREN [*with genuine amazement*]

Respect! Treat my own daughter with respect! What next, pray!

---

423 *anyhow. If* MS has a brief exchange between these sentences:
    CROFTS
      I didnt say you were. I said you were afraid of him.
    MRS WARREN
      Its a good thing you didnt say so.

429 *Kitty* Again, the audience cannot be certain that this is her real given name. Shaw might have taken it from Kitty O'Shea, whose adulterous affair with Charles Stewart Parnell, the leader of the Irish Parliamentary Party, led to his downfall and death in 1891, and the division of the Irish nationalist movement for years to come. See the Introduction, pp. xxii–xxiii.

436–7 'Only this – that I strongly advise you – in fact, Kitty, I beg you most earnestly to remember that Vivie is a grown woman, and to treat her with every respect' (MS).

439 MS continues the exchange:
    PRAED (desperately)
      <u>Dont</u> you understand?
    MRS WARREN
      No; and I dont think you understand either. Youre coming it just a little too strong this time.

17

VIVIE [*appearing at the cottage door and calling to* MRS WARREN]   440
    Mother: will you come to my room before tea?

MRS WARREN
    Yes, dearie. [*She laughs indulgently at* PRAED'*s gravity, and pats*
    him on the cheek as she passes him on her way to the porch] Dont
    be cross, Praddy. [*She follows* VIVIE *into the cottage*]   445

CROFTS [*furtively*]
    I say, Praed.

PRAED
    Yes.

CROFTS   450
    I want to ask you a rather particular question.

PRAED
    Certainly. [*He takes* MRS WARREN'*s chair and sits close to*
    CROFTS]

CROFTS   455
    Thats right: they might hear us from the window. Look here:
    did Kitty ever tell you who that girl's father is?

PRAED
    Never.

CROFTS   460
    Have you any suspicion of who it might be?

PRAED
    None.

CROFTS [*not believing him*]
    I know, of course, that you perhaps might feel bound not to tell   465
    if she had said anything to you. But it's very awkward to be
    uncertain about it now that we shall be meeting the girl every
    day. We dont exactly know how we ought to feel towards her.

PRAED
    What difference can that make? We take her on her own merits.   470
    What does it matter who her father was?

441   Shaw directs: 'sing it out' (RN). 'Mother: will you come up to my room and take
       your bonnet off before tea?' (GR).

443–539 Shaw replaced the scene between Praed and Crofts with the following s.d.: '*She laughs*
       indulgently at Praed and pats him on the cheek as she passes him on her way to the
       porch. She follows Vivie into the cottage, Crofts accompanying her. Praed is following
       slowly when he is hailed by a young gentleman who has just appeared in the common
       & is making for the gate. He is a pleasant, pretty, smartly dressed, and entirely good-
       for-nothing young fellow, not long turned 20, with a charming voice and agreeably
       disrespectful manner. He carries a very light sporting magazine rifle' (LC1).

444–5   *Dont be cross, Praddy* This line does not appear in GR.

CROFTS [*suspiciously*]

    Then you know who he was?

PRAED [*with a touch of temper*]

    I said no just now. Did you not hear me?   475

CROFTS

    Look here, Praed. I ask you as a particular favor. If you *do* know [*movement of protest from* PRAED] – I only say, if you know, you might at least set my mind at rest about her. The fact is, I feel attracted.   480

PRAED [*sternly*]

    What do you mean?

CROFTS

    Oh, dont be alarmed: it's quite an innocent feeling. Thats what puzzles me about it. Why, for all I know, *I* might be her father.   485

PRAED

    You! Impossible!

CROFTS [*catching him up cunningly*]

    You know for certain that I'm not?

PRAED   490

    I know nothing about it, I tell you, any more than you. But really, Crofts – oh no, it's out of the question. Theres not the least resemblance.

CROFTS

    As to that, theres no resemblance between her and her mother   495 that I can see. I suppose she's not *your* daughter, is she?

PRAED [*rising indignantly*]

    Really, Crofts – !

CROFTS

    No offence, Praed. Quite allowable as between two men of the   500 world.

481–2   The s.d. and Praed's line do not appear in GR.

    485   *Why . . . father* 'All I ask you to tell me – and I consider it a right to know it, mind – is, am I her father?' (MS).

    487   *Impossible!* Praed continues: 'Oh no, nonsense!' (GR).

497–501   Instead of protesting, the s.d. in GR states: '*He meets the question with an indignant stare.*' Because Praed is less expressive in his indignation, Crofts does not calm him down.

497–503   no s.d. in MS. As opposed to admonishing Crofts, Praed's calm response simply reads: 'No, I can answer for that.'

500–1   These lines were added in 1926 (LC2).

PRAED [*recovering himself with an effort and speaking gently and gravely*]

Now listen to me, my dear Crofts. [*He sits down again*] I have nothing to do with that side of Mrs Warren's life, and never 505 had. She has never spoken to me about it; and of course I have never spoken to her about it. Your delicacy will tell you that a handsome woman needs *some* friends who are not – well, not on that footing with her. The effect of her own beauty would become a torment to her if she could not escape from it 510 occasionally. You are probably on much more confidential terms with Kitty than I am. Surely you can ask her the question yourself.

CROFTS

I *have* asked her, often enough. But she's so determined to keep 515 the child all to herself that she would deny that it ever had a father if she could. [*Rising*] I'm thoroughly uncomfortable about it, Praed.

PRAED [*rising also*]

Well, as you are, at all events, old enough to be her father, I dont 520 mind agreeing that we both regard Miss Vivie in a parental way, as a young girl whom we are bound to protect and help. What do you say?

CROFTS [*aggressively*]

I'm no older than you, if you come to that. 525

PRAED

Yes you are, my dear fellow: you were born old. I was born a boy: Ive never been able to feel the assurance of a grown-up man in my life. [*He folds his chair and carries it to the porch*]

MRS WARREN [*calling from within the cottage*] 530

Prad-dee! George! Tea-ea-ea-ea!

CROFTS [*hastily*]

She's calling us. [*He hurries in*]

---

514 GR has Crofts '*rising impatiently*' before he speaks, not '*rising*' in mid-speech.

517 Before s.d.: 'She made the greatest favor of bringing me down here to see the girl, though I've been asking her to do it for three years past. No, there's nothing to be got out of her about it – nothing that one can believe, anyhow' (MS). GR replicates the MS, but without the first sentence.

522 *protect and help* GR adds the line: 'All the more, as the real father, whoever he was, was probably a blackguard.'

529 no s.d. in GR

PRAED *shakes his head bodingly, and is following* CROFTS
when he is hailed by a young gentleman who has just appeared on   535
the common, and is making for the gate. He is pleasant, pretty,
smartly dressed, cleverly good-for-nothing, not long turned 20,
with a charming voice and agreeably disrespectful manners. He
carries a light sporting magazine rifle.

THE YOUNG GENTLEMAN   540

Hallo! Praed!

PRAED

Why, Frank Gardner! [FRANK *comes in and shakes hands*
cordially] What on earth are you doing here?

FRANK   545

Staying with my father.

PRAED

The Roman father?

FRANK

He's rector here. I'm living with my people this autumn for the   550
sake of economy. Things came to a crisis in July: the Roman
father had to pay my debts. He's stony broke in consequence;
and so am I. What are you up to in these parts? Do you know
the people here?

PRAED   555

Yes: I'm spending the day with a Miss Warren.

FRANK [*enthusiastically*]

What! Do you know Vivie? Isnt she a jolly girl? I'm teaching her
to shoot with this. [*Putting down the rifle*] I'm so glad she
knows you: youre just the sort of fellow she ought to know. [*He*   560
smiles, and raises the charming voice almost to a singing tone as
he exclaims] It's *ever* so jolly to find you here, Praed.

536–9 'Son of the Rev. Samuel. A pleasant and entirely good-for-nothing young gentleman
not long turned 20. Agreeably disrespectful in his attitude to life in general. Imper-
turbably polite' (MS). Note the absence of the rifle.

537   *cleverly* 'entirely' (GR)

539   *a light sporting magazine rifle* s.d. '*a very light sporting rifle*' (GR)

541   *Hallo! Praed!* Shaw directs the actor to 'play out' and 'announce yourself' (RN).

543   *Frank Gardner* Frank's given name emphasises his tendency to be direct. His sur-
name reinforces the links of characters to the earth.

548   As Frank's father is not a Roman Catholic priest, it is likely that use of the term
'Roman' here is ironic in its relation to the qualities considered characteristic of
Ancient Roman patricians: strict, courageous, honest, and honourable. The Reverend
Samuel Gardner exemplifies none of these traits. MS reads: 'The Roman father,
whose solemn letters you used to read to me?'

553   *I. What* Between these sentences, MS adds: 'I've got just twelve and ten pence to last
me until October.' Frank has more than enough to live on.

PRAED

I'm an old friend of her mother. Mrs Warren brought me over
to make her daughter's acquaintance.   565

FRANK

The mother! Is *she* here?

PRAED

Yes: inside, at tea.

MRS WARREN [*calling from within*]   570

Prad-dee-ee-ee-eee! The tea-cake'll be cold.

PRAED [*calling*]

Yes, Mrs Warren. In a moment. Ive just met a friend here.

MRS WARREN

A what?   575

PRAED [*louder*]

A friend.

MRS WARREN

Bring him in.

PRAED   580

All right. [*To* FRANK] Will you accept the invitation?

FRANK [*incredulous, but immensely amused*]

Is that Vivie's mother?

PRAED

Yes.   585

FRANK

By Jove! What a lark! Do you think she'll like me?

PRAED

Ive no doubt youll make yourself popular, as usual. Come in
and try. [*Moving towards the house*]   590

FRANK

Stop a bit. [*Seriously*] I want to take you into my confidence.

PRAED

Pray dont. It's only some fresh folly, like the barmaid at Redhill.

FRANK   595

It's ever so much more serious than that. You say youve only
just met Vivie for the first time?

PRAED

Yes.

---

587 *Jove! What* Between these sentences, MS adds: 'She must be ever so free and easy to
     rip out like that.'
594 *Redhill* another small town in Surrey

FRANK [*rhapsodically*]   600

Then you can have no idea what a girl she is. Such character!
Such sense! And her cleverness! Oh, my eye, Praed, but I can tell
you she is clever! And – need I add? – she loves me.

CROFTS [*putting his head out of the window*]

I say, Praed: what are you about? Do come along. [*He disappears*]   605

FRANK

Hallo! Sort of chap that would take a prize at a dog show, aint
he? Who's he?

PRAED

Sir George Crofts, an old friend of Mrs Warren's. I think we had   610
better come in.

> *On their way to the porch they are interrupted by a call from
> the gate. Turning, they see an elderly clergyman looking over it.*

THE CLERGYMAN [*calling*]

Frank!   615

FRANK

Hallo! [*To* PRAED] The Roman father. [*To the clergyman*] Yes,
gov'nor: all right: presently. [*To* PRAED] Look here, Praed: youd
better go in to tea. I'll join you directly.

PRAED   620

Very good. [*He goes into the cottage*]

> *The clergyman remains outside the gate, with his hands on the
> top of it. The* REV. SAMUEL GARDNER, *a beneficed clergyman of
> the Established Church, is over 50. Externally he is pretentious,
> booming, noisy, important. Really he is that obsolescent social*   625
> *phenomenon the fool of the family dumped on the Church by his
> father the patron, clamorously asserting himself as father and clergy-
> man without being able to command respect in either capacity.*

REV. S.

Well, sir. Who are your friends here, if I may ask?   630

---

603   *And . . . me* 'And the most loving little heart that –' (GR)
620   s.d. before Praed enters the cottage: '*He raises his hat to the clergyman who acknow-
      ledges the salute distantly*' (GR).
622   In GR, the clergyman remains '*stiffly outside the gate*'.
623–4   *beneficed clergyman of the Establish Church* He is provided with a house and stipend
      as a clergyman in the established Church of England.
624–7   *Externally . . . himself* s.d.: '*He is a pretentious, booming, noisy person, hopelessly
      asserting himself*' (GR).

FRANK

Oh, it's all right, gov'nor! Come in.

REV. S.

No, sir; not until I know whose garden I am entering.

FRANK   635

It's all right. It's Miss Warren's.

REV. S.

I have not seen her at church since she came.

FRANK

Of course not: she's a third wrangler. Ever so intellectual. Took   640
a higher degree than you did; so why should she go to hear you
preach?

REV. S.

Dont be disrespectful, sir.

FRANK   645

Oh, it dont matter: nobody hears us. Come in. [*He opens the
gate, unceremoniously pulling his father with it into the garden*] I
want to introduce you to her. Do you remember the advice you
gave me last July, gov'nor?

REV. S. [*severely*]   650

Yes. I advised you to conquer your idleness and flippancy, and
to work your way into an honorable profession and live on it
and not upon me.

FRANK

No: thats what you thought of afterwards. What you actually   655
said was that since I had neither brains nor money, I'd better
turn my good looks to account by marrying somebody with
both. Well, look here. Miss Warren has brains: you cant deny
that.

REV. S.   660

Brains are not everything.

FRANK

No, of course not: theres the money –

---

632   *gov'nor* While the title of Governor is a mark of respect, the habit of young men
      referring to their fathers as 'governor' is often seen as familiar, even disrespectful.
658   *both. Well* Between these sentences, MS reads:

>   REV. S.
>   If I uttered such a sentiment it must have been in a moment of great
>   irritation.
>   FRANK
>   Yes, it certainly was. You can talk practically enough when youre roused.

REV. S. [*interrupting him austerely*]

I was not thinking of money, sir. I was speaking of higher   665
things. Social position, for instance.

FRANK

I dont care a rap about that.

REV. S.

But I do, sir.   670

FRANK

Well, nobody wants *you* to marry her. Anyhow, she has what
amounts to a high Cambridge degree; and she seems to have as
much money as she wants.

REV. S. [*sinking into a feeble vein of humor*]   675

I greatly doubt whether she has as much money as *you* will
want.

FRANK

Oh, come: I havnt been so very extravagant. I live ever so
quietly; I dont drink; I dont bet much; and I never go regularly   680
on the razzle-dazzle as you did when you were my age.

REV. S. [*booming hollowly*]

Silence, sir.

FRANK

Well, you told me yourself, when I was making ever such an ass   685
of myself about the barmaid at Redhill, that you once offered a
woman £50 for the letters you wrote to her when –

REV. S. [*terrified*]

Sh-sh-sh, Frank, for Heaven's sake! [*He looks round apprehensively. Seeing no one within earshot he plucks up courage to boom   690
again, but more subduedly*] You are taking an ungentlemanly
advantage of what I confided to you for your own good, to save
you from an error you would have repented all your life long.
Take warning by your father's follies, sir; and dont make them
an excuse for your own.   695

---

680   *I dont bet much* 'I dont gamble' (MS)
681   *razzle-dazzle* a boisterous outing, or a binge
687   *£50* MS has £500. The lesser amount diminishes the importance and potentially
scandalous nature of the letters, but it nicely mirrors the amount that Vivie is paid
when she ties the third wrangler.
688–91   'Silence sir, silence' and no s.d. (MS)

FRANK

Did you ever hear the story of the Duke of Wellington and his letters?

REV. S.

No, sir; and I dont want to hear it. 700

FRANK

The old Iron Duke didnt throw away £50: not he. He just wrote: 'Dear Jenny: publish and be damned! Yours affectionately, Wellington.' Thats what you should have done.

REV. S. [*piteously*] 705

Frank, my boy: when I wrote those letters I put myself into that woman's power. When I told you about them I put myself, to some extent, I am sorry to say, in your power. She refused my money with these words, which I shall never forget. 'Knowledge is power,' she said; 'and I never sell power.' Thats more than 710 twenty years ago; and she has never made use of her power or caused me a moment's uneasiness. You are behaving worse to me than she did, Frank.

FRANK

Oh yes I dare say! Did you ever preach at her the way you 715 preach at me every day?

REV. S. [*wounded almost to tears*]

I leave you, sir. You are incorrigible. [*He turns towards the gate*]

FRANK [*utterly unmoved*]

Tell them I shant be home to tea, will you, gov'nor, like a good 720 fellow? [*He moves towards the cottage door and is met by* PRAED *and* VIVIE *coming out*]

VIVIE [*to* FRANK]

Is that your father, Frank? I do so want to meet him.

---

697   Frank begins: 'I speak in self defence, governor. I'm the last man in the world to remind you of your frailties if you'd only let mine alone' (MS).

697–704   *the Duke of Wellington* Arthur Wellesley (1769–1852), the first Duke of Wellington who is also known as the Iron Duke, was the British army commander during the Napoleonic wars and later became Prime Minister (1828–30). His wife was Catherine Pakenham, though she is more commonly known as Kitty. The blackmailer was Harriette Wilson, a famous courtesan who published the details of her affairs with Wellington and other members of Britain's aristocracy, including Lord Byron.

705   'more seriously' (MS)

707   *them* 'her' (GR)

717–19   no s.d. in MS

FRANK   725
  Certainly. [*Calling after his father*] Gov'nor. Youre wanted. [*The
  parson turns at the gate, fumbling nervously at his hat.* PRAED
  *crosses the garden to the opposite side, beaming in anticipation of
  civilities*] My father: Miss Warren.

VIVIE [*going to the clergyman and shaking his hand*]   730
  Very glad to see you here, Mr Gardner. [*Calling to the cottage*]
  Mother: come along: youre wanted.

      MRS WARREN *appears on the threshold, and is immediately
      transfixed recognizing the clergyman.*

VIVIE [*continuing*]   735
  Let me introduce –

MRS WARREN [*swooping on the* REVEREND SAMUEL]
  Why, it's Sam Gardner, gone into the Church! Well, I never!
  Dont you know us, Sam? This is George Crofts, as large as life
  and twice as natural. Dont you remember me?   740

REV. S. [*very red*]
  I really – er –

MRS WARREN
  Of course you do. Why, I have a whole album of your letters
  still: I came across them only the other day.   745

REV. S. [*miserably confused*]
  Miss Vavasour, I believe.

MRS WARREN [*correcting him quickly in a loud whisper*]
  Tch! Nonsense! Mrs Warren: dont you see my daughter there?

726–9 no s.d. in MS
   729 *civilities* s.d. continues: '*Crofts prowls about near the hammock, poking it with his stick
         to make it swing. Mrs Warren halts on the threshold, staring hard at the clergyman*' (GR).
   736 Vivie is not cut off so quickly in GR. She begins her introductions, naming each
         man, and before Mrs Warren speaks, Shaw adds s.d.: '*As the men are raising their
         hats to one another, Vivie is interrupted by an exclamation from her mother, who
         swoops down on the Reverend Samuel.*' Mrs Warren's memory was possibly tripped
         by Gardner's name in the earlier version.
   747 *Miss Vavasour* A vavasour is a feudal tenant who ranks just below and owes allegiance
         to a baron. The Earl of Oxford fell from the good graces of Queen Elizabeth I in
         part because of his affair with Ann Vavasour. Lilian Vavasour is the heroine of Tom
         Taylor and Augustus Dubourg's *New Men and Old Acres* (1869), which Shaw saw in
         1876 when Ellen Terry starred in the role. For a discussion of these references, see
         the letters to the editor from Irving McKee and Sidney P. Albert in *The Shavian* 3.6
         (Winter 1966–7) and 3.7 (Spring–Summer 1967). Sir Vavasour, a baronet in
         Benjamin Disraeli's novel *Sybil* (1845), might be a further candidate as original for
         the name. Dan H. Laurence suggests that Miss Vavasour 'is a name commonly
         associated with prostitution at the end of the 19th century. Hence its effectiveness
         as a curtain line when addressed at Kitty Warren' (DLVF).

ACT II

Inside the cottage after nightfall. Looking eastward from within instead of westward from without, the latticed window, with its curtains drawn, is now seen in the middle of the front wall of the cottage, with the porch door to the left of it. In the left-hand side wall is the door leading to the kitchen. Farther back against the same wall is a dresser 5
with a candle and matches on it, and FRANK*'s rifle standing beside them, with the barrel resting in the plate-rack. In the centre a table stands with a lighted lamp on it.* VIVIE*'s books and writing materials are on a table to the right of the window, against the wall. The fireplace is on the right, with a settle: there is no fire. Two of the chairs* 10
are set right and left of the table.

The cottage door opens, shewing a fine starlit night without; and MRS WARREN*, her shoulders wrapped in a shawl borrowed from* VIVIE*, enters, followed by* FRANK*, who throws his cap on the window seat. She has had enough of walking, and gives a gasp of relief as she* 15
unpins her hat; takes it off; sticks the pin through the crown; and puts it on the table.

MRS WARREN

> O Lord! I dont know which is the worst of the country, the walking or the sitting at home with nothing to do. I could do 20
> with a whisky and soda now very well, if only they had such a thing in this place.

FRANK

> Perhaps Vivie's got some.

This entire Act is cut from LC1.

1–17 'Inside the Cottage. Night. Lamp on the table. Door in scene R leading to garden. Another door L.U.E. leading to main room. Enter Mrs Warren with Frank. They have been taking a walk together' (MS). L.U.E. means that the door is a left upper entrance on the stage.
5 *kitchen* s.d. '*wing*' (GR)
10 *settle* chair or bench, usually with a high back
14–15 *who . . . seat* not in GR
19–20 *O Lord . . . to do* 'It's a blessing to get out of that hot sun' (MS)
23 s.d.: '*helping her to take off her shawl, and giving her shoulders the most delicate possible little caress with his fingers as he does so*' (GR), replaced later by s.d. on lines 30–1
25 s.d.: '*glancing back at him for an instant from the corner of her eye as she detects the pressure*' (GR)

MRS WARREN   25

Nonsense! What would a young girl like her be doing with such
things! Never mind: it dont matter. I wonder how she passes
her time here! I'd a good deal rather be in Vienna.

FRANK

Let me take you there. [*He helps her to take off her shawl, gallantly*   30
giving her shoulders a very perceptible squeeze as he does so]

MRS WARREN

Ah! would you? I'm beginning to think youre a chip of the old
block.

FRANK   35

Like the gov'nor, eh? [*He hangs the shawl on the nearest chair,*
and sits down]

MRS WARREN

Never you mind. What do you know about such things? Youre
only a boy. [*She goes to the hearth, to be farther from temptation*]   40

FRANK

Do come to Vienna with me? It'd be ever such larks.

MRS WARREN

No, thank you. Vienna is no place for you – at least not until
youre a little older. [*She nods at him to emphasize this piece of*   45
advice. He makes a mock-piteous face, belied by his laughing eyes.
She looks at him; then comes back to him] Now, look here, little
boy [*taking his face in her hands and turning it up to her*]: I
know you through and through by your likeness to your father,
better than you know yourself. Dont you go taking any silly   50
ideas into your head about me. Do you hear?

FRANK [*gallantly wooing her with his voice*]

Cant help it, my dear Mrs Warren: it runs in the family.

She pretends to box his ears; then looks at the pretty laughing
upturned face for a moment, tempted. At last she kisses him, and   55
immediately turns away, out of patience with herself.

MRS WARREN

There! I shouldnt have done that. I *am* wicked. Never you

28   *Vienna* 'Monte Carlo' (MS). Same in line 42
33   *Ah! would you?* 'Get out!' (GR).
33–4   *chip of the old block* This was the standard expression in Shaw's day. 'Chip *off* the old
       block' is the more frequently used form in recent years.
36   s.d. before Frank hangs it on the chair: '*folds the shawl neatly*' (GR)
40   s.d. not in GR
44–5   *Vienna . . . older* not in MS

mind, my dear; it's only a motherly kiss. Go and make love to
Vivie.   60

FRANK

So I have.

MRS WARREN [*turning on him with a sharp note of alarm in her
voice*]

What!   65

FRANK

Vivie and I are ever such chums.

MRS WARREN

What do you mean? Now see here: I wont have any young scamp
tampering with my little girl. Do you hear? I wont have it.   70

FRANK [*quite unabashed*]

My dear Mrs Warren: dont you be alarmed. My intentions are
honorable: ever so honorable; and your little girl is jolly well
able to take care of herself. She dont need looking after half so
much as her mother. She aint so handsome, you know.   75

MRS WARREN [*taken aback by his assurance*]

Well, you have got a nice healthy two inches thick of cheek all
over you. I dont know where you got it. Not from your father,
anyhow.

CROFTS [*in the garden*]   80

The gipsies, I suppose?

REV. S. [*replying*]

The broomsquires are far worse.

MRS WARREN [*to FRANK*]

S-sh! Remember! youve had your warning.   85

    CROFTS *and the* REVEREND SAMUEL *come in from the garden,
the clergyman continuing his conversation as he enters.*

REV. S.

The perjury at the Winchester assizes is deplorable.

MRS WARREN   90

Well? what became of you two? And wheres Praddy and Vivie?

77–8   *two inches thick of cheek all over you* To have cheek is to be insolent. To have two
     inches of cheek would make Frank extremely insolent.

80–3   These lines were added for the 1926 production (LC2).

81   *gipsies* Gypsies first appeared in England in the early sixteenth century.

83   *broomsquires* makers of brooms

89   *Winchester assizes* Winchester is a city in Hampshire, which lies to the southwest of
     Surrey. Assizes were periodic sessions of the High Court of Justice held in the counties
     until they were abolished in 1971. Scholars have not traced this reference to any mean-
     ingful source. However, Mrs Warren's sister Liz now lives in Winchester (II.729–30).

CROFTS [*putting his hat on the settle and his stick in the chimney corner*]

    They went up the hill. We went to the village. I wanted a drink. [*He sits down on the settle, putting his legs up along the seat*]   95

MRS WARREN

    Well, she oughtnt to go off like that without telling me. [*To* FRANK] Get your father a chair, Frank: where are your manners? [FRANK *springs up and gracefully offers his father his chair; then takes another from the wall and sits down at the table, in the*   100 *middle, with his father on his right and* MRS WARREN *on his left*] George: where are you going to stay to-night? You cant stay here. And whats Praddy going to do?

CROFTS

    Gardner'll put me up.   105

MRS WARREN

    Oh, no doubt youve taken care of yourself! But what about Praddy?

CROFTS

    Dont know. I suppose he can sleep at the inn.   110

MRS WARREN

    Havnt you room for him, Sam?

REV. S.

    Well – er – you see, as rector here, I am not free to do as I like. Er – what is Mr Praed's social position?   115

MRS WARREN

    Oh, he's all right: he's an architect. What an old stick-in-the-mud you are, Sam!

FRANK

    Yes, it's all right, gov'nor. He built that place down in Wales for   120 the Duke. Caernarvon Castle they call it. You must have heard

---

117   *architect* As a member of this skilled profession, Praed would be considered socially acceptable to visit a beneficed clergyman.

120–1   *He built . . . call it* Caernarvon Castle was built in its present-day form in the late thirteenth and early fourteenth centuries. In the earlier edition, this line read: 'He built that place down in Monmouthshire for the Duke of Beaufort – Tintern Abbey they call it' (GR). In his favourable report of the play on 17 August 1924, Lord Cromer's sole demand was that 'some fictitious name' be substituted for the Duke of Beaufort (LCP Corr 1924/5632 *Mrs Warren's Profession*, BL). See Appendix V, p. 150. Tintern Abbey, founded in 1131, is best known today as the source of inspiration for William Wordsworth's final poem in *Lyrical Ballads* (1798). The joke here is twofold: it has long been a ruin and the Reverend Samuel's inability to recognise the places of either version marks him as a Philistine (see note to IV.219). On 28 August 1893, while writing the play on vacation in Monmouth, where he was of it. [*He winks with lightning smartness at* MRS WARREN, *and regards his father blandly*]

REV. S.

Oh, in that case, of course we shall only be too happy. I suppose   125
he knows the Duke personally.

FRANK

Oh, ever so intimately! We can stick him in Georgina's old room.

MRS WARREN   130

Well, thats settled. Now if those two would only come in and let
us have supper. Theyve no right to stay out after dark like this.

CROFTS [*aggressively*]

What harm are they doing you?

MRS WARREN   135

Well, harm or not, I dont like it.

FRANK

Better not wait for them, Mrs Warren. Praed will stay out as
long as possible. He has never known before what it is to stray
over the heath on a summer night with my Vivie.   140

CROFTS [*sitting up in some consternation*]

I say, you know! Come!

REV. S. [*rising, startled out of his professional manner into real force
and sincerity*]

Frank, once for all, it's out of the question. Mrs Warren will tell   145
you that it's not to be thought of.

CROFTS

Of course not.

FRANK [*with enchanting placidity*]

Is that so, Mrs Warren?   150

MRS WARREN [*reflectively*]

Well, Sam, I dont know. If the girl wants to get married, no
good can come of keeping her unmarried.

staying with the Webbs, Shaw visited Beaufort Castle. The next day, and again on 31
August, he visited Tintern Abbey. *Diaries*, p. 985.

138–40   'Let's take advantage of this chance to settle <u>my</u> affair. Sir George Crofts wont mind
our talking it over before him, and I really cant hold in any longer. Vivie and I are
ever so fond of one another. I suppose you dont object to my proposing formally
Mrs Warren?' (MS).

140   *heath* an open tract of wilderness, generally covered with low-lying shrubs and plants

141   *sitting . . . consternation* 'remonstrating' (MS)

REV. S. [*astounded*]

But married to *him*! – your daughter to my son! Only think: it's   155
impossible.

CROFTS

Of course it's impossible. Dont be a fool, Kitty.

MRS WARREN [*nettled*]

Why not? Isnt my daughter good enough for your son?   160

REV. S.

But surely, my dear Mrs Warren, you know the reasons –

MRS WARREN [*defiantly*]

I know no reasons. If you know any, you can tell them to the
lad, or to the girl, or to your congregation, if you like.   165

REV. S. [*collapsing helplessly into his chair*]

You know very well that I couldnt tell anyone the reasons. But
my boy will believe me when I tell him there *are* reasons.

FRANK

Quite right, Dad: he will. But has your boy's conduct ever been   170
influenced by your reasons?

CROFTS

You cant marry her; and thats all about it. [*He gets up and
stands on the hearth, with his back to the fireplace, frowning determinedly*]   175

MRS WARREN [*turning on him sharply*]

What have you got to do with it, pray?

FRANK [*with his prettiest lyrical cadence*]

Precisely what I was going to ask myself, in my own graceful
fashion.   180

CROFTS [*to* MRS WARREN]

I suppose you dont want to marry the girl to a man younger
than herself and without either a profession or twopence to
keep her on. Ask Sam, if you dont believe me. [*To the parson*]
How much more money are you going to give him?   185

---

158   *Dont be a fool, Kitty* Shaw directs Crofts to 'come at her' (RN).
165   In MS, Mrs Warren adds: 'No doubt they'll give them every attention.'
182   Crofts begins in MS: 'I dont know whether I've got anything to do with it or not. You
know that better than I do. But I suppose . . .'

REV. S.

Not another penny. He has had his patrimony; and he spent the last of it in July. [MRS WARREN's *face falls*]

CROFTS [*watching her*]

There! I told you. [*He resumes his place on the settle and puts up* 190
his legs on the seat again, as if the matter were finally disposed of]

FRANK [*plaintively*]

This is ever so mercenary. Do you suppose Miss Warren's going to marry for money? If we love one another –

MRS WARREN 195

Thank you. Your love's a pretty cheap commodity, my lad. If you have no means of keeping a wife, that settles it: you cant have Vivie.

FRANK [*much amused*]

What do you say, gov'nor, eh? 200

REV. S.

I agree with Mrs Warren.

FRANK

And good old Crofts has already expressed his opinion.

CROFTS [*turning angrily on his elbow*] 205

Look here: I want none of *your* cheek.

FRANK [*pointedly*]

I'm *ever* so sorry to surprise you, Crofts, but you allowed yourself the liberty of speaking to me like a father a moment ago. One father is enough, thank you. 210

CROFTS [*contemptuously*]

Yah! [*He turns away again*]

FRANK [*rising*]

Mrs Warren: I cannot give my Vivie up, even for your sake.

---

187   *patrimony* inheritance
196   *Your love's a pretty cheap commodity, my lad* Shaw directs Mrs Warren to 'look at him reminiscent of the previous scene' (RN).
210   In MS, Frank adds: 'Nothing but the respect due to the presence of a lady and a clergyman prevented me from telling you to [go to] the devil.'
213–20   In MS:

> FRANK
>
> Come; I'll lay any of you three to two that I win Vivie! Have a flutter, governor.

MRS WARREN [*muttering*]   215

    Young scamp!

FRANK [*continuing*]

    And as you no doubt intend to hold out other prospects to her,
    I shall lose no time in placing my case before her. [*They stare at*
    him; and he begins to declaim gracefully]   220

        He either fears his fate too much,
        Or his deserts are small,
        That dares not put it to the touch
        To gain or lose it all.

    The cottage door opens whilst he is reciting; and VIVIE *and*   225
PRAED *come in. He breaks off.* PRAED *puts his hat on the dresser.*
There is an immediate improvement in the company's behavior.
CROFTS *takes down his legs from the settle and pulls himself*
together as PRAED *joins him at the fireplace.* MRS WARREN *loses*
her ease of manner and takes refuge in querulousness.   230

MRS WARREN

    Wherever have you been, Vivie?

VIVIE [*taking off her hat and throwing it carelessly on the table*]

    On the hill.

MRS WARREN   235

    Well, you shouldnt go off like that without letting me know.
    How could I tell what had become of you? And night coming
    on too!

REV. S.

    Silence, Sir.

MRS WARREN

    It'd serve you right to take you at your word & make you pay.

FRANK

    My dear Mrs Warren, I'll offer you six to one, ten to one, a hundred to one,
    what you please.

A flutter is a slang expression for a gambling bet.

221–4   Frank slightly misquotes 'My Dear and Only Love', a poem by James Graham
      (1612–50), the fifth Earl and first Marquess of Montrose. The stanza reads: 'He either
      fears his fate too much, / Or his deserts are small, / That puts it not unto the touch
      / To win or lose it all.'

  230   *querulousness* the state of complaining

VIVIE [*going to the door of the kitchen and opening it, ignoring her mother*]   240

Now, about supper? [*All rise except* MRS WARREN] We shall be rather crowded in here, I'm afraid.

MRS WARREN

Did you hear what I said, Vivie?

VIVIE [*quietly*]   245

Yes, mother. [*Reverting to the supper difficulty*] How many are we? [*Counting*] One, two, three, four, five, six. Well, two will have to wait until the rest are done: Mrs Alison has only plates and knives for four.

PRAED   250

Oh, it doesnt matter about me. I –

VIVIE

You have had a long walk and are hungry, Mr Praed: you shall have your supper at once. I can wait myself. I want one person to wait with me. Frank: are you hungry?   255

FRANK

Not the least in the world. Completely off my peck, in fact.

MRS WARREN [*to* CROFTS]

Neither are you, George. You can wait.

CROFTS   260

Oh, hang it, Ive eaten nothing since tea-time. Cant Sam do it?

FRANK

Would you starve my poor father?

REV. S. [*testily*]

Allow me to speak for myself, sir. I am perfectly willing to wait.   265

VIVIE [*decisively*]

Theres no need. Only two are wanted. [*She opens the door of the kitchen*] Will you take my mother in, Mr Gardner. [*The parson takes* MRS WARREN; *and they pass into the kitchen.* PRAED *and* CROFTS *follow. All except* PRAED *clearly disapprove of the arrange-*   270
ment, but do not know how to resist it. VIVIE *stands at the door looking in at them*] Can you squeeze past to that corner, Mr

239–42   Instead of Vivie, it is Praed who responds: 'We've been inspecting the screen Professor Tyndall has put up to prevent people from looking at his house. A perfect outrage – a most unsocial outrage' (MS). John Tyndall (1820–93) was an Irish scientist who was best known for his popular lectures that explained science for the average person. He died in Hindhead, Surrey, on 4 December, one month after Shaw completed *Mrs Warren's Profession.*

241   s.d. not in GR

Praed: it's rather a tight fit. Take care of your coat against the white-wash: thats right. Now, are you all comfortable?

PRAED [*within*]   275

Quite, thank you.

MRS WARREN [*within*]

Leave the door open, dearie. [VIVIE *frowns; but* FRANK *checks her with a gesture, and steals to the cottage door, which he softly sets wide open*] Oh Lor, what a draught! Youd better shut it,   280 dear.

VIVIE *shuts it with a slam, and then, noting with disgust that her mother's hat and shawl are lying about, takes them tidily to the window seat, whilst* FRANK *noiselessly shuts the cottage door.*

FRANK [*exulting*]   285

Aha! Got rid of em. Well, Vivvums: what do you think of my guvernor?

VIVIE [*preoccupied and serious*]

Ive hardly spoken to him. He doesnt strike me as being a particularly able person.   290

FRANK

Well, you know, the old man is not altogether such a fool as he looks. You see, he was shoved into the Church rather; and in trying to live up to it he makes a much bigger ass of himself than he really is. I dont dislike him as much as you might   295 expect. He means well. How do you think youll get on with him?

VIVIE [*rather grimly*]

I dont think my future life will be much concerned with him, or with any of that old circle of my mother's, except perhaps   300 Praed. [*She sits down on the settle*] What do you think of my mother?

FRANK

Really and truly?

---

280   *Lor* a clipped form of 'Lord'.

282–4 *Vivie . . . whilst* 'Vivie shuts it promptly' (GR)

293–5 *You see . . . really is* 'You see, being rector here, he's supposed to be a regular good holy man – better than anybody else, at least, and ever so learned. Well, you know, the governor aint all that; and in trying to live up to it he makes a much bigger ass of himself than he really is. No, the governor isnt so bad, poor old chap' (MS).

301   In GR, Vivie does not sit down. As a result, Frank does not sit beside her (309) and neither of them needs to rise (332–4).

37

VIVIE   305
  Yes, really and truly.
FRANK
  Well, she's ever so jolly. But she's rather a caution, isnt she? And
  Crofts! Oh, my eye, Crofts! [*He sits beside her*]
VIVIE   310
  What a lot, Frank!
FRANK
  What a crew!
VIVIE [*with intense contempt for them*]
  If I thought that *I* was like that – that I was going to be a waster,   315
  shifting along from one meal to another with no purpose, and
  no character, and no grit in me, I'd open an artery and bleed to
  death without one moment's hesitation.
FRANK
  Oh no, you wouldnt. Why should they take any grind when   320
  they can afford not to? I wish I had their luck. No: what I object
  to is their form. It isnt the thing: it's slovenly, ever so slovenly.
VIVIE
  Do you think your form will be any better when youre as old as
  Crofts, if you dont work?   325
FRANK
  Of course I do. Ever so much better. Vivvums mustnt lecture:
  her little boy's incorrigible. [*He attempts to take her face caress-
  ingly in his hands*]
VIVIE [*striking his hands down sharply*]   330
  Off with you: Vivvums is not in a humor for petting her little
  boy this evening. [*She rises and comes forward to the other side
  of the room*]
FRANK [*following her*]
  How unkind!   335
VIVIE [*stamping at him*]
  Be serious. I'm serious.
FRANK
  Good. Let us talk learnedly. Miss Warren: do you know that all
  the most advanced thinkers are agreed that half the diseases of   340
  modern civilization are due to starvation of the affections in
  the young. Now, *I* –

308   *a caution* an extraordinary or eccentric person; 'a character'
315   *If I thought* Shaw directs: 'dont drop it, grind it' (RN).

VIVIE [*cutting him short*]

> You are very tiresome. [*She opens the inner door*] Have you
> room for Frank there? He's complaining of starvation.   345

MRS WARREN [*within*]

> Of course there is. [*Clatter of knives and glasses as she moves
> things on the table*] Here! theres room now beside me. Come
> along, Mr Frank.

FRANK   350

> Her little boy will be ever so even with his Vivvums for this. [*He
> passes into the kitchen*]

MRS WARREN [*within*]

> Here, Vivie: come on you too, child. You must be famished. [*She
> enters, followed by* CROFTS, *who holds the door open for* VIVIE   355
> *with marked deference. She goes out without looking at him; and
> he shuts the door after her*] Why, George, you cant be done:
> youve eaten nothing. Is there anything wrong with you?

CROFTS

> Oh, all I wanted was a drink. [*He thrusts his hands in his pockets,   360
> and begins prowling about the room, restless and sulky*]

MRS WARREN

> Well, I like enough to eat. But a little of that cold beef and
> cheese and lettuce goes a long way. [*With a sigh of only half
> repletion she sits down lazily on the settle*]   365

CROFTS

> What do you go encouraging that young pup for?

MRS WARREN [*on the alert at once*]

> Now see here, George: what are you up to about that girl? Ive
> been watching your way of looking at her. Remember: I know   370
> you and what your looks mean.

CROFTS

> Theres no harm in looking at her, is there?

MRS WARREN

> I'd put you out and pack you back to London pretty soon if I   375
> saw any of your nonsense. My girl's little finger is more to me
> than your whole body and soul. [CROFTS *receives this with a
> sneering grin.* MRS WARREN, *flushing a little at her failure to*

---

350   s.d.: '*aside to Vivie, as he goes*' (GR)
358   *Is there anything wrong with you?* not in GR
363   *cold beef* 'bread' (MS)

impose on him in the character of a theatrically devoted mother,
adds in a lower key] Make your mind easy: the young pup has   380
no more chance than you have.

CROFTS

Maynt a man take an interest in a girl?

MRS WARREN

Not a man like you.   385

CROFTS

How old is she?

MRS WARREN

Never you mind how old she is.

CROFTS   390

Why do you make such a secret of it?

MRS WARREN

Because I choose.

CROFTS

Well, I'm not fifty yet; and my property is as good as ever it   395
was –

MRS WARREN [*interrupting him*]

Yes; because youre as stingy as youre vicious.

CROFTS [*continuing*]

And a baronet isnt to be picked up every day. No other man in   400
my position would put up with you for a mother-in-law. Why
shouldnt she marry me?

MRS WARREN

You!

CROFTS   405

We three could live together quite comfortably. I'd die before
her and leave her a bouncing widow with plenty of money.
Why not? It's been growing in my mind all the time Ive been
walking with that fool inside there.

---

383   Crofts continues in MS: '– a fatherly interest?'

385   'No' (MS)

400   *baronet* literally, a lesser baron; in practice an honour which does not grant privilege
or bestow a seat in the House of Lords. It is nonetheless superior to a knighthood
in that it is a hereditary title.

404   Shaw directs: 'You!!!! not enough surprise' (RN).

MRS WARREN [*revolted*]   410

Yes: it's the sort of thing that *would* grow in your mind.

He halts in his prowling; and the two look at one another, she steadfastly, with a sort of awe behind her contemptuous disgust: he stealthily, with a carnal gleam in his eye and a loose grin.

CROFTS [*suddenly becoming anxious and urgent as he sees no sign*   415
of sympathy in her]

Look here, Kitty: youre a sensible woman: you neednt put on any moral airs. I'll ask no more questions; and you need answer none. I'll settle the whole property on her; and if you want a cheque for yourself on the wedding day, you can name any   420
figure you like – in reason.

MRS WARREN

So it's come to that with you, George, like all the other worn-out old creatures!

CROFTS [*savagely*]   425

Damn you!

Before she can retort the door of the kitchen is opened; and the voices of the others are heard returning. CROFTS, *unable to recover his presence of mind, hurries out of the cottage. The clergyman appears at the kitchen door.*   430

REV. S. [*looking around*]

Where is Sir George?

410–16   In MS, there is no opening s.d. The dialogue then follows until Crofts pleads with Kitty:

    MRS WARREN

        Yes, it's the sort of thing that would grow in your mind. (lowering her voice) How do you know that the girl maynt be your own daughter, eh?

    CROFTS (lowering his)

        How do you know that that maynt be one of the fascinations of the thing? What harm if she is? (becoming urgent)

414   *loose grin* GR continues: '*tempting her*'.

423–4   Shaw directs: 'Dont scold – dead slow' (RN). GR begins with the ejaculation 'Faugh!'

424   In MS, Kitty continues: 'If you want a young girl to marry, you'd better go into fashionable society: you'll find plenty of mothers there that will only be too glad to give you their daughters for the sake of the baronetcy & the property. But I havent reached that height of fashion yet. So just drop it now; and dont be an old fool.'

426   *Damn you!* See also III.569–71. The Lord Chamberlain did not require that the expletives be removed. However, there are instances where the characters swallow worse ones (III.480–9; IV.569–70).

427   Kitty '*turns on him fiercely*' before she is interrupted by the door opening (GR)

MRS WARREN

Gone out to have a pipe. [*The clergyman takes his hat from the table, and joins* MRS WARREN *at the fireside. Meanwhile* VIVIE *comes in, followed by* FRANK, *who collapses into the nearest chair with an air of extreme exhaustion.* MRS WARREN *looks round at* VIVIE *and says, with her affectation of maternal patronage even more forced than usual*] Well, dearie: have you had a good supper?

VIVIE

You know what Mrs Alison's suppers are. [*She turns to* FRANK *and pets him*] Poor Frank! was all the beef gone? did it get nothing but bread and cheese and ginger beer? [*Seriously, as if she had done quite enough trifling for one evening*] Her butter is really awful. I must get some down from the stores.

FRANK

Do, in Heaven's name!

VIVIE *goes to the writing-table and makes a memorandum to order the butter.* PRAED *comes in from the kitchen, putting up his handkerchief, which he has been using as a napkin.*

REV. S.

Frank, my boy: it is time for us to be thinking of home. Your mother does not know yet that we have visitors.

PRAED

I'm afraid we're giving trouble.

FRANK [*rising*]

Not the least in the world: my mother will be delighted to see you. She's a genuinely intellectual artistic woman; and she sees nobody here from one year's end to another except the gov'nor; so you can imagine how jolly dull it pans out for her. [*To his father*] Youre not intellectual or artistic: are you, pater? So take Praed home at once; and I'll stay here and entertain Mrs Warren. Youll pick up Crofts in the garden. He'll be excellent company for the bull-pup.

PRAED [*taking his hat from the dresser, and coming close to* FRANK]

Come with us, Frank. Mrs Warren has not seen Miss Vivie for a long time; and we have prevented them from having a moment together yet.

435

440

445

450

455

460

465

---

434   s.d. begins: '*She goes to the fireplace, turning her back on him to compose herself*' (GR).

444   *ginger beer* a carbonated, sometimes mildly alcoholic drink that was rather popular at the time

462   *pater* Latin for 'father'. See I.347.

FRANK [*quite softened, and looking at* PRAED *with romantic*   470
admiration]

    Of course. I forgot. Ever so thanks for reminding me. Perfect
gentleman, Praddy. Always were. My ideal through life. [*He rises
to go, but pauses a moment between the two older men, and puts
his hand on* PRAED'*s shoulder*] Ah, if you had only been my   475
father instead of this unworthy old man! [*He puts his other
hand on his father's shoulder*]

REV. S. [*blustering*]

    Silence, sir, silence: you are profane.

MRS WARREN [*laughing heartily*]   480

    You should keep him in better order, Sam. Goodnight. Here:
take George his hat and stick with my compliments.

REV. S. [*taking them*]

    Goodnight. [*They shake hands. As he passes* VIVIE *he shakes
hands with her also and bids her goodnight. Then, in booming*   485
command, to FRANK] Come along, sir, at once. [*He goes out*]

MRS WARREN

    Byebye, Praddy.

PRAED

    Byebye, Kitty.   490

        *They shake hands affectionately and go out together, she
accompanying him to the garden gate.*

FRANK [*to* VIVIE]

    Kissums?

VIVIE [*fiercely*]   495

    No. I hate you. [*She takes a couple of books and some paper from
the writing-table, and sits down with them at the middle table, at
the end next the fireplace*]

FRANK [*grimacing*]

    Sorry. [*He goes for his cap and rifle.* MRS WARREN *returns. He*   500
takes her hand] Good-night, *dear* Mrs Warren. [*He kisses her
hand. She snatches it away, her lips tightening, and looks more
than half disposed to box his ears. He laughs mischievously and
runs off, clapping-to the door behind him*]

487–90   Mrs Warren and Praed shake hands silently in GR.
493–500 Instead of this exchange, GR has s.d.: '*Frank silently begs a kiss from Vivie; but she,
          dismissing him with a stern glance, takes a couple of books and some paper from the
          writing-table, and sits down with them at the middle table, so as to have the benefit of
          the lamp.*'
   501   Frank '*squeezes*' her hand (GR).
   504   *clapping-to* slamming

MRS WARREN [*resigning herself to an evening of boredom now that*   505
  the men are gone]
  Did you ever in your life hear anyone rattle on so? Isnt he
  a tease? [*She sits at the table*] Now that I think of it, dearie,
  dont you go encouraging him. I'm sure he's a regular good-for-
  nothing.   510

VIVIE [*rising to fetch more books*]
  I'm afraid so. Poor Frank! I shall have to get rid of him; but I
  shall feel sorry for him, though he's not worth it. That man
  Crofts does not seem to me to be good for much either: is he?
  [*She throws the books on the table rather roughly*]   515

MRS WARREN [*galled by* VIVIE *'s indifference*]
  What do you know of men, child, to talk that way about them?
  Youll have to make up your mind to see a good deal of Sir
  George Crofts, as he's a friend of mine.

VIVIE [*quite unmoved*]   520
  Why? [*She sits down and opens a book*] Do you expect that we
  shall be much together? You and I, I mean?

MRS WARREN [*staring at her*]
  Of course: until youre married. Youre not going back to college
  again.   525

VIVIE
  Do you think my way of life would suit you? I doubt it.

MRS WARREN
  Your way of life! What do you mean?

VIVIE [*cutting a page of her book with the paper knife on her*   530
  chatelaine]
  Has it really never occurred to you, mother, that I have a way of
  life like other people?

MRS WARREN
  What nonsense is this youre trying to talk? Do you want to   535
  shew your independence, now that youre a great little person at
  school? Dont be a fool, child.

VIVIE [*indulgently*]
  Thats all you have to say on the subject, is it, mother?

MRS WARREN [*puzzled, then angry*]   540
  Dont you keep on asking me questions like that. [*Violently*]

511–13   s.d. not in GR. The next three sentences instead read: 'Yes: I'm afraid poor Frank *is*
         a thorough good-for-nothing' (GR)
516   *indifference* GR has '*cool tone*'.
521   s.d. not in GR

Hold your tongue. [VIVIE *works on, losing no time, and saying nothing*] You and your way of life, indeed! What next? [*She looks at* VIVIE *again. No reply*] Your way of life will be what I please, so it will. [*Another pause*] Ive been noticing these airs in you   545
ever since you got that tripos or whatever you call it. If you think I'm going to put up with them youre mistaken; and the sooner you find it out, the better. [*Muttering*] All I have to say on the subject, indeed! [*Again raising her voice angrily*] Do you know who youre speaking to, Miss?   550

VIVIE [*looking across at her without raising her head from her book*]
    No. Who are you? What are you?

MRS WARREN [*rising breathless*]
    You young imp!

VIVIE   555
    Everybody knows my reputation, my social standing, and the profession I intend to pursue. I know nothing about you. What is that way of life which you invite me to share with you and Sir George Crofts, pray?

MRS WARREN   560
    Take care. I shall do something I'll be sorry for after, and you too.

VIVIE [*putting aside her books with cool decision*]
    Well, let us drop the subject until you are better able to face it. [*Looking critically at her mother*] You want some good walks and a little lawn tennis to set you up. You are shockingly out of   565
    condition: you were not able to manage twenty yards uphill today without stopping to pant; and your wrists are mere rolls of fat. Look at mine. [*She holds out her wrists*]

MRS WARREN [*after looking at her helplessly, begins to whimper*]
    Vivie –   570

VIVIE [*springing up sharply*]
    Now pray dont begin to cry. Anything but that. I really cannot stand whimpering. I will go out of the room if you do.

---

548   Instead of s.d., MS reads: 'I didnt pay for your education to have it thrown at my head.'

548–50   *All . . . Miss* Shaw added this in the MS, but he originally wrote, then struck out:
    MRS WARREN
        Remember who I am and learn to keep your place.
    VIVIE
        I think I know my place quite accurately. It has been ascertained at Cambridge. My friends will answer for my social standing. I am much indebted to you for my education, but you will not lose by it, as it will enable me to keep myself in future. I shall be no further expense to you.

MRS WARREN [*piteously*]

Oh, my darling, how can you be so hard on me? Have I no 575
rights over you as your mother?

VIVIE

Are you my mother?

MRS WARREN [*appalled*]

Am I your mother! Oh, Vivie! 580

VIVIE

Then where are our relatives? my father? our family friends?
You claim the rights of a mother: the right to call me fool and
child; to speak to me as no woman in authority over me at
college dare speak to me; to dictate my way of life; and to force 585
on me the acquaintance of a brute whom anyone can see to be
the most vicious sort of London man about town. Before I give
myself the trouble to resist such claims, I may as well find out
whether they have any real existence.

MRS WARREN [*distracted, throwing herself on her knees*] 590

Oh no, no. Stop, stop. I *am* your mother: I swear it. Oh, you
cant mean to turn on me – my own child! it's not natural. You
believe me, dont you? Say you believe me.

VIVIE

Who was my father? 595

MRS WARREN

You dont know what youre asking. I cant tell you.

VIVIE [*determinedly*]

Oh yes you can, if you like. I have a right to know; and you
know very well that I have that right. You can refuse to tell me, 600
if you please; but if you do, you will see the last of me tomorrow
morning.

MRS WARREN

Oh, it's too horrible to hear you talk like that. You wouldnt –
you *couldnt* leave me. 605

VIVIE [*ruthlessly*]

Yes, without a moment's hesitation, if you trifle with me about
this. [*Shivering with disgust*] How can I feel sure that I may not
have the contaminated blood of that brutal waster in my veins?

---

589   In MS, Vivie continues: 'or whether you merely adopted me as an apprentice to your
own way of life, whatever that may be.'
600–1   *You . . . please* Shaw directs: 'threatening inflection' (RN).

MRS WARREN   610

    No, no. On my oath it's not he, nor any of the rest that you have
ever met. I'm certain of that, at least.

       VIVIE*'s eyes fasten sternly on her mother as the significance of
*   this flashes on her.*

VIVIE [*slowly*]   615

    You are certain of that, at *least*. Ah! You mean that that is all you
are certain of. [*Thoughtfully*] I see. [MRS WARREN *buries her
face in her hands*] Dont do that, mother: you know you dont
feel it a bit. [MRS WARREN *takes down her hands and looks up
deplorably at* VIVIE, *who takes out her watch and says*] Well, that   620
is enough for tonight. At what hour would you like breakfast?
Is half-past eight too early for you?

MRS WARREN [*wildly*]

    My God, what sort of woman are you?

VIVIE [*coolly*]   625

    The sort the world is mostly made of, I should hope. Otherwise
I dont understand how it gets its business done. Come [*taking
her mother by the wrist, and pulling her up pretty resolutely*]: pull
yourself together. Thats right.

MRS WARREN [*querulously*]   630

    Youre very rough with me, Vivie.

VIVIE

    Nonsense. What about bed? It's past ten.

MRS WARREN [*passionately*]

    Whats the use of my going to bed? Do you think I could sleep?   635

VIVIE

    Why not? I shall.

MRS WARREN

    You! youve no heart. [*She suddenly breaks out vehemently in her
natural tongue – the dialect of a woman of the people – with all*   640
*her affectations of maternal authority and conventional manners
gone, and an overwhelming inspiration of true conviction and
scorn in her*] Oh, I wont bear it: I wont put up with the injustice
of it. What right have you to set yourself up above me like this?
You boast of what you are to me – to *me*, who gave you the   645

---

635   Shaw directs: 'fierce' (RN).
643–4 *Oh, I . . . injustice of it* Shaw directs: 'play to it – she's going off the deep end' (RN).

chance of being what you are. What chance had I? Shame on you for a bad daughter and a stuck-up prude!

VIVIE [*sitting down with a shrug, no longer confident; for her replies, which have sounded sensible and strong to her so far, now begin to ring rather woodenly and even priggishly against the new tone of her mother*]   650

Dont think for a moment I set myself above you in any way. You attacked me with the conventional authority of a mother: I defended myself with the conventional superiority of a respectable woman. Frankly, I am not going to stand any of your nonsense; and when you drop it I shall not expect you to stand any of mine. I shall always respect your right to your own opinions and your own way of life.   655

MRS WARREN

My own opinions and my own way of life! Listen to her talking! Do you think I was brought up like you? able to pick and choose my own way of life? Do you think I did what I did because I liked it, or thought it right, or wouldnt rather have gone to college and been a lady if I'd had the chance?   660

VIVIE   665

Everybody has some choice, mother. The poorest girl alive may not be able to choose between being Queen of England or Principal of Newnham; but she can choose between ragpicking and flowerselling, according to her taste. People are always blaming their circumstances for what they are. I dont believe in circumstances. The people who get on in this world are the people who get up and look for the circumstances they want, and, if they cant find them, make them.   670

---

647   *prude* Mrs Warren has yet to reveal her past to Vivie, but she already charges her with being someone who is extremely modest in sexual matters.

648   *sitting down with a shrug* GR has '*cool and determined*' ()

660   *My ... talking* Shaw directs: 'get in the scorn' (RN).

662   *life?* Before she continues, MS adds: 'You're very clever and as hard as nails, stone into the bargain; but you're a greater little prig than you think.'

668   *Principal* the head, dean, or provost of the college

668–9 *ragpicking and flowerselling* Shaw appears to have drawn on this early reference in creating the character Eliza Doolittle in *Pygmalion*, a play that has many references to women of the lower classes being associated with prostitution. See Celia Marshik, *British Modernism and Censorship* (Cambridge: Cambridge University Press, 2006), pp. 46–87.

671   *circumstances* In MS Vivie qualifies her remarks, the sentence continuing: '– at least not after a certain point.'

MRS WARREN

Oh, it's easy to talk, very easy, isnt it? Here! would you like to   675
know what *my* circumstances were?

VIVIE

Yes: you had better tell me. Wont you sit down?

MRS WARREN

Oh, I'll sit down: dont you be afraid. [*She plants her chair farther*   680
forward with brazen energy, and sits down. VIVIE *is impressed in*
spite of herself] D'you know what your gran'mother was?

VIVIE

No.

MRS WARREN   685

No you dont. I do. She called herself a widow and had a fried-
fish shop down by the Mint, and kept herself and four daughters out of it. Two of us were sisters: that was me and Liz; and
we were both good-looking and well made. I suppose our
father was a well-fed man: mother pretended he was a gentle-   690
man; but I dont know. The other two were only half sisters:
undersized, ugly, starved looking, hard working, honest poor
creatures: Liz and I would have half-murdered them if mother
hadnt half-murdered *us* to keep our hands off them. They were
the respectable ones. Well, what did they get by their respec-   695
tability? I'll tell you. One of them worked in a whitelead factory
twelve hours a day for nine shillings a week until she died of
lead poisoning. She only expected to get her hands a little
paralyzed; but she died. The other was always held up to us as
a model because she married a Government laborer in the   700

---

680   For this scene, Shaw directs: 'Dont meditate on the past sentimentally – rub it into
       Vivie' (RN).   687   *the Mint* In Shaw's time, the Royal Mint was located at
       Tower Hill, London. In 1967, its operations were moved to Llantrisant, Wales.

696–9   *One of them worked . . . but she died* Whitelead was used in the production of lead-
       based paints. Because of the accumulative effects of its high toxicity, it is banned in
       many countries. Paralysis from lead poisoning tends to first attack the fingers, hands
       and wrists; this is referred to as 'wrist drop'.

697   *shillings* silver coins used prior to the decimalisation of British currency in 1971. A
       shilling was worth one-twentieth of a pound, or twelve pence.

Deptford victualling yard, and kept his room and the three
children neat and tidy on eighteen shillings a week – until he
took to drink. That was worth being respectable for, wasnt it?

VIVIE [*now thoughtfully attentive*]

Did you and your sister think so?   705

MRS WARREN

Liz didnt, I can tell you: she had more spirit. We both went to a
church school – that was part of the ladylike airs we gave ourselves to be superior to the children that knew nothing and
went nowhere – and we stayed there until Liz went out one   710
night and never came back. I know the schoolmistress thought
I'd soon follow her example; for the clergyman was always
warning me that Lizzie'd end by jumping off Waterloo Bridge.
Poor fool: that was all he knew about it! But I was more afraid
of the whitelead factory than I was of the river; and so would   715
you have been in my place. That clergyman got me a situation
as scullery maid in a temperance restaurant where they sent out
for anything you liked. Then I was waitress; and then I went to
the bar at Waterloo station: fourteen hours a day serving drinks
and washing glasses for four shillings a week and my board.   720
That was considered a great promotion for me. Well, one cold,
wretched night, when I was so tired I could hardly keep myself
awake, who should come up for a half of Scotch but Lizzie, in a

---

701   *Deptford victualling yard* The Admiralty Victualling Yard, the storage facility for the
      famous Deptford dockyards, was established in 1742. It was renamed the Royal Victoria
      Yard in 1858 and redeveloped into the Pepys Estate, a social housing project, in the
      1960s. Deptford lies along the south bank of the River Thames, in the East End of
      London.

708   *church school* school run by the Church of England and governed by a culture of
      strict morality

713   *Waterloo Bridge* Built in 1817, Waterloo Bridge joins the South Bank to the Victoria
      Embankment. It was demolished in 1936 and replaced in 1945 by the present
      structure.

717–18 *scullery maid . . . anything you liked* The scullery is a little room attached to the
      kitchen where the washing and other dirty work is done. A temperance restaurant
      would have been closely aligned with the church and would not allow alcohol on its
      premises. Kitty appears to suggest that alcohol could be procured for customers if
      they so wished.

719   *Waterloo station* Built in 1848 to the south of Waterloo Bridge, it remains one of
      Britain's largest main-line railway stations.

723   *half of Scotch* a half-gill (one-eighth of a pint) of Scotch whisky

long fur cloak, elegant and comfortable, with a lot of sovereigns
in her purse.   725

VIVIE [*grimly*]

My aunt Lizzie!

MRS WARREN

Yes; and a very good aunt to have, too. She's living down at
Winchester now, close to the cathedral, one of the most respec-   730
table ladies there. Chaperones girls at the county ball, if you
please. No river for Liz, thank you! You remind me of Liz a little:
she was a first-rate business woman – saved money from the
beginning – never let herself look too like what she was – never
lost her head or threw away a chance. When she saw I'd grown   735
up good-looking she said to me across the bar 'What are you
doing there, you little fool? wearing out your health and your
appearance for other people's profit!' Liz was saving money
then to take a house for herself in Brussels; and she thought we
two could save faster than one. So she lent me some money and   740
gave me a start; and I saved steadily and first paid her back, and
then went into business with her as her partner. Why shouldnt
I have done it? The house in Brussels was real high class: a
much better place for a woman to be in than the factory where
Anne Jane got poisoned. None of our girls were ever treated as   745
I was treated in the scullery of that temperance place, or at the
Waterloo bar, or at home. Would you have had me stay in them
and become a worn out old drudge before I was forty?

VIVIE [*intensely interested by this time*]

No; but why did you choose that business? Saving money and   750
good management will succeed in any business.

MRS WARREN

Yes, saving money. But where can a woman get the money to

---

725   *sovereigns* A sovereign was a gold coin worth a pound, replaced by paper currency
        well before decimalisation in 1971.
727   *My aunt Lizzie!* Shaw suggests that the actress says this as 'my aunt Lizzie' (RN).
730   *Winchester . . . cathedral* At 169 metres, the cathedral of Winchester is the longest in
        England. Shaw might have been making allusion to the great size of the cathedral as
        reflecting the town's supposed piety and the irony of Liz being respected there. See
        also the earlier reference to the Winchester assizes (II.89).
731–2 *Chaperones . . . please* Shaw directs: 'Liz chaperoning must not drop into light
        comedy' and that there should be 'no mockery – brag' (RN).
745   *None of our girls* Shaw directs: 'None of our girls' (RN).
748   *worn out old drudge* Shaw directs: 'worn out old drudge' (RN).

save in any other business? Could you save out of four shillings
a week and keep yourself dressed as well? Not you. Of course, if   755
youre a plain woman and cant earn anything more; or if you
have a turn for music, or the stage, or newspaper-writing: thats
different. But neither Liz nor I had any turn for such things: all
we had was our appearance and our turn for pleasing men. Do
you think we were such fools as to let other people trade in our   760
good looks by employing us as shopgirls, or barmaids, or
waitresses, when we could trade in them ourselves and get all
the profits instead of starvation wages? Not likely.

VIVIE

You were certainly quite justified – from the business point of   765
view.

MRS WARREN

Yes; or any other point of view. What is any respectable girl
brought up to do but to catch some rich man's fancy and get
the benefit of his money by marrying him? – as if a marriage   770
ceremony could make any difference in the right or wrong of
the thing! Oh, the hypocrisy of the world makes me sick! Liz
and I had to work and save and calculate just like other people;
elseways we should be as poor as any good-for-nothing drunken
waster of a woman that thinks her luck will last for ever. [With   775
great energy] I despise such people: theyve no character; and if
theres a thing I hate in a woman, it's want of character.

VIVIE

Come now, mother: frankly! Isnt it part of what you call
character in a woman that she should greatly dislike such a way   780
of making money?

MRS WARREN

Why, of course. Everybody dislikes having to work and make
money; but they have to do it all the same. I'm sure Ive often
pitied a poor girl, tired out and in low spirits, having to try to   785
please some man that she doesnt care two straws for – some
half-drunken fool that thinks he's making himself agreeable
when he's teasing and worrying and disgusting a woman so
that hardly any money could pay her for putting up with it. But
she has to bear with disagreeables and take the rough with the   790
smooth, just like a nurse in a hospital or anyone else. It's not
work that any woman would do for pleasure, goodness knows;

776   *I despise such people* Shaw directs: 'let out for the grand climax' (RN).

though to hear the pious people talk you would suppose it was a bed of roses.

VIVIE   795

Still, you consider it worth while. It pays.

MRS WARREN

Of course it's worth while to a poor girl, if she can resist temptation and is good-looking and well conducted and sensible. It's far better than any other employment open to her. I   800
always thought that oughtnt to be. It *cant* be right, Vivie, that there shouldnt be better opportunities for women. I stick to that: it's wrong. But it's so, right or wrong; and a girl must make the best of it. But of course it's not worth while for a lady. If you took to it youd be a fool; but I should have been a fool if I'd   805
taken to anything else.

VIVIE [*more and more deeply moved*]

Mother: suppose we were both as poor as you were in those wretched old days, are you quite sure that you wouldnt advise me to try the Waterloo bar, or marry a laborer, or even go into   810
the factory?

MRS WARREN [*indignantly*]

Of course not. What sort of mother do you take me for! How could you keep your self-respect in such starvation and slavery? And whats a woman worth? whats life worth? without self-   815
respect! Why am I independent and able to give my daughter a first-rate education, when other women that had just as good opportunities are in the gutter? Because I always knew how to respect myself and control myself. Why is Liz looked up to in a cathedral town? The same reason. Where would we be now if   820
we'd minded the clergyman's foolishness? Scrubbing floors for one and sixpence a day and nothing to look forward to but the workhouse infirmary. Dont you be led astray by people who dont know the world, my girl. The only way for a woman to provide for herself decently is for her to be good to some man   825
that can afford to be good to her. If she's in his own station of life, let her make him marry her; but if she's far beneath him she cant expect it: why should she? it wouldnt be for her own

---

798–9   MS does not mention resisting temptation.
823   *workhouse infirmary* Workhouses were places of last resort for the sick, infirm, and impoverished, and deliberately provided harsh conditions to discourage people from relying upon public assistance. In the first half of the twentieth century, workhouses were gradually replaced by modern social welfare services, and abolished in 1948.

happiness. Ask any lady in London society that has daughters; and she'll tell you the same, except that I tell you straight and she'll tell you crooked. Thats all the difference. 830

VIVIE [*fascinated, gazing at her*]

My dear mother: you are a wonderful woman: you are stronger than all England. And are you really and truly not one wee bit doubtful – or – or – ashamed? 835

MRS WARREN

Well, of course, dearie, it's only good manners to be ashamed of it: it's expected from a woman. Women have to pretend to feel a great deal that they dont feel. Liz used to be angry with me for plumping out the truth about it. She used to say that when 840 every woman could learn enough from what was going on in the world before her eyes, there was no need to talk about it to her. But then Liz was such a perfect lady! She had the true instinct of it; while I was always a bit of a vulgarian. I used to be so pleased when you sent me your photos to see that you 845 were growing up like Liz: youve just her ladylike, determined way. But I cant stand saying one thing when everyone knows I mean another. Whats the use in such hypocrisy? If people arrange the world that way for women, theres no good pretending it's arranged the other way. No: I never was a bit ashamed really. I 850 consider I had a right to be proud of how we managed everything so respectably, and never had a word against us, and how the girls were so well taken care of. Some of them did very well: one of them married an ambassador. But of course now I darent talk about such things: whatever would they think of us! 855 [*She yawns*] Oh dear! I do believe I'm getting sleepy after all. [*She stretches herself lazily, thoroughly relieved by her explosion, and placidly ready for her night's rest*]

VIVIE

I believe it is I who will not be able to sleep now. [*She goes to the* 860 *dresser and lights the candle. Then she extinguishes the lamp, darkening the room a good deal*] Better let in some fresh air before locking up. [*She opens the cottage door, and finds that it is broad moonlight*] What a beautiful night! Look! [*She draws*

833–4 *you are stronger than all England* 'you are standing against the whole world' (MS).
845 *photos* 'photographs' (GR)
847–8 *But . . . another* Shaw directs: '<u>reckless</u>' (RN)
850 'No' not in GR

aside the curtains of the window. The landscape is seen bathed in   865
the radiance of the harvest moon rising over Blackdown]

MRS WARREN [with a perfunctory glance at the scene]

Yes, dear; but take care you dont catch your death of cold from
the night air.

VIVIE [contemptuously]   870

Nonsense.

MRS WARREN [querulously]

Oh yes: everything I say is nonsense, according to you.

VIVIE [turning to her quickly]

No: really that is not so, mother. You have got completely the   875
better of me tonight, though I intended it to be the other way.
Let us be good friends now.

MRS WARREN [shaking her head a little ruefully]

So it *has* been the other way. But I suppose I must give in to it.
I always got the worst of it from Liz; and now I suppose it'll be   880
the same with you.

VIVIE

Well, never mind. Come: goodnight, dear old mother. [She
takes her mother in her arms]

MRS WARREN [fondly]   885

I brought you up well, didnt I, dearie?

VIVIE

You did.

MRS WARREN

And youll be good to your poor old mother for it, wont you?   890

VIVIE

I will, dear. [Kissing her] Goodnight.

MRS WARREN [with unction]

Blessings on my own dearie darling! a mother's blessing!

    She embraces her daughter protectingly, instinctively looking   895
upward for divine sanction.

---

866   *harvest moon* the full moon nearest the autumnal equinox, the first day of autumn
866   *Blackdown* a hill in the Haslemere area
888   'You did, darling, and I shall never forget it' (MS)
893   *with unction* struck out s.d. in MS: 'with a burst of emotion'
895–6   'embraces her fondly. Vivie gives her the candle, and attends her affectionately to
       the door R. Left alone, she shuts the window shutters & bars them. Then she goes to
       the door & stares thoughtfully out into the moonlight as the act drop falls' (MS).
896   *for divine sanction* GR has 'as if to call down a blessing'.

ACT III

*In the Rectory garden next morning, with the sun shining from a
cloudless sky. The garden wall has a five-barred wooden gate, wide
enough to admit a carriage, in the middle. Beside the gate hangs a
bell on a coiled spring, communicating with a pull outside. The
carriage drive comes down the middle of the garden and then swerves* 5
*to its left, where it ends in a little gravelled circus opposite the Rectory
porch. Beyond the gate is seen the dusty high road, parallel with the
wall, bounded on the farther side by a strip of turf and an unfenced
pine wood. On the lawn, between the house and the drive, is a clipped
yew tree, with a garden bench in its shade. On the opposite side the* 10
*garden is shut in by a box hedge; and there is a sundial on the turf,
with an iron chair near it. A little path leads off through the box
hedge, behind the sundial.*

FRANK, *seated on the chair near the sundial, on which he has
placed the morning papers, is reading* The Standard. *His father comes* 15
from the house, red-eyed and shivery, and meets FRANK'S *eye with
misgiving.*

FRANK [*looking at his watch*]

Half-past eleven. Nice hour for a rector to come down to
breakfast! 20

REV. S.

Dont mock, Frank: dont mock. I am a little – er – [*shivering*] –

FRANK

Off color?

REV. S. [*repudiating the expression*] 25

No, sir: *unwell* this morning. Wheres your mother?

---

1   *Rectory* the residence of a rector, in this case the Reverend Samuel Gardner's house

1–2 *from a cloudless sky* GR has '*and the birds in full song*'.

6   *circus* a circle

10   *yew tree* The yew is an evergreen tree. In *The Second Mrs Tanqueray*, Hugh Ardale
      conceals himself behind a yew tree so he is not spotted on his tryst with Ellean.

11   *sundial* The sundial, one of the earliest time-keeping devices, traces its origins back
      to the eighth century BC in Egypt. Sundials were still used in the nineteenth century
      to reset mechanical clocks.

15   *The Standard* a leading evening newspaper founded in 1827, now known as the
      London Evening Standard

FRANK

Dont be alarmed: she's not here. Gone to town by the 11.13
with Bessie. She left several messages for you. Do you feel equal
to receiving them now, or shall I wait til youve breakfasted?   30

REV. S.

I *have* breakfasted, sir. I am surprised at your mother going to
town when we have people staying with us. Theyll think it very
strange.

FRANK   35

Possibly she has considered that. At all events, if Crofts is going
to stay here, and you are going to sit up every night with him
until four, recalling the incidents of your fiery youth, it is
clearly my mother's duty, as a prudent housekeeper, to go up to
the stores and order a barrel of whisky and a few hundred   40
siphons.

REV. S.

I did not observe that Sir George drank excessively.

FRANK

You were not in a condition to, gov'nor.   45

REV. S.

Do you mean to say that *I* – ?

FRANK [*calmly*]

I never saw a beneficed clergyman less sober. The anecdotes you
told about your past career were so awful that I really dont   50
think Praed would have passed the night under your roof if it
hadnt been for the way my mother and he took to one another.

REV. S.

Nonsense, sir. I am Sir George Crofts' host. I must talk to him
about something; and he has only one subject. Where is Mr   55
Praed now?

FRANK

He is driving my mother and Bessie to the station.

REV. S.

Is Crofts up yet?   60

FRANK

Oh, long ago. He hasnt turned a hair: he's in much better

---

41   *siphons* pressurised bottles that generally contain carbonated water used to mix with
        drinks, in this case whisky
54–5   *I am ... subject* Not in MS

practice than you. Has kept it up ever since, probably. He's taken himself off somewhere to smoke.

FRANK *resumes his paper. The parson turns disconsolately* 65
towards the gate; then comes back irresolutely.

REV. S.

Er – Frank.

FRANK

Yes. 70

REV. S.

Do you think the Warrens will expect to be asked here after yesterday afternoon?

FRANK

Theyve been asked already. 75

REV. S. [*appalled*]

What!!!

FRANK

Crofts informed us at breakfast that you told him to bring Mrs Warren and Vivie over here today, and to invite them to make 80 this house their home. My mother then found she must go to town by the 11.13 train.

REV. S. [*with despairing vehemence*]

I never gave any such invitation. I never thought of such a thing. 85

FRANK [*compassionately*]

How do you know, gov'nor, what you said and thought last night?

PRAED [*coming in through the hedge*]

Good morning. 90

REV. S.

Good morning. I must apologize for not having met you at breakfast. I have a touch of – of –

FRANK

Clergyman's sore throat, Praed. Fortunately not chronic. 95

---

65   *parson* synonym for 'clergyman'
76–7   not in GR
81   *My mother* In GR, this sentence begins: 'It was after that communication that'.
88   Frank continues: 'Hallo! heres Praed back again' (GR).
89   *the hedge* GR has '*the gate*'.
95   *Clergyman's sore throat* a medical term of the period used to describe an inflammation of the pharynx due to overuse of the voice

PRAED [*changing the subject*]

Well, I must say your house is in a charming spot here. Really most charming.

REV. S.

Yes: it is indeed. Frank will take you for a walk, Mr Praed, if you   100
like. I'll ask you to excuse me: I must take the opportunity to write my sermon while Mrs Gardner is away and you are all amusing yourselves. You wont mind, will you?

PRAED

Certainly not. Dont stand on the slightest ceremony with me.   105

REV. S.

Thank you. I'll – er – er – [*He stammers his way to the porch and vanishes into the house*]

PRAED

Curious thing it must be writing a sermon every week.   110

FRANK

Ever so curious, if *he* did it. He buys em. He's gone for some soda water.

PRAED

My dear boy: I wish you would be more respectful to your   115
father. You know you can be so nice when you like.

FRANK

My dear Praddy: you forget that I have to live with the governor. When two people live together – it dont matter whether theyre father and son or husband and wife or brother and sister   120
– they cant keep up the polite humbug thats so easy for ten minutes on an afternoon call. Now the governor, who unites to many admirable domestic qualities the irresoluteness of a sheep and the pompousness and aggressiveness of a jackass –

PRAED   125

No, pray, pray, my dear Frank, remember! He is your father.

FRANK

I give him due credit for that. [*Rising and flinging down his paper*] But just imagine his telling Crofts to bring the Warrens

---

109   s.d.: '*sitting down on the turf near Frank, and hugging his ankles*' (GR)
112   *He buys em* Shaw warns: 'dont laugh' (RN).
116   *father. You* Between these sentences, MS adds: 'The things you say to him are really dreadful. And you have a way of bringing me into the conversation and making me your accomplice, as if I were saying the things too.'
121   *humbug* slang for deception or fraud
128–35   s.d. not in GR

over here! He must have been ever so drunk. You know, my   130
dear Praddy, my mother wouldnt stand Mrs Warren for a
moment. Vivie mustnt come here until she's gone back to town.

PRAED

But your mother doesnt know anything about Mrs Warren,
does she? [*He picks up the paper and sits down to read it*]   135

FRANK

I dont know. Her journey to town looks as if she did. Not that
my mother would mind in the ordinary way: she has stuck like
a brick to lots of women who had got into trouble. But they
were all nice women. Thats what makes the real difference. Mrs   140
Warren, no doubt, has her merits; but she's ever so rowdy; and
my mother simply wouldnt put up with her. So – hallo! [*This
exclamation is provoked by the reappearance of the clergyman,
who comes out of the house in haste and dismay*]

REV. S.   145

Frank: Mrs Warren and her daughter are coming across the
heath with Crofts: I saw them from the study windows. What
am I to say about your mother?

FRANK

Stick on your hat and go out and say how delighted you are to   150
see them; and that Frank's in the garden; and that mother and
Bessie have been called to the bedside of a sick relative, and
were ever so sorry they couldnt stop; and that you hope Mrs
Warren slept well; and – and – say any blessed thing except the
truth, and leave the rest to Providence.   155

REV. S.

But how are we to get rid of them afterwards?

FRANK

Theres no time to think of that now. Here! [*He bounds into the
house*]   160

REV. S.

He's so impetuous. I dont know what to do with him, Mr Praed.

149   s.d.: '*jumping up energetically*' (GR)
154–5   *any . . . Providence* Shaw notes that this is the 'climax' of the speech (RN). Providence
        is divine direction, or the will of God.
161–2   The Reverend Samuel's line does not appear in GR.

FRANK [*returning with a clerical felt hat, which he claps on his father's head*]

Now: off with you. [*Rushing him through the gate*] Praed and   165
I'll wait here, to give the thing an unpremeditated air. [*The clergyman, dazed but obedient, hurries off*]

FRANK

We must get the old girl back to town somehow, Praed. Come!
Honestly, dear Praddy, do you like seeing them together?   170

PRAED

Oh, why not?

FRANK [*his teeth on edge*]

Dont it make your flesh creep ever so little? that wicked old
devil, up to every villainy under the sun, I'll swear, and Vivie –   175
ugh!

PRAED

Hush, pray. Theyre coming.

The clergyman and CROFTS *are seen coming along the road,
followed by* MRS WARREN *and* VIVIE *walking affectionately together.*   180

FRANK

Look: she actually has her arm round the old woman's waist.
It's her right arm: she began it. She's gone sentimental, by God!
Ugh! ugh! Now do you feel the creeps? [*The clergyman opens
the gate; and* MRS WARREN *and* VIVIE *pass him and stand in the*   185
middle of the garden looking at the house. FRANK, *in an ecstasy
of dissimulation, turns gaily to* MRS WARREN, *exclaiming*] Ever
so delighted to see you, Mrs Warren. This quiet old rectory
garden becomes you perfectly.

MRS WARREN   190

Well, I never! Did you hear that, George? He says I look well in
a quiet old rectory garden.

REV. S. [*still holding the gate for* CROFTS, *who loafs through it,
heavily bored*]

You look well everywhere, Mrs Warren.   195

---

165   s.d. not in GR
167   s.d. continues: '*Praed gets up from the turf, and dusts himself*' (GR).
170   Frank's question ends '– Vivie and the old lady?' (GR).

FRANK

Bravo, gov'nor! Now look here: lets have a treat before lunch.
First lets see the church. Everyone has to do that. It's a regular
old thirteenth century church, you know; the gov'nor's ever so
fond of it, because he got up a restoration fund and had it   200
completely rebuilt six years ago. Praed will be able to shew its
points.

PRAED [*rising*]

Certainly, if the restoration has left any to shew.

REV. S. [*mooning hospitably at them*]   205

I shall be pleased, I'm sure, if Sir George and Mrs Warren really
care about it.

MRS WARREN

Oh, come along and get it over.

CROFTS [*turning back towards the gate*]   210

Ive no objection.

REV. S.

Not that way. We go through the fields, if you dont mind.
Round here. [*He leads the way by the little path through the box
hedge*]   215

CROFTS

Oh, all right. [*He goes with the parson*]

    PRAED *follows with* MRS WARREN. VIVIE *does not stir: she
watches them until they have gone, with all the lines of purpose in
her face marking it strongly.*   220

FRANK

Aint you coming?

VIVIE

No. I want to give you a warning, Frank. You were making fun
of my mother just now when you said that about the rectory   225
garden. That is barred in future. Please treat my mother with as
much respect as you treat your own.

---

197   *treat* 'time of it' (GR)

198–9 *regular old thirteenth century church* The phrasing offers further proof of Frank's
       disrespect for tradition. The church would have been built in the same period as
       Caernarvon Castle (II.120–1).

205   *mooning* listless, without energy

209   Mrs Warren continues: 'Itll do George good: I'll lay *he* doesnt trouble church much'
       (GR).

FRANK

My dear Viv: she wouldnt appreciate it: the two cases require
different treatment. But what on earth has happened to you?   230
Last night we were perfectly agreed as to your mother and her
set. This morning I find you attitudinizing sentimentally with
your arm round your parent's waist.

VIVIE [*flushing*]

Attitudinizing!   235

FRANK

That was how it struck me. First time I ever saw you do a
second-rate thing.

VIVIE [*controlling herself*]

Yes, Frank: there has been a change; but I dont think it a change   240
for the worse. Yesterday I was a little prig.

FRANK

And today?

VIVIE [*wincing; then looking at him steadily*]

Today I know my mother better than you do.   245

FRANK

Heaven forbid!

VIVIE

What do you mean?

FRANK   250

Viv: theres a freemasonry among thoroughly immoral people
that you know nothing of. You've too much character. *Thats* the
bond between your mother and me: thats why I know her
better than youll ever know her.

229–86   *the two . . . suppose* expurgated in LC1
229–30   *the two . . . treatment* 'She's not like my mother: the same treatment wouldnt do for
        both cases' (GR).
246–54   MS reads:

    FRANK

      I congratulate her. How has she made you think so?

    VIVIE

       Is it so easy to make me think things without good reason?

    FRANK

      Yesterday it wasnt. But there's evidently been an explosion caused by a sudden
      and violent expansion of the sympathies. My old unique Vivie – my strong
      headed one – my third wrangler – has been blown up; and nothing remains but
      an attitude – a second rate attitude: you can make an attitude believe anything.

251   *freemasonry* the teachings and actions of the order of Free and Accepted Masons, the
      world's largest secret organisation. Frank suggests that, as immoral people, he and
      Mrs Warren have a secret understanding of one another and a set of beliefs apart
      from the larger society.

VIVIE   255

You are wrong: you know nothing about her. If you knew the
circumstances against which my mother had to struggle –

FRANK [*adroitly finishing the sentence for her*]

I should know why she is what she is, shouldnt I? What
difference would that make? Circumstances or no circum-   260
stances, Viv, you wont be able to stand your mother.

VIVIE [*very angrily*]

Why not?

FRANK

Because she's an old wretch, Viv. If you ever put your arm   265
round her waist in my presence again, I'll shoot myself there
and then as a protest against an exhibition which revolts me.

VIVIE

Must I choose between dropping your acquaintance and
dropping my mother's?   270

FRANK [*gracefully*]

That would put the old lady at ever such a disadvantage. No,
Viv: your infatuated little boy will have to stick to you in any
case. But he's all the more anxious that you shouldnt make
mistakes. It's no use, Viv: your mother's impossible. She may be   275
a good sort; but she's a bad lot, a very bad lot.

VIVIE [*hotly*]

Frank – ! [*He stands his ground. She turns away and sits down on
the bench under the yew tree, struggling to recover her self-
command. Then she says*] Is she to be deserted by all the world   280
because she's what you call a bad lot? Has she no right to live?

FRANK

No fear of that, Viv: she wont ever be deserted. [*He sits on the
bench beside her*]

VIVIE   285

But I am to desert her, I suppose.

FRANK [*babyishly, lulling her and making love to her with his voice*]

Mustnt go live with her. Little family group of mother and
daughter wouldnt be a success. Spoil *our* little group.

VIVIE [*falling under the spell*]   290

What little group?

259–60   *What difference would that make?* In MS, Shaw wrote, then struck out: 'But what
       exactly has that got to do with it? If you only knew the circumstances half the
       convicts in Britain had to struggle against, you would wonder that they are each decent
       fellows as no doubt they are. But that dont make 'em any the pleasanter to live with.'

FRANK

The babes in the wood: Vivie and little Frank. [*He nestles against her like a weary child*] Lets go and get covered up with leaves. 295

VIVIE [*rhythmically, rocking him like a nurse*]

Fast asleep, hand in hand, under the trees.

FRANK

The wise little girl with her silly little boy.

VIVIE 300

The dear little boy with his dowdy little girl.

FRANK

Ever so peaceful, and relieved from the imbecility of the little boy's father and the questionableness of the little girl's –

VIVIE [*smothering the word against her breast*] 305

Sh-sh-sh-sh! little girl wants to forget all about her mother. [*They are silent for some moments, rocking one another. Then* VIVIE *wakes up with a shock, exclaiming*] What a pair of fools we are! Come: sit up. Gracious! your hair. [*She smooths it*] I wonder do all grown up people play in that childish way when 310 nobody is looking. I never did it when I was a child.

FRANK

Neither did I. You are my first playmate. [*He catches her hand to kiss it, but checks himself to look round first. Very unexpectedly, he sees* CROFTS *emerging from the box hedge*] Oh damn! 315

VIVIE

Why damn, dear?

FRANK [*whispering*]

Sh! Here's this brute Crofts. [*He sits farther away from her with an unconcerned air*] 320

CROFTS

Could I have a few words with you, Miss Vivie?

VIVIE

Certainly.

CROFTS [*to* FRANK] 325

Youll excuse me, Gardner. Theyre waiting for you in the church, if you dont mind.

293–5   *The babes . . . leaves* The traditional tale *The Babes in the Wood* tells of a brother and sister who are abandoned in the woods and are covered in leaves by birds. S.d.: '*He slips his arm round her waist and nestles against her like a weary child*' (GR).

FRANK [*rising*]

Anything to oblige you, Crofts – except church. If you should happen to want me, Vivvums, ring the gate bell. [*He goes into the house with unruffled suavity*]   330

CROFTS [*watching him with a crafty air as he disappears, and speaking to* VIVIE *with an assumption of being on privileged terms with her*]

Pleasant young fellow that, Miss Vivie. Pity he has no money, isnt it?   335

VIVIE

Do you think so?

CROFTS

Well, whats he to do? No profession. No property. Whats he good for?   340

VIVIE

I realize his disadvantages, Sir George.

CROFTS [*a little taken aback at being so precisely interpreted*]

Oh, it's not that. But while we're in this world we're in it; and money's money. [VIVIE *does not answer*] Nice day, isnt it?   345

VIVIE [*with scarcely veiled contempt for this effort at conversation*]

Very.

CROFTS [*with brutal good humor, as if he liked her pluck*]

Well, thats not what I came to say. [*Sitting down beside her*] Now listen, Miss Vivie. I'm quite aware that I'm not a young lady's man.   350

VIVIE

Indeed, Sir George?

CROFTS   355

No; and to tell you the honest truth I dont want to be either. But when I say a thing I mean it; when I feel a sentiment I feel it in earnest; and what I value I pay hard money for. Thats the sort of man I am.

VIVIE   360

It does you great credit, I'm sure.

---

330   Frank continues: 'and a domestic will appear' (GR).
350   s.d.: '*Affecting frankness*' (GR)

CROFTS

> Oh, I dont mean to praise myself. I have my faults, Heaven knows: no man is more sensible of that than I am. I know I'm not perfect: thats one of the advantages of being a middle-aged 365 man; for I'm not a young man, and I know it. But my code is a simple one, and, I think, a good one. Honor between man and man; fidelity between man and woman; and no cant about this religion or that religion, but an honest belief that things are making for good on the whole. 370

VIVIE [*with biting irony*]

> 'A power, not ourselves, that makes for righteousness,' eh?

CROFTS [*taking her seriously*]

> Oh certainly. Not ourselves, of course. *You* understand what I mean. Well, now as to practical matters. You may have an idea 375 that Ive flung my money about; but I havnt: I'm richer today than when I first came into the property. Ive used my knowledge of the world to invest my money in ways that other men have overlooked; and whatever else I may be, I'm a safe man from the money point of view. 380

VIVIE

> It's very kind of you to tell me all this.

CROFTS

> Oh well, come, Miss Vivie: you neednt pretend you dont see what I'm driving at. I want to settle down with a Lady Crofts. I 385 suppose you think me very blunt, eh?

VIVIE

> Not at all: I am much obliged to you for being so definite and business-like. I quite appreciate the offer: the money, the

---

364   *sensible* aware

367   *simple one* Before continuing, MS adds 'and an old one'.

372   '*A power . . . righteousness*' from Matthew Arnold's *Literature and Dogma* (1873). The exact phrase is 'the eternal *not ourselves* that makes for righteousness' (original emphasis). See Arnold, *Literature and Dogma* (London: Nelson, 1873), p. 322.

375   *mean* s.d. before Crofts continues: '*He sits down beside her, as one who has found a kindred spirit*' (GR).

385   *I want . . . Lady Crofts* In MS, Shaw added this after striking out: 'It's rather sudden, perhaps; but I've no time to lose with Master Frank: it's only fair to you to let you know what choices are open to you in case young Gardner should try to trap you into an engagement.' Upon marriage to a baronet, a woman automatically takes the title 'Lady'.

position, *Lady Crofts*, and so on. But I think I will say no, if you 390
dont mind. I'd rather not. [*She rises, and strolls across to the sundial to get out of his immediate neighborhood*]

CROFTS [*not at all discouraged, and taking advantage of the additional room left him on the seat to spread himself comfortably, as if a few preliminary refusals were part of the inevitable routine of* 395
courtship]

I'm in no hurry. It was only just to let you know in case young Gardner should try to trap you. Leave the question open.

VIVIE [*sharply*]

My no is final. I wont go back from it. 400

CROFTS *is not impressed. He grins; leans forward with his elbows on his knees to prod with his stick at some unfortunate insect in the grass; and looks cunningly at her. She turns away impatiently.*

CROFTS 405

I'm a good deal older than you. Twenty-five years: quarter of a century. I shant live for ever; and I'll take care that you shall be well off when I'm gone.

VIVIE

I am proof against even that inducement, Sir George. Dont you 410
think youd better take your answer? There is not the slightest chance of my altering it.

CROFTS [*rising, after a final slash at a daisy, and coming nearer to her*]

Well, no matter. I could tell you some things that would change 415
your mind fast enough; but I wont, because I'd rather win you by honest affection. I was a good friend to your mother: ask her whether I wasnt. She'd never have made the money that paid for your education if it hadnt been for my advice and help, not to mention the money I advanced her. There are not many men 420
would have stood by her as I have. I put not less than £40,000 into it, from first to last.

390   *Lady Crofts* Shaw directs: 'dont turn away – hold him hard' (RN).

401   *Crofts is not impressed* GR has '*She looks authoritatively at him.*'

413–14   *coming nearer to her* GR has '*beginning to walk to and fro*'.

413–574   expurgated in LC1

422   MS continues with the following which Shaw struck out:

VIVIE

Was that the investment you spoke of just now that made you a safe man from the money point of view?

VIVIE [*staring at him*]

Do you mean to say you were my mother's business partner?

CROFTS 425

Yes. Now just think of all the trouble and the explanations it would save if we were to keep the whole thing in the family, so to speak. Ask your mother whether she'd like to have to explain all her affairs to a perfect stranger.

VIVIE 430

I see no difficulty, since I understand that the business is wound up, and the money invested.

CROFTS [*stopping short, amazed*]

Wound up! Wind up a business thats paying 35 per cent in the worst years! Not likely. Who told you that? 435

VIVIE [*her color quite gone*]

Do you mean that it is still – ? [*She stops abruptly, and puts her hand on the sundial to support herself. Then she gets quickly to the iron chair and sits down*] What business are you talking about? 440

CROFTS

Well, the fact is it's not what would be considered exactly a high-class business in my set – the county set, you know – *our* set it will be if you think better of my offer. Not that theres any mystery about it: dont think that. Of course you know by your 445 mother's being in it that it's perfectly straight and honest. Ive known her for many years; and I can say of her that she'd cut off her hands sooner than touch anything that was not what it ought to be. I'll tell you all about it if you like. I dont know whether youve found in travelling how hard it is to find a really 450 comfortable private hotel.

CROFTS

Well, yes it was. Now for reasons which I'm not at liberty to mention, it would be very hard to explain all this to a stranger if you wanted to marry one – in fact, it couldnt be done. With me it's different: I stand your mother's friend, I became as good as her business partner; and no explanations are needed with me: we can keep it all in the family. See the hold that would give you on me.

VIVIE

And the hold it would give you on me, perhaps.

442–51 Shaw first wrote, then struck out: 'Oh well, I'll explain all about it when we're married: it'll be an additional bond between us. As your mother is in it, you may feel sure that it is alright' (MS).

VIVIE [*sickened, averting her face*]

Yes: go on.

CROFTS

Well, thats all it is. Your mother has a genius for managing such   455
things. We've got two in Brussels, one in Ostend, one in Vienna,
and two in Budapest. Of course there are others besides ourselves in it; but we hold most of the capital; and your mother's
indispensable as managing director. Youve noticed, I daresay,
that she travels a good deal. But you see you cant mention such   460
things in society. Once let out the word hotel and everybody
says you keep a public-house. You wouldnt like people to say
that of your mother, would you? Thats why we're so reserved
about it. By the way, youll keep it to yourself, wont you? Since
it's been a secret so long, it had better remain so.   465

VIVIE

And this is the business you invite me to join you in?

CROFTS

Oh no. My wife shant be troubled with business. Youll not be in
it more than youve always been.   470

VIVIE

I always been! What do you mean?

CROFTS

Only that youve always lived on it. It paid for your education
and the dress you have on your back. Dont turn up your nose at   475
business, Miss Vivie: where would your Newnhams and Girtons
be without it?

VIVIE [*rising, almost beside herself*]

Take care. I know what this business is.

CROFTS [*starting, with a suppressed oath*]   480

Who told you?

---

455   *genius* Shaw directs: '<u>genius</u>' (RN).
456–7   'We've got two in Brussels, one in Berlin, one in Vienna, and two in Buda-Pesth'
(GR); Shaw uses Berlin instead of Ostend later in the play as well (IV.361). Following
this list of cities in which they have brothels, for the 1926 production Shaw had
Crofts add that although their business is presently restricted in London 'our
prospects are rather rosy' (LC2), before continuing to note that others were also
involved in the business.
469   Shaw directs: '<u>my</u> wife' (RN).
476   *Girtons* Founded in 1869, Girton was the first women's college at Cambridge
University.
479   'Sir George Crofts: you will understand my opinion of you without my further
explanation when I tell you that I found out last night the real nature of this
business'(MS)

VIVIE

Your partner. My mother.

CROFTS [*black with rage*]

The old –   485

VIVIE

Just so.

He swallows the epithet and stands for a moment swearing and raging foully to himself. But he knows that his cue is to be sympathetic. He takes refuge in generous indignation.   490

CROFTS

She ought to have had more consideration for you. I'd never have told you.

VIVIE

I think you would probably have told me when we were   495
married: it would have been a convenient weapon to break me in with.

CROFTS [*quite sincerely*]

I never intended that. On my word as a gentleman I didnt.

VIVIE *wonders at him. Her sense of the irony of his protest*   500
cools and braces her. She replies with contemptuous self-possession.

VIVIE

It does not matter. I suppose you understand that when we leave here today our acquaintance ceases.

CROFTS   505

Why? Is it for helping your mother?

VIVIE

My mother was a very poor woman who had no reasonable choice but to do as she did. You were a rich gentleman; and you did the same for the sake of 35 per cent. You are a pretty   510
common sort of scoundrel, I think. That is my opinion of you.

---

483   Shaw directs: 'Your <u>partner</u> my <u>mother</u>' (RN).
485   Shaw changed the line to read: 'The old bitch' (LC2). However, the censor crossed
       out the expletive in red pencil. Lord Cromer, the Lord Chamberlain, wrote to Shaw
       on 1 March 1926 that he would allow all of the revisions Shaw had made to the
       script save for this one, which he demanded be returned to the original as it appears
       above (LCP Corr 1924/5632 *Mrs Warren's Profession*, BL).
486–90 s.d.: 'Vivie looks quickly at him & he swallows the epithet & stands evidently swear-
       ing & raging foully to himself. At last, with a revolting effort to appear sympathetic,
       he says' (MS).
503   *matter* Before continuing, MS adds: 'What you have just told me changes my plans
       rather suddenly.'
510–11 *pretty common sort of* 'most abhorrent' (MS)

CROFTS [*after a stare: not at all displeased, and much more at his ease on these frank terms than on their former ceremonious ones*]
Ha! ha! ha! ha! Go it, little missie, go it: it doesnt hurt me and it amuses you. Why the devil shouldnt I invest my money that   515
way? I take the interest on my capital like other people: I hope you dont think I dirty my own hands with the work. Come! you wouldnt refuse the acquaintance of my mother's cousin the Duke of Belgravia because some of the rents he gets are earned in queer ways. You wouldnt cut the Archbishop of Canterbury,   520
I suppose, because the Ecclesiastical Commissioners have a few publicans and sinners among their tenants. Do you remember your Crofts scholarship at Newnham? Well, that was founded by my brother the M.P. He gets his 22 per cent out of a factory with 600 girls in it, and not one of them getting wages enough   525
to live on. How d'ye suppose they manage when they have no family to fall back on? Ask your mother. And do you expect me to turn my back on 35 per cent when all the rest are pocketing what they can, like sensible men? No such fool! If youre going to pick and choose your acquaintances on moral principles,   530
youd better clear out of this country, unless you want to cut yourself out of all decent society.
VIVIE [*conscience stricken*]
You might go on to point out that I myself never asked where the money I spent came from. I believe I am just as bad as you.   535
CROFTS [*greatly reassured*]
Of course you are; and a very good thing too! What harm does it do after all? [*Rallying her jocularly*] So you dont think me such a scoundrel now you come to think it over. Eh?

---

519   *Duke of Belgravia* Belgravia is an affluent and fashionable area of central London. Like the unnamed Duke mentioned earlier (II.120–6), this is a fictitious individual; the authorities therefore never demanded a change in name as they did with the Duke of Beaufort.

520   *Archbishop of Canterbury* the head of the Church of England

521   *Ecclesiastical Commissioners* a body created by Act of Parliament in 1836. They were responsible for the administration of church property, the profit from which was used to augment the clergy's income, until they were replaced by the Church Commissioners in 1948.

524   *M.P.* Member of Parliament

526–7   *How . . . on* 'How d'ye suppose most of them manage?' (GR).

535   *I believe . . . you* Shaw directs: 'reassure him' (RN). 'You are quite right: the contamination is everywhere' (MS).

VIVIE   540

I have shared profits with you; and I admitted you just now to
the familiarity of knowing what I think of you.

CROFTS [*with serious friendliness*]

To be sure you did. You wont find me a bad sort: I dont go in
for being superfine intellectually; but Ive plenty of honest   545
human feeling; and the old Crofts breed comes out in a sort of
instinctive hatred of anything low, in which I'm sure youll
sympathize with me. Believe me, Miss Vivie, the world isnt such
a bad place as the croakers make out. As long as you dont fly
openly in the face of society, society doesnt ask any incon-   550
venient questions; and it makes precious short work of the cads
who do. There are no secrets better kept than the secrets
everybody guesses. In the class of people I can introduce you to,
no lady or gentleman would so far forget themselves as to
discuss my business affairs or your mother's. No man can offer   555
you a safer position.

---

541   Before this line, MS adds:

    VIVIE

      You seem such a little crawling thing in the whole great welter of wickedness
      that I feel as if I had no loathing to spare for you.

    CROFTS

      That's all right. Remember, I stand to my offer. When you get tired of your
      loathing, you can think over it. Youre not really angry with me, you know.

549   *croakers* people who prophesy evil and doom

556   After this line, MS adds:

    VIVIE

      And everybody, on your own showing, can offer me just as safe a one. How old
      are you?

    CROFTS

      Eh?

    VIVIE

      How old are you? You do not expect me to marry you without knowing your
      age, I presume.

    CROFTS

      Oh, of course not. Well, I told you I was 25 years older than you. I've been
      honest with you, Vivie.

    VIVIE

      Yes, in the way of self-revelation. And now, since you have got to the point of
      addressing me as if you were one of my intimate friends, may I ask how long
      you intend to stay down here?

    CROFTS

      As long as you like. If I run up to town for a few hours it will only be to buy a
      few little things that I'd like you to accept from me to shew our good under-
      standing.

VIVIE [*studying him curiously*]

I suppose you really think youre getting on famously with me.

CROFTS

Well, I hope I may flatter myself that you think better of me   560
than you did at first.

VIVIE [*quietly*]

I hardly find you worth thinking about at all now. When I think
of the society that tolerates you, and the laws that protect you!
when I think of how helpless nine out of ten young girls would   565
be in the hands of you and my mother! the unmentionable
woman and her capitalist bully –

CROFTS [*livid*]

Damn you!

VIVIE   570

You need not. I feel among the damned already.

> *She raises the latch of the gate to open it and go out. He follows*
> *her and puts his hand heavily on the top bar to prevent its*
> *opening.*

CROFTS [*panting with fury*]   575

Do you think I'll put up with this from you, you young devil?

VIVIE [*unmoved*]

Be quiet. Some one will answer the bell. [*Without flinching a*
step she strikes the bell with the back of her hand. It clangs
harshly; and he starts back involuntarily. Almost immediately   580
FRANK *appears at the porch with his rifle*]

FRANK [*with cheerful politeness*]

Will you have the rifle, Viv; or shall I operate?

VIVIE

Frank: have you been listening?   585

---

563   *now* s.d. before Vivie continues: '*She rises and turns towards the gate, pausing on her*
         way to contemplate him and say almost gently, but with intense conviction' (GR).

568   *livid* 'white' (MS)

576   MS continues: 'Say another word, and –'.

580–647   Shaw directs Frank to play the scene with the rifle 'very cool' (RN).

585–7   *Frank . . . assure you* MS reads:

>   VIVIE
>   I thought you were at the church.
>   CROFTS
>   No, he's been listening.

FRANK [*coming down into the garden*]

Only for the bell, I assure you; so that you shouldnt have to wait. I think I shewed great insight into your character, Crofts.

CROFTS

For two pins I'd take that gun from you and break it across your head. 590

FRANK [*stalking him cautiously*]

Pray dont. I'm ever so careless in handling firearms. Sure to be a fatal accident, with a reprimand from the coroner's jury for my negligence. 595

VIVIE

Put the rifle away, Frank: it's quite unnecessary.

FRANK

Quite right, Viv. Much more sportsmanlike to catch him in a trap. [CROFTS, *understanding the insult, makes a threatening* 600 *movement*] Crofts: there are fifteen cartridges in the magazine here; and I am a dead shot at the present distance and at an object of your size.

CROFTS

Oh, you neednt be afraid. I'm not going to touch you. 605

FRANK

Ever so magnanimous of you under the circumstances! Thank you!

CROFTS

I'll just tell you this before I go. It may interest you, since youre 610 so fond of one another. Allow me, Mister Frank, to introduce you to your half-sister, the eldest daughter of the Reverend

---

FRANK

Not at all, I assure you. When I got half way to the church I felt so sure you'd have to ring that I came back and sat down in the breakfast room & told the servants to leave the bell to me;

586 s.d. not in GR

600–1 Instead of s.d., MS reads: 'At the same time, as he's a big man, and I'm not celebrated for my physical prowess, I decline to lay down my arms.'

611–14 *Allow me . . . road* 'This young lady's mother was convicted five times of shoplifting before she took to her present trade of training young girls to the profession of larceny. [*He goes through the gates*]' (LC1).

Samuel Gardner. Miss Vivie: your half-brother. Good morning.
[*He goes out through the gate and along the road*]

FRANK [*after a pause of stupefaction, raising the rifle*]   615

Youll testify before the coroner that it's an accident, Viv. [*He
takes aim at the retreating figure of* CROFTS. VIVIE *seizes the
muzzle and pulls it round against her breast*]

VIVIE

Fire now. You may.   620

FRANK [*dropping his end of the rifle hastily*]

Stop! take care. [*She lets it go. It falls on the turf*] Oh, youve given
your little boy such a turn. Suppose it had gone off! ugh! [*He
sinks on the garden seat, overcome*]

VIVIE   625

Suppose it had: do you think it would not have been a relief to
have some sharp physical pain tearing through me?

FRANK [*coaxingly*]

Take it ever so easy, dear Viv. Remember: even if the rifle scared
that fellow into telling the truth for the first time in his life, that   630
only makes us the babes in the wood in earnest. [*He holds out
his arms to her*] Come and be covered up with leaves again.

VIVIE [*with a cry of disgust*]

Ah, not that, not that. You make all my flesh creep.

FRANK   635

Why, whats the matter?

VIVIE

Goodbye. [*She makes for the gate*]

---

638   The end of Act III was first written as it is transcribed in Appendix VII (pp. 166–7).
      Shaw included a revised version at the end of MS, after the play had been completed
      on 2 November 1893. It inserted a short exchange that would not make it into GR:
         VIVIE
            All the morning a cloud of horror has been gathering over me like a storm after
            the moonlight of last night. I must get away from it all – from the spell of that
            ghastly moonlight – from the very air breathed by my mother and that man –
         FRANK
            But not from little Frank. There was no cloud over the babes in the wood just
            now.
         VIVIE
            Oh, how can you remind me of it – how can you bear to think of it! Never
            that again – never whilst we live: it is all tainted – horrible: Goodbye. (makes
            for the gate)

FRANK [*jumping up*]

    Hallo! Stop! Viv! Viv! [*She turns in the gateway*] Where are you   640
going to? Where shall we find you?

VIVIE

    At Honoria Fraser's chambers, 67 Chancery Lane, for the rest of
my life. [*She goes off quickly in the opposite direction to that taken
by* CROFTS]   645

FRANK

    But I say – wait – dash it! [*He runs after her*]

ACT IV

Honoria Fraser's chambers in Chancery Lane. An office at the top of
New Stone Buildings, with a plate-glass window, distempered walls,
electric light, and a patent stove. Saturday afternoon. The chimneys
of Lincoln's Inn and the western sky beyond are seen through the
window. There is a double writing table in the middle of the room,   5
with a cigar box, ash pans, and a portable electric reading lamp
almost snowed up in heaps of papers and books. This table has knee
holes and chairs right and left and is very untidy. The clerk's desk,
closed and tidy, with its high stool, is against the wall, near a door
communicating with the inner rooms. In the opposite wall is the door   10
leading to the public corridor. Its upper panel is of opaque glass, let-
tered in black on the outside, FRASER AND WARREN. *A baize screen*
hides the corner between this door and the window.

    FRANK, *in a fashionable light-colored coaching suit, with his stick,*
gloves, and white hat in his hands, is pacing up and down the office.   15
Somebody tries the door with a key.

FRANK [*calling*]
    Come in. It's not locked.

  1–24   *Honoria . . . see you* 'Fireplace. Arm chair before it in which Frank is sitting with his
           hat & stick between his knees & his legs stretched out, fast asleep. Enter Vivie at door
           R, with her hat & jacket on. Not seeing him, she takes them off & hangs them up
           behind the screen; then comes back & sits down to work at the table. Frank's hat &
           stick topple over. She looks up, sees the hat & swings the arm chair vigorously round.
           They stare at one another' (MS).
     1   *An office* 'A newish office' (LC1)
     2   *New Stone Buildings* so named to differentiate them from the Old Stone Buildings
          located off Chancery Lane
     2   *distempered* painted
     3   *patent stove* open stove
     4   *Lincoln's Inn* Along with Middle Temple, Inner Temple, and Gray's Inn, Lincoln's
          Inn is one of the four institutions that have historically been responsible for legal
          education in Britain. Together, they are called the Inns of Court and since the Middle
          Ages have held the exclusive right of admitting barristers to the bar, which allows
          them to practise law. As the s.d. notes, Lincoln's Inn is located just to the west of
          Chancery Lane.
     8   *clerk* secretary
    12   *baize* a coarse woollen fabric
    14   *coaching suit* suit for travelling, usually made from a resistant material like wool

VIVIE *comes in, in her hat and jacket. She stops and stares at him.*   20

VIVIE [*sternly*]

What are you doing here?

FRANK

Waiting to see you. Ive been here for hours. Is this the way you attend to your business? [*He puts his hat and stick on the table,*   25 *and perches himself with a vault on the clerk's stool, looking at her with every appearance of being in a specially restless, teasing, flip- pant mood*]

VIVIE

Ive been away exactly twenty minutes for a cup of tea. [*She takes*   30 *off her hat and jacket and hangs them up behind the screen*] How did you get in?

FRANK

The staff had not left when I arrived. He's gone to play cricket on Primrose Hill. Why dont you employ a woman, and give   35 your sex a chance?

VIVIE

What have you come for?

FRANK [*springing off the stool and coming close to her*]

Viv: lets go and enjoy the Saturday half-holiday somewhere,   40 like the staff. What do you say to Richmond, and then a music hall, and a jolly supper?

VIVIE

Cant afford it. I shall put in another six hours work before I go to bed.   45

---

30   *twenty* '35' (MS)

34   *cricket* 'football' (GR)

35   *Primrose Hill* a public open space located to the north of Regent's Park, notable for its view of central London to the southeast. Shaw took regular walks on Primrose Hill while composing the play and even wrote parts of it there. *Diaries*, pp. 968–71, 973–4.

35–6 *Why . . . chance* 'How did you get in? Did I open the door in my sleep?' (MS).

40   *the Saturday half-holiday* In late-Victorian Britain, many people worked on Saturday morning but were free for the afternoon.

41   *Richmond* a town in Surrey to the southwest of London, located along the River Thames. There have been several productions of *Mrs Warren's Profession* in Rich- mond over the years.

41–2 *music hall* Music halls were places of popular entertainment that allowed drinking and smoking and normally catered to the working and middle classes.

79

FRANK

Cant afford it, cant we? Aha! Look here. [*He takes out a handful of sovereigns and makes them chink*] Gold, Viv: gold!

VIVIE

Where did you get it?   50

FRANK

Gambling, Viv: gambling. Poker.

VIVIE

Pah! It's meaner than stealing it. No: I'm not coming. [*She sits down to work at the table, with her back to the glass door, and*   55 *begins turning over the papers*]

FRANK [*remonstrating piteously*]

But, my dear Viv, I want to talk to you ever so seriously.

VIVIE

Very well: sit down in Honoria's chair and talk here. I like ten   60 minutes chat after tea. [*He murmurs*] No use groaning: I'm inexorable. [*He takes the opposite seat disconsolately*] Pass that cigar box, will you?

FRANK [*pushing the cigar box across*]

Nasty womanly habit. Nice men dont do it any longer.   65

VIVIE

Yes: they object to the smell in the office; and weve had to take to cigarets. See! [*She opens the box and takes out a cigaret, which she lights. She offers him one; but he shakes his head with a wry face. She settles herself comfortably in her chair, smoking*]   70 Go ahead.

FRANK

Well, I want to know what youve done – what arrangements youve made.

VIVIE   75

Everything was settled twenty minutes after I arrived here. Honoria has found the business too much for her this year; and

---

60–1   *ten minutes* 'half an hour's' (MS)
  61   *tea* an afternoon or evening meal. Despite the name, tea is not invariably served.
62–70   *Pass . . . smoking* not in MS
73–4   *what arrangements youve made* 'what our relations are to be in future?' (LC1)
75–165   expurgated in LC1

she was on the point of sending for me and proposing a
partnership when I walked in and told her I hadnt a farthing in
the world. So I installed myself and packed her off for a fort- 80
night's holiday. What happened at Haslemere when I left?

FRANK

Nothing at all. I said youd gone to town on particular business.

VIVIE

Well? 85

FRANK

Well, either they were too flabbergasted to say anything, or else
Crofts had prepared your mother. Anyhow, she didnt say any-
thing; and Crofts didnt say anything; and Praddy only stared.
After tea they got up and went; Ive not seen them since. 90

VIVIE [*nodding placidly with one eye on a wreath of smoke*]
Thats all right.

FRANK [*looking round disparagingly*]
Do you intend to stick in this confounded place?

VIVIE [*blowing the wreath decisively away, and sitting straight up*] 95
Yes. These two days have given me back all my strength and
self-possession. I will never take a holiday again as long as I live.

FRANK [*with a very wry face*]
Mps! You look quite happy. And as hard as nails.

VIVIE [*grimly*] 100
Well for me that I am!

FRANK [*rising*]
Look here, Viv: we must have an explanation. We parted the
other day under a complete misunderstanding. [*He sits on the
table, close to her*] 105

VIVIE [*putting away the cigaret*]
Well: clear it up.

---

79   *farthing* a quarter of a penny. Largely because inflation had made it useless, the
     farthing was phased out before the decimalisation of British currency.
80–1 *fortnight* a period of two weeks. The term comes from a contraction of 'fourteen
     nights'.
96–7 *all my strength and self-possession* Shaw directs: 'hard as nails' (RN).

FRANK

You remember what Crofts said?

VIVIE   110

Yes.

FRANK

That revelation was supposed to bring about a complete change
in the nature of our feeling for one another. It placed us on the
footing of brother and sister.   115

VIVIE

Yes.

FRANK

Have you ever had a brother?

VIVIE   120

No.

FRANK

Then you dont know what being brother and sister feels like?
Now I have lots of sisters; and the fraternal feeling is quite familiar to me. I assure you my feeling for you is not the least in the   125
world like it. The girls will go their way; I will go mine; and we
shant care if we never see one another again. Thats brother and
sister. But as to you, I cant be easy if I have to pass a week without seeing you. Thats not brother and sister. It's exactly what I
felt an hour before Crofts made his revelation. In short, dear   130
Viv, it's love's young dream.

VIVIE [*bitingly*]

The same feeling, Frank, that brought your father to my
mother's feet. Is that it?

FRANK [*so revolted that he slips off the table for a moment*]   135

I very strongly object, Viv, to have my feelings compared to any
which the Reverend Samuel is capable of harboring; and I
object still more to a comparison of you to your mother.
[*Resuming his perch*] Besides, I dont believe the story. I have
taxed my father with it, and obtained from him what I consider   140
tantamount to a denial.

VIVIE

What did he say?

---

124   *sisters* Frank adds: 'Jessie and Georgina and the rest' (GR). These are the names that
       Frank notes later in the scene, though Jessie becomes Bessie (IV.422).
135   '*revolted*' (GR). Thus, the next s.d. (IV.139) did not appear.

FRANK

He said he was sure there must be some mistake. 145

VIVIE

Do you believe him?

FRANK

I am prepared to take his word as against Crofts'.

VIVIE 150

Does it make any difference? I mean in your imagination or conscience; for of course it makes no real difference.

FRANK [*shaking his head*]

None whatever to me.

VIVIE 155

Nor to me.

FRANK [*staring*]

But this is ever so surprising! [*He goes back to his chair*] I thought our whole relations were altered in your imagination and conscience, as you put it, the moment those words were 160 out of that brute's muzzle.

VIVIE

No: it was not that. I didnt believe him. I only wish I could.

FRANK

Eh? 165

VIVIE

I think brother and sister would be a very suitable relation for us.

FRANK

You really mean that? 170

VIVIE

Yes. It's the only relation I care for, even if we could afford any other. I mean that.

FRANK [*raising his eyebrows like one on whom a new light has dawned, and rising with quite an effusion of chivalrous sentiment*] 175

My dear Viv: why didnt you say so before? I am ever so sorry for persecuting you. I understand, of course.

151   In MS, Vivie begins: 'And I am prepared to take my mother's word.'
158   s.d. not in GR
175   *rising* 'GR has *speaking*'.

VIVIE [*puzzled*]

Understand what?

FRANK   180

Oh, I'm not a fool in the ordinary sense: only in the Scriptural sense of doing all the things the wise man declared to be folly, after trying them himself on the most extensive scale. I see I am no longer Vivvums's little boy. Dont be alarmed: I shall never call you Vivvums again – at least unless you get tired of your   185 new little boy, whoever he may be.

VIVIE

My new little boy!

FRANK [*with conviction*]

Must be a new little boy. Always happens that way. No other   190 way, in fact.

VIVIE

None that you know of, fortunately for you.

Someone knocks at the door.

FRANK   195

My curse upon yon caller, whoe'er he be!

VIVIE

It's Praed. He's going to Italy and wants to say goodbye. I asked him to call this afternoon. Go and let him in.

FRANK   200

We can continue our conversation after his departure for Italy. I'll stay him out. [*He goes to the door and opens it*] How are you, Praddy? Delighted to see you. Come in.

PRAED, *dressed for travelling, comes in, in high spirits.*

181–3   *Oh ... scale* probably a reference to Solomon, the warrior king who is often regarded as the greatest leader of Israel. He was well known in later life for his wisdom, much of which is imparted in the Book of Proverbs. Solomon's aphorisms are told from the point of view of a father counselling his son, whereas Frank has shown that he will not heed his father, who has probably recited many of the book's verses in his sermons.

196   The Shakespearean diction of this line might be traced to *Henry VI, Part 1*. At the opening of Act I, Scene iii, the Duke of Gloucester appears at the gates of the Tower of London but the warders refuse him entry when he is announced, one of them stating: 'Whoe'er he be, you may not be let in.' Frank's curse foreshadows Mrs Warren's parting curse upon Vivie (IV.740–2) and Kitty's cursing of honest work (IV.750–2).

204   s.d. continues: '*excited by the beginning of his journey*' (GR).

PRAED   205

How do you do, Miss Warren? [*She presses his hand cordially,
though a certain sentimentality in his high spirits jars on her*] I
start in an hour from Holborn Viaduct. I wish I could persuade
you to try Italy.

VIVIE   210

What for?

PRAED

Why, to saturate yourself with beauty and romance, of course.
    VIVIE, *with a shudder, turns her chair to the table, as if the
work waiting for her there were a support to her.* PRAED *sits*   215
opposite to her. FRANK *places a chair near* VIVIE, *and drops
lazily and carelessly into it, talking at her over his shoulder.*

FRANK

No use, Praddy. Viv is a little Philistine. She is indifferent to my
romance, and insensible to my beauty.   220

VIVIE

Mr Praed: once for all, there is no beauty and no romance in
life for me. Life is what it is; and I am prepared to take it as it is.

PRAED [*enthusiastically*]

You will not say that if you come with me to Verona and on to   225
Venice. You will cry with delight at living in such a beautiful
world.

FRANK

This is most eloquent, Praddy. Keep it up.

PRAED   230

Oh I assure you *I* have cried – I shall cry again, I hope – at fifty!
At your age, Miss Warren, you would not need to go so far as
Verona. Your spirits would absolutely fly up at the mere sight of
Ostend. You would be charmed with the gaiety, the vivacity, the
happy air of Brussels.   235

VIVIE [*springing up with an exclamation of loathing*]
Agh!

---

208   *Holborn Viaduct* Opened in 1874, Holborn Viaduct Station was a central London
      terminus which served continental as well as local trains; it was closed in 1990 and
      replaced by City Thameslink Station.

219   *Philistine* a nation of people who were often in conflict with the Israelites. It is a
      term commonly used to denote those who are uneducated and indifferent or even
      hostile towards art and culture.

236–7 s.d. instead of this reaction: '*Vivie recoils*' (GR). Neither Praed nor Frank then rises
      (IV. 238–40), meaning that they do not have to sit again (IV.259–65).

PRAED [*rising*]

Whats the matter?

FRANK [*rising*]   240

Hallo, Viv!

VIVIE [*to* PRAED, *with deep reproach*]

Can you find no better example of your beauty and romance
than Brussels to talk to me about?

PRAED [*puzzled*]   245

Of course it's very different from Verona. I dont suggest for a
moment that –

VIVIE [*bitterly*]

Probably the beauty and romance come to much the same in
both places.   250

PRAED [*completely sobered and much concerned*]

My dear Miss Warren: I – [*looking inquiringly at* FRANK] Is
anything the matter?

FRANK

She thinks your enthusiasm frivolous, Praddy. She's had ever   255
such a serious call.

VIVIE [*sharply*]

Hold your tongue, Frank. Dont be silly.

FRANK [*sitting down*]

Do you call this good manners, Praed?   260

PRAED [*anxious and considerate*]

Shall I take him away, Miss Warren? I feel sure we have disturbed you at your work.

VIVIE

Sit down: I'm not ready to go back to work yet. [PRAED *sits*]   265
You both think I have an attack of nerves. Not a bit of it. But
there are two subjects I want dropped, if you dont mind. One
of them [*to* FRANK] is love's young dream in any shape or
form: the other [*to* PRAED] is the romance and beauty of life,
especially Ostend and the gaiety of Brussels. You are welcome   270
to any illusions you may have left on these subjects: I have
none. If we three are to remain friends, I must be treated as a
woman of business, permanently single [*to* FRANK] and
permanently unromantic [*to* PRAED].

258   Shaw directs: 'make him jump' (RN).
263   s.d.: '*He is about to rise*' (GR).
270   *especially . . . Brussels* 'especially as exemplified by the gaiety of Brussels' (GR)

86

FRANK   275

    I also shall remain permanently single until you change your
    mind. Praddy: change the subject. Be eloquent about some-
    thing else.

PRAED [*diffidently*]

    I'm afraid theres nothing else in the world that I *can* talk about   280
    about. The Gospel of Art is the only one I can preach. I know
    Miss Warren is a great devotee of the Gospel of Getting On; but
    we cant discuss that without hurting your feelings, Frank, since
    you are determined not to get on.

FRANK   285

    Oh, dont mind my feelings. Give me some improving advice by
    all means: it does me ever so much good. Have another try to
    make a successful man of me, Viv. Come: lets have it all: energy,
    thrift, foresight, self-respect, character. Dont you hate people
    who have no character, Viv?   290

VIVIE [*wincing*]

    Oh, stop, stop: let us have no more of that horrible cant. Mr
    Praed: if there are really only those two gospels in the world, we
    had better all kill ourselves; for the same taint is in both,
    through and through.   295

FRANK [*looking critically at her*]

    There is a touch of poetry about you today, Viv, which has
    hitherto been lacking.

PRAED [*remonstrating*]

    My dear Frank: arnt you a little unsympathetic?   300

VIVIE [*merciless to herself*]

    No: it's good for me. It keeps me from being sentimental.

FRANK [*bantering her*]

    Checks your strong natural propensity that way, dont it?

VIVIE [*almost hysterically*]   305

    Oh yes: go on: dont spare me. I was sentimental for one
    moment in my life – beautifully sentimental – by moonlight;
    and now –

286–90   Shaw directs Vivie: 'During Frank's character speech look like vinegar on a hot iron'
        (RN).

   308   In MS, Vivie continues: 'I have to extricate myself from the tie I formed in that
        instant of folly.'

FRANK [*quickly*]

    I say, Viv: take care. Dont give yourself away. 310

VIVIE

    Oh, do you think Mr Praed does not know all about my mother? [*Turning on* PRAED] You had better have told me that morning, Mr Praed. You are very old fashioned in your delicacies, after all. 315

PRAED

    Surely it is you who are a little old fashioned in your prejudices, Miss Warren. I feel bound to tell you, speaking as an artist, and believing that the most intimate human relationships are far beyond and above the scope of the law, that though I know that 320 your mother is an unmarried woman, I do not respect her the less on that account. I respect her more.

FRANK [*airily*]

    Hear! Hear!

VIVIE [*staring at him*] 325

    Is that *all* you know?

PRAED

    Certainly that is all.

VIVIE

    Then you neither of you know anything. Your guesses are inno- 330 cence itself compared to the truth.

PRAED [*rising, startled and indignant, and preserving his politeness with an effort*]

    I hope not. [*More emphatically*] I hope not, Miss Warren.

309–28   MS reads:

       FRANK (quickly)

         I say, Viv: take care. If you've any secret, dont give it away to us in a tantrum.

       PRAED

         Quite right, Frank, quite right.

       VIVIE (turning on Praed)

         Surely <u>you</u> know that I am speaking of my mother. You know the truth about her; and he had better know. You must tell him for me. <u>I</u> cannot utter such a thing.

       PRAED

         But I cannot – I know nothing – at least, nothing unpardonable – nothing that need be told now.

       FRANK

         My dear Viv: dont you think you may safely trust us to our powers of guessing?

314–82   *You are . . . easy* expurgated and replaced in LC1 by:

       VIVIE

         I know now that my mother is a convicted thief.

FRANK [*whistles*]   335
  Whew!
VIVIE
  You are not making it easy for me to tell you, Mr Praed.
PRAED [*his chivalry drooping before their conviction*]
  If there *is* anything worse – that is, anything else – are you sure   340
  you are right to tell us, Miss Warren?
VIVIE
  I am sure that if I had the courage I should spend the rest of my
  life in telling everybody – stamping and branding it into them
  until they all felt their part in its abomination as I feel mine.   345
  There is nothing I despise more than the wicked convention that
  protects these things by forbidding a woman to mention them.
  And yet I cant tell you. The two infamous words that describe
  what my mother is are ringing in my ears and struggling on my
  tongue; but I cant utter them: the shame of them is too horrible   350
  for me. [*She buries her face in her hands. The two men, astonished, stare at one another and then at her. She raises her head
  again desperately and snatches a sheet of paper and a pen*] Here:
  let me draft you a prospectus.
FRANK   355
  Oh, she's mad. Do you hear, Viv? mad. Come! pull yourself
  together.
VIVIE
  You shall see. [*She writes*] 'Paid up capital: not less than £40,000
  standing in the name of Sir George Crofts, Baronet, the chief   360

PRAED
  But she has repented, and atoned for that slip of her youth and poverty.
VIVIE
  You are mistaken. She no longer steals; but she teaches others to steal.
PRAED
  Great Heaven! And you have the courage to tell us this.
  In addition to the change in Mrs Warren's profession, her repentance here is particu-
  larly noteworthy.
335–9 These lines read only as s.d.: '*Frank's face shows that he does not share Praed's
       incredulity. Vivie utters an exclamation of impatience. Praed's chivalry droops before
       their conviction. He adds, slowly*' (GR).
345   *part in its abomination* 'share in its shame and horror' (GR)
350–1 *the shame . . . for me* 'my instinct is too strong for me' (GR).
353   *snatches* GR has '*takes*'.

89

shareholder. Premises at Brussels, Ostend, Vienna, and Budapest. Managing director: Mrs Warren'; and now dont let us forget *her* qualifications: the two words. [*She writes the words and pushes the paper to them*] There! Oh no: dont read it: dont! [*She snatches it back and tears it to pieces; then seizes her head in her hands and hides her face on the table*]   365

FRANK, *who has watched the writing over her shoulder, and opened his eyes very widely at it, takes a card from his pocket; scribbles the two words on it; and silently hands it to* PRAED, *who reads it with amazement, and hides it hastily in his pocket.*   370

FRANK [*whispering tenderly*]

Viv, dear: thats all right. I read what you wrote: so did Praddy. We understand. And we remain, as this leaves us at present, yours ever so devotedly.

PRAED   375

We do indeed, Miss Warren. I declare you are the most splendidly courageous woman I ever met.

This sentimental compliment braces VIVIE. *She throws it away from her with an impatient shake, and forces herself to stand up, though not without some support from the table.*   380

FRANK

Dont stir, Viv, if you dont want to. Take it easy.

VIVIE

Thank you. You can always depend on me for two things: not to cry and not to faint. [*She moves a few steps towards the door*   385 *of the inner room, and stops close to* PRAED *to say*] I shall need much more courage than that when I tell my mother that we have come to the parting of the ways. Now I must go into the next room for a moment to make myself neat again, if you dont mind.   390

PRAED

Shall we go away?

VIVIE

No: I'll be back presently. Only for a moment. [*She goes into the other room,* PRAED *opening the door for her*]   395

---

363   *the two words* The actress Ellen Terry wrote to Shaw asking him what the two words were. He responded: 'Prostitute and Procuress' (File 5, Box 21, HRC).

370   *and hides . . . pocket* GR has '*Frank then remorsefully stoops over Vivie*'.

386   *room* GR has '*rooms*'. Like the cottage, Vivie's office becomes more modest through revisions.

PRAED

What an amazing revelation! I'm extremely disappointed in Crofts: I am indeed.

FRANK

I'm not in the least. I feel he's perfectly accounted for at last. But what a facer for me, Praddy! I cant marry her now. 400

PRAED [*sternly*]

Frank! [*The two look at one another,* FRANK *unruffled,* PRAED *deeply indignant*] Let me tell you, Gardner, that if you desert her now you will behave very despicably. 405

FRANK

Good old Praddy! Ever chivalrous! But you mistake: it's not the moral aspect of the case: it's the money aspect. I really cant bring myself to touch the old woman's money now.

PRAED 410

And was that what you were going to marry on?

FRANK

What else? *I* havnt any money, nor the smallest turn for making it. If I married Viv now she would have to support me; and I should cost her more than I am worth. 415

PRAED

But surely a clever bright fellow like you can make something by your own brains.

FRANK

Oh yes, a little. [*He takes out his money again*] I made all that 420 yesterday in an hour and a half. But I made it in a highly speculative business. No, dear Praddy: even if Bessie and Georgina marry millionaires and the governor dies after cutting them off with a shilling, I shall have only four hundred a year. And he wont die until he's three score and ten: he hasnt originality 425 enough. I shall be on short allowance for the next twenty years. No short allowance for Viv, if I can help it. I withdraw gracefully and leave the field to the gilded youth of England. So thats settled. I shant worry her about it: I'll just send her a little note after we're gone. She'll understand. 430

397–400   *I'm . . . last* expurgated in LC1
   401   *facer* setback
   425   *three score and ten* 'The days of our years are threescore years and ten' (Psalms 90:10). A score is a group or set of twenty, so 'threescore years and ten' equals seventy years.

PRAED [*grasping his hand*]

Good fellow, Frank! I heartily beg your pardon. But must you never see her again?

FRANK

Never see her again! Hang it all, be reasonable. I shall come 435
along as often as possible, and be her brother. I can *not* understand the absurd consequences you romantic people expect
from the most ordinary transactions. [*A knock at the door*] I
wonder who this is. Would you mind opening the door? If it's a
client it will look more respectable than if I appeared. 440

PRAED

Certainly. [*He goes to the door and opens it.* FRANK *sits down in*
VIVIE*'s chair to scribble a note*] My dear Kitty: come in: come in.

MRS WARREN *comes in, looking apprehensively round for*
VIVIE. *She has done her best to make herself matronly and* 445
dignified. The brilliant hat is replaced by a sober bonnet, and the
gay blouse covered by a costly black silk mantle. She is pitiably
anxious and ill at ease: evidently panic-stricken.

MRS WARREN [*to* FRANK]

What! *Youre* here, are you? 450

FRANK [*turning in his chair from his writing, but not rising*]

Here, and charmed to see you. You come like a breath of spring.

MRS WARREN

Oh, get out with your nonsense. [*In a low voice*] Wheres Vivie?

FRANK *points expressively to the door of the inner room, but* 455
says nothing.

MRS WARREN [*sitting down suddenly and almost beginning to cry*]

Praddy: wont she see me, dont you think?

444–54   Mrs Warren is not described in MS, but she enters with the Reverend Samuel. Shaw
wrote a brief exchange before striking it out and excluding the clergyman from the
act:

    MRS WARREN (to Frank)

      What! <u>Youre</u> here, are you?

    FRANK (without rising)

      Here and charmed to see you. What have you brought my father up to town for?
      An elopement, eh?

    REV. S.

      Spare Mrs Warren your pleasantries, sir.

    FRANK

      She likes 'em. Dont you Mrs Warren?

    MRS WARREN

      Not today, thank you. I'm too worried. Where's Vivie?

PRAED

My dear Kitty: dont distress yourself. Why should she not?   460

MRS WARREN

Oh, you never can see why not: youre too innocent. Mr Frank: did she say anything to you?

FRANK [*folding his note*]

She *must* see you, if [*very expressively*] you wait til she comes in.   465

MRS WARREN [*frightened*]

Why shouldnt I wait?

> FRANK *looks quizzically at her; puts his note carefully on the inkbottle, so that* VIVIE *cannot fail to find it when next she dips her pen; then rises and devotes his attention entirely to her.*   470

FRANK

My dear Mrs Warren: suppose you were a sparrow – ever so tiny and pretty a sparrow hopping in the roadway – and you saw a steam roller coming in your direction, would you wait for it?

MRS WARREN   475

Oh, dont bother me with your sparrows. What did she run away from Haslemere like that for?

FRANK

I'm afraid she'll tell you if you rashly await her return.

MRS WARREN   480

Do you want me to go away?

FRANK

No: I always want you to stay. But I *advise* you to go away.

MRS WARREN

What! And never see her again!   485

FRANK

Precisely.

MRS WARREN [*crying again*]

Praddy: dont let him be cruel to me. [*She hastily checks her tears and wipes her eyes*] She'll be so angry if she sees Ive been crying.   490

FRANK [*with a touch of real compassion in his airy tenderness*]

You know that Praddy is the soul of kindness, Mrs Warren. Praddy: what do *you* say? Go or stay?

---

462   *Oh, you never can see* Shaw directs: 'Oh you never can see anything – not you never can see anything' (RN).

462   *innocent* 'amiable' (GR)

479   *if you rashly await her return* 'if you wait until she comes back' (GR)

PRAED [*to* MRS WARREN]

    I really should be very sorry to cause you unnecessary pain; but   495
I think perhaps you had better not wait. The fact is – [VIVIE *is
heard at the inner door*]

FRANK

    Sh! Too late. She's coming.

MRS WARREN   500

    Dont tell her I was crying. [VIVIE *comes in. She stops gravely on
seeing* MRS WARREN, *who greets her with hysterical cheerfulness*]
Well, dearie. So here you are at last.

VIVIE

    I am glad you have come: I want to speak to you. You said you   505
were going, Frank, I think.

FRANK

    Yes. Will you come with me, Mrs Warren? What do you say to
a trip to Richmond, and the theatre in the evening? There is
safety in Richmond. No steam roller there.   510

VIVIE

    Nonsense, Frank. My mother will stay here.

MRS WARREN [*scared*]

    I dont know: perhaps I'd better go. We're disturbing you at your
work.   515

VIVIE [*with quiet decision*]

    Mr Praed: please take Frank away. Sit down, mother. [MRS
WARREN *obeys helplessly*]

PRAED

    Come, Frank. Goodbye, Miss Vivie.   520

VIVIE [*shaking hands*]

    Goodbye. A pleasant trip.

PRAED

    Thank you: thank you. I hope so.

FRANK [*to* MRS WARREN]   525

    Goodbye: youd ever so much better have taken my advice. [*He
shakes hands with her. Then airily to* VIVIE] Byebye, Viv.

VIVIE

    Goodbye. [*He goes out gaily without shaking hands with her*]

---

508   *Yes* MS adds: 'You will find a little note on the desk from me. It's of no importance:
any time will do to read it.'

PRAED [*sadly*]   530
   Goodbye, Kitty.
MRS WARREN [*snivelling*]
   – oodbye!

> PRAED *goes.* VIVIE, *composed and extremely grave, sits down*
> *in Honoria's chair, and waits for her mother to speak.* MRS   535
> WARREN, *dreading a pause, loses no time in beginning.*

MRS WARREN
   Well, Vivie, what did you go away like that for without saying a
   word to me? How could you do such a thing! And what have
   you done to poor George? I wanted him to come with me; but   540
   he shuffled out of it. I could see that he was quite afraid of you.
   Only fancy: he wanted me not to come. As if [*trembling*] I
   should be afraid of you, dearie. [VIVIE *'s gravity deepens*] But of
   course I told him it was all settled and comfortable between us,
   and that we were on the best of terms. [*She breaks down*] Vivie: 545
   whats the meaning of this? [*She produces a commercial envelope,*
   and fumbles at the enclosure with trembling fingers] I got it from
   the bank this morning.

VIVIE
   It is my month's allowance. They sent it to me as usual the other   550
   day. I simply sent it back to be placed to your credit, and asked
   them to send you the lodgment receipt. In future I shall support myself.

MRS WARREN [*not daring to understand*]
   Wasnt it enough? Why didnt you tell me? [*With a cunning*   555
   gleam in her eye] I'll double it: I was intending to double it.
   Only let me know how much you want.

VIVIE
   You know very well that that has nothing to do with it. From
   this time I go my own way in my own business and among my   560
   own friends. And you will go yours. [*She rises*] Goodbye.

MRS WARREN [*rising, appalled*]
   Goodbye?

VIVIE
   Yes: Goodbye. Come: dont let us make a useless scene: you   565

530–3   not in GR
546–7   *She . . . fingers* GR has '*She produces a paper from an envelope; comes to the table; and*
        hands it across.'
   552   *lodgment receipt* deposit receipt.

understand perfectly well. Sir George Crofts has told me the whole business.

MRS WARREN [*angrily*]

Silly old – [*She swallows an epithet, and turns white at the narrowness of her escape from uttering it*]   570

VIVIE

Just so.

MRS WARREN

He ought to have his tongue cut out. But I thought it was ended: you said you didnt mind.   575

VIVIE [*steadfastly*]

Excuse me: I *do* mind.

MRS WARREN

But I explained –

VIVIE   580

You explained how it came about. You did not tell me that it is still going on. [*She sits*]

   MRS WARREN, *silenced for a moment, looks forlornly at* VIVIE, *who waits, secretly hoping that the combat is over. But the cunning expression comes back into* MRS WARREN*'s face; and she*   585
bends across the table, sly and urgent, half whispering.

MRS WARREN

Vivie: do you know how rich I am?

VIVIE

I have no doubt you are very rich.   590

MRS WARREN

But you dont know all that means: youre too young. It means a new dress every day; it means theatres and balls every night; it means having the pick of all the gentlemen in Europe at your feet; it means a lovely house and plenty of servants; it means   595
the choicest of eating and drinking; it means everything you like, everything you want, everything you can think of. And what are you here? A mere drudge, toiling and moiling early and late

---

566–82   *Sir George . . . going on* This passage is expurgated in LC1.

571–2   not in GR

574–5   *But I thought it was ended* 'But I explained it all to you' (GR). Mrs Warren's next line (578–9) does not appear in GR.

581–2   *You did not . . . going on* 'That does not alter it' (GR). And she does not sit.

597   *everything you can think of* 'one continual round of pleasure and variety and power' (MS)

for your bare living and two cheap dresses a year. Think over it.
[*Soothingly*] Youre shocked, I know. I can enter into your feelings;   600
and I think they do you credit; but trust me, nobody will blame
you: you may take my word for that. I know what young girls
are; and I know youll think better of it when youve turned it
over in your mind.

VIVIE   605

So thats how it's done, is it? You must have said all that to many
a woman, mother, to have it so pat.

MRS WARREN [*passionately*]

What harm am I asking you to do? [VIVIE *turns away contemptuously.* MRS WARREN *continues desperately*] Vivie: listen to me: 610
you dont understand: youve been taught wrong on purpose:
you dont know what the world is really like.

VIVIE [*arrested*]

Taught wrong on purpose! What do you mean?

MRS WARREN   615

I mean that youre throwing away all your chances for nothing.
You think that people are what they pretend to be: that the way
you were taught at school and college to think right and proper
is the way things really are. But it's not: it's all only a pretence,
to keep the cowardly slavish common run of people quiet. Do   620
you want to find that out, like other women, at forty, when
youve thrown yourself away and lost your chances; or wont you
take it in good time now from your own mother, that loves you
and swears to you that it's truth: gospel truth? [*Urgently*] Vivie:
the big people, the clever people, the managing people, all   625
know it. They do as I do, and think what I think. I know plenty
of them. I know them to speak to, to introduce you to, to make

609–73   *What harm ... the same?* MS has a much briefer exchange:
            MRS WARREN (passionately)
                What harm am I asking you to do? (Vivie turns away contemptuously and Mrs
                W again becomes conciliatory) Well, I wont ask you any more – I promise I
                wont. Dont be too hard Vivie: it's not good – it's not right to have no mercy on
                your own mother. Surely you wont cut me off from you altogether.
            VIVIE
                Cannot you find something else to do than what you are doing? Your sister,
                you told me, has left all that behind her.

97

friends of for you. I dont mean anything wrong: thats what you
dont understand: your head is full of ignorant ideas about me.
What do the people that taught you know about life or about   630
people like me? When did they ever meet me, or speak to me,
or let anyone tell them about me? the fools! Would they ever
have done anything for you if I hadnt paid them? Havnt I told
you that I want you to be respectable? Havnt I brought you up
to be respectable? And how can you keep it up without my   635
money and my influence and Lizzie's friends? Cant you see that
youre cutting your own throat as well as breaking my heart in
turning your back on me?

VIVIE

I recognize the Crofts philosophy of life, mother. I heard it all   640
from him that day at the Gardners'.

MRS WARREN

You think I want to force that played-out old sot on you! I dont,
Vivie: on my oath I dont.

VIVIE   645

It would not matter if you did: you would not succeed. [MRS
WARREN *winces, deeply hurt by the implied indifference towards
her affectionate intention.* VIVIE, *neither understanding this nor
concerning herself about it, goes on calmly*] Mother: you dont at
all know the sort of person I am. I dont object to Crofts more   650
than to any other coarsely built man of his class. To tell you the
truth, I rather admire him for being strongminded enough to
enjoy himself in his own way and make plenty of money
instead of living the usual shooting, hunting, dining-out,
tailoring, loafing life of his set merely because all the rest do it.   655
And I'm perfectly aware that if I'd been in the same circumstances as my aunt Liz, I'd have done exactly what she did. I
dont think I'm more prejudiced or straitlaced than you: I think
I'm less. I'm certain I'm less sentimental. I know very well that
fashionable morality is all a pretence, and that if I took your   660
money and devoted the rest of my life to spending it fashion-
ably, I might be as worthless and vicious as the silliest woman
could possibly want to be without having a word said to me

635–6   *And how ... friends* expurgated in LC1
643   *sot* a fool or a drunkard. In this case, it could mean both.
650–64 *I dont ... about it* expurgated in LC1

about it. But I dont want to be worthless. I shouldnt enjoy
trotting about the park to advertize my dressmaker and   665
carriage builder, or being bored at the opera to shew off a
shopwindowful of diamonds.

MRS WARREN [*bewildered*]

But –

VIVIE   670

Wait a moment: Ive not done. Tell me why you continue your
business now that you are independent of it. Your sister, you
told me, has left all that behind her. Why dont you do the same?

MRS WARREN

Oh, it's all very easy for Liz: she likes good society, and has the   675
air of being a lady. Imagine *me* in a cathedral town! Why, the
very rooks in the trees would find me out even if I could stand
the dulness of it. I must have work and excitement, or I should
go melancholy mad. And what else is there for me to do? The
life suits me: I'm fit for it and not for anything else. If I didnt   680
do it somebody else would; so I dont do any real harm by it.
And then it brings in money; and I like making money. No: it's
no use: I cant give it up – not for anybody. But what need you
know about it? I'll never mention it. I'll keep Crofts away. I'll
not trouble you much: you see I have to be constantly running   685
about from one place to another. Youll be quit of me altogether
when I die.

VIVIE

No: I am my mother's daughter. I am like you: I must have
work, and must make more money than I spend. But my work   690
is not your work, and my way not your way. We must part. It
will not make much difference to us: instead of meeting one
another for perhaps a few months in twenty years, we shall
never meet: thats all.

664–7   *I shouldn't . . . diamonds* This typifies a number of courtesan narratives, most
          glaringly Alexandre Dumas, *fils' La Dame aux Camélias* and Émile Zola's *Nana*.

673   *Why . . . same?* not in MS

677   *rooks* birds of the crow family that nest in treetops

684–5   *I'll not trouble you much* Shaw directs: 'more urgent – to provoke her "No: I'm my
          mother's"' (RN).

687   MS continues: 'Oh dont leave me altogether, darling – dont, dont.'

688–96   not in MS

689   Shaw directs: 'The No is ↑ not ↓' (RN).

MRS WARREN [*her voice stifled in tears*]   695

Vivie: I meant to have been more with you: I did indeed.

VIVIE

It's no use, mother: I am not to be changed by a few cheap tears
and entreaties any more than you are, I daresay.

MRS WARREN [*wildly*]   700

Oh, you call a mother's tears cheap.

VIVIE

They cost you nothing; and you ask me to give you the peace
and quietness of my whole life in exchange for them. What use
would my company be to you if you could get it? What have we   705
two in common that could make either of us happy together?

MRS WARREN [*lapsing recklessly into her dialect*]

We're mother and daughter. I want my daughter. Ive a right to
you. Who is to care for me when I'm old? Plenty of girls have
taken to me like daughters and cried at leaving me; but I let   710
them all go because I had you to look forward to. I kept myself
lonely for you. Youve no right to turn on me now and refuse to
do your duty as a daughter.

VIVIE [*jarred and antagonized by the echo of the slums in her
mother's voice*]   715

My duty as a daughter! I thought we should come to that
presently. Now once for all, mother, you want a daughter and
Frank wants a wife. I dont want a mother; and I dont want a
husband. I have spared neither Frank nor myself in sending
him about his business. Do you think I will spare *you*?   720

MRS WARREN [*violently*]

Oh, I know the sort you are: no mercy for yourself or anyone
else. *I* know. My experience has done that for me anyhow: I can
tell the pious, canting, hard, selfish woman when I meet her.
Well, keep yourself to yourself: *I* dont want you. But listen to 725
this. Do you know what I would do with you if you were a baby
again? aye, as sure as theres a Heaven above us.

VIVIE

Strangle me, perhaps.

MRS WARREN   730

No: I'd bring you up to be a real daughter to me, and not what
you are now, with your pride and your prejudices and the

703–4   *the peace . . . for them* 'in exchange for them the little happiness and honor that is left
to me' (MS)

100

college education you stole from me: yes, stole: deny it if you can: what was it but stealing? I'd bring you up in my own house, I would.   735

VIVIE [*quietly*]

In one of your own houses.

MRS WARREN [*screaming*]

Listen to her! listen to how she spits on her mother's grey hairs! Oh, may you live to have your own daughter tear and trample   740 on you as you have trampled on me. And you will: you will. No woman ever had luck with a mother's curse on her.

VIVIE

I wish you wouldnt rant, mother. It only hardens me. Come: I suppose I am the only young woman you ever had in your   745 power that you did good to. Dont spoil it all now.

MRS WARREN

Yes, Heaven forgive me, it's true; and you are the only one that ever turned on me. Oh, the injustice of it! the injustice! the injustice! I always wanted to be a good woman. I tried honest   750 work; and I was slave-driven until I cursed the day I ever heard of honest work. I was a good mother; and because I made my daughter a good woman she turns me out as if I was a leper. Oh, if I only had my life to live over again! I'd talk to that lying clergyman in the school. From this time forth, so help me   755 Heaven in my last hour, I'll do wrong and nothing but wrong. And I'll prosper on it.

VIVIE

Yes: it's better to choose your line and go through with it. If I had been you, mother, I might have done as you did; but I   760 should not have lived one life and believed in another. You are a conventional woman at heart. That is why I am bidding you goodbye now. I am right, am I not?

MRS WARREN [*taken aback*]

Right to throw away all my money?   765

VIVIE

No: right to get rid of you! I should be a fool not to! Isnt that so?

---

744   *I wish ... Come:* '(judging her) Then dont curse me, mother' (MS).
760   *I might ... but* not in MS
761–2   *You are ... heart* not in MS

MRS WARREN [*sulkily*]

Oh well, yes, if you come to that, I suppose you are. But Lord help the world if everybody took to doing the right thing! And now I'd better go than stay where I'm not wanted. [*She turns to the door*]   770

VIVIE [*kindly*]

Wont you shake hands?

MRS WARREN [*after looking at her fiercely for a moment with a savage impulse to strike her*]   775

No, thank you. Goodbye.

VIVIE [*matter-of-factly*]

Goodbye. [MRS WARREN *goes out, slamming the door behind her. The strain on* VIVIE*'s face relaxes; her grave expression*   780 *breaks up into one of joyous content; her breath goes out in a half sob, half laugh of intense relief. She goes buoyantly to her place at the writing-table; pushes the electric lamp out of the way; pulls over a great sheaf of papers; and is in the act of dipping her pen in the ink when she finds* FRANK*'s note. She opens it unconcernedly*   785 *and reads it quickly, giving a little laugh at some quaint turn of expression in it*] And goodbye, Frank. [*She tears the note up and tosses the pieces into the wastepaper basket without a second thought. Then she goes at her work with a plunge, and soon becomes absorbed in its figures*]   790

790   *its* GR has '*her*'.

APPENDIX I

SHAW'S REVIEW OF ARTHUR WING PINERO'S
THE SECOND MRS TANQUERAY

Shaw reviewed the published text of Arthur Wing Pinero's The Second Mrs
Tanqueray *in* The Saturday Review *on 23 February 1895. It appeared just
after his reviews of Oscar Wilde's* The Importance of Being Earnest *and
another play which, he claimed, was so hackneyed that he had simply forgotten what it was. Pinero's play was originally performed in 1893 at the St
James's Theatre, where it caused a great sensation during its very successful run.*

I am indebted to Mr Heinemann[1] for a copy of *The Second Mrs Tanquery*,
which he has just published in a five-shilling volume, with an excellent
photographic portrait of the author by Mr Hollyer.[2] Those who did not see
the play at the St James's Theatre can now examine the literary basis of the
work that so immoderately fascinated playgoing London in 1893. But they
must not expect the play to be as imposing in the library as it was on the
stage. Its merit there was relative to the culture of the playgoing public.
Paula Tanqueray is an astonishingly well-drawn figure as stage figures go
nowadays, even allowing for the fact that there is no cheaper subject for the
character draughtsman than the ill-tempered sensual woman seen from
the point of view of the conventional man. But off the stage her distinction
vanishes. The novels of Anthony Trollope, Charles Lever, Bulwer Lytton,
Charles Reade,[3] and many other novelists, whom nobody praised thirty
years ago in the terms in which Mr Pinero is praised now, are full of feats
of character-drawing in no way inferior – to say the least – to Mr Pinero's.
The theatre was not ready for that class of work then: it is now; and
accordingly Mr Pinero, who in literature is a humble and somewhat

---

1   William Heinemann (1863–1920) founded the Heinemann publishing house in London
    in 1890.
2   Frederick Hollyer (1838–1933) was well known for his photographs of paintings,
    drawings, and famous people of the late Victorian and Edwardian periods, including
    Shaw himself.
3   Anthony Trollope (1815–82) was a prolific English author. Charles Lever (1806–72) was
    a popular Irish novelist. Edward Bulwer-Lytton (1803–73) was an English politician and
    writer; he is perhaps best known today as opening his novel *Paul Clifford* (1830) with 'It
    was a dark and stormy night.' Charles Reade (1814–84) was an English novelist and
    playwright whose greatest stage success came with *Drink* (1879), an adaptation of Émile
    Zola's *L'Assommoir*.

belated follower of the novelists of the middle of that nineteenth century, and who has never written a line from which it could be guessed that he is a contemporary of Ibsen, Tolstoi, Meredith, or Sarah Grand,[4] finds himself at the dawn of the twentieth hailed as a man of new ideas, of daring originality, of supreme literary distinction, and even – which is perhaps oddest – of consummate stage craft. Stage craft, after all, is very narrowly limited by the physical conditions of stage representation; but when one turns over the pages of *The Second Mrs Tanqueray*, and notes the naïve machinery of the exposition in the first act, in which two whole actors are wasted on sham parts, and the hero, at his own dinner party, is compelled to get up and go ignominiously into the next room 'to write some letters' when something has to be said behind his back; when one follows Cayley Drummle, the confidant to whom both Paula and her husband explain themselves for the benefit of the audience; when one counts the number of doors which Mr Pinero needs to get his characters on and off the stage, and how they have finally to be supplemented by the inevitable 'French windows' (two of them); and when the activity of the postman is taken into consideration, it is impossible to avoid the conclusion that what most of our critics mean by mastery of stage craft is recklessness in the substitution of dead machinery and lay figures for vital action and real characters. I do not deny that an author may be driven by his own limitations to ingenuities which Shakespear[5] had on occasion to cultivate, just as a painter without hands or feet learns to surpass Michael Angelo in the art of drawing with the brush held in the mouth; but I regard such ingenuity as an extremity to be deplored, not as an art to be admired. In *The Second Mrs Tanqueray* I find little except a scaffold for the situation of a step-daughter and step-mother finding themselves in the positions respectively of affianced wife and discarded mistress to the same man. Obviously, the only necessary conditions of this situation are that the persons concerned shall be respectable enough to be shocked by it, and that the step-mother shall be an improper person. Mr Pinero has not got above this minimum. He is, of course, sufficiently skilled in fiction to give

4   Henrik Ibsen (1828–1906), a Norwegian playwright, reviled by critics and loved by the avant-garde, pioneered the New Drama. Leo Tolstoi (1828–1910), whose last name was spelled Tolstoi in British circles at the time that Shaw wrote his review, was the Russian author of *War and Peace* (1869) and *Anna Karenina* (1877). George Meredith (1828–1909) was an English novelist and poet. Sarah Grand (1854–1943) was an English writer who became a prototype for the New Woman. Her feminist novel *The Heavenly Twins* (1893) influenced Shaw's *You Never Can Tell* (1897). Of this list of writers, she is the only one who could truly be considered a contemporary of Pinero (1855–1934) given that the others belong to an earlier generation.

5   Shaw always spelled Shakespeare's name withhout the 'e' at the end.

Ellean, Mrs Cortelyon, Ardale, Tanqueray, and Cayley Drummle a passable air of being human beings. He has even touched up Cayley into a Thackerayan *flâneur*[6] in order to secure toleration of his intrusiveness. But who will pretend that any of these figures are more than the barest accessories to the main situation? To compare them with the characters in Robertson's *Caste*[7] would be almost as ridiculous as to compare *Caste* with *A Doll's House*.[8] The two vulgar characters produce the requisite jar – a pitilessly disagreeable jar – and that is all. Still, all the seven seem good as far as they go; and that very little way may suggest that Mr Pinero might have done good creative work if he had carried them further. Unfortunately for this surmise, he has carried Paula further; and with what result? The moment the point is reached at which the comparatively common gift of 'an eye for the character' has to be supplemented by the higher dramatic gift of sympathy with character – of the power of seeing the world from the point of view of others instead of merely describing or judging them from one's own point of view in terms of the conventional systems of morals, Mr Pinero breaks down. I remember that when I saw the play acted I sat up very attentively when Tanqueray said to Paula, 'I know what you were at Ellean's age. You hadnt a thought that wasnt a wholesome one; you hadnt an impulse that didnt tend towards good; you never harbored a notion you couldnt have gossiped about to a parcel of children. And this was a very few years back, etc. etc.' On the reply to that fatuous but not unnatural speech depended the whole question of Mr Pinero's rank as a dramatist. One can imagine how, in a play by a master-hand, Paula's reply would have opened Tanqueray's foolish eyes to the fact that a woman of that sort is already the same at three as she is at thirty-three, and that however she may have found by experience that her nature is in conflict with the ideals of differently constituted people, she remains perfectly valid to herself, and despises herself, if she sincerely does so at all, for the hypocrisy that the world forces on her instead of for being what she is. What reply does Mr Pinero put into her mouth? Here it is, with the stage directions: 'A few – years ago! (*She walks slowly towards the door, then suddenly drops upon the ottoman in a paroxysm of weeping.*) O God! A few

---

6   William Makepeace Thackeray (1811–63) was an English novelist whose best known work is *Vanity Fair* (1848). A *flâneur*, a term coined by French author Charles Baudelaire (1821–67), means a gentleman stroller, one who is economically able to travel and leisurely take in the sights and sounds. In this case, a *flâneur* is similar to a dandy. Thackeray published several books about the many places to which he travelled.

7   T.W. Robertson (1829–71) was an Irish playwright and director who helped create the genre of 'the problem play' and bring realist writing and acting to the stage. Shaw reviewed a revival of *Caste* (1867) in *The Saturday Review* on 19 June 1897.

8   *A Doll's House* (1879) was written by Ibsen.

years ago!' That is to say, she makes her reply from the Tanqueray–Ellean–Pinero point of view, and thus betrays the fact that she is a work of prejudiced observation instead of comprehension, and that the other characters only owe their faint humanity to the fact that they are projections of Mr Pinero's own personal amiabilities and beliefs and conventions. Mr Pinero, then, is no interpreter of character, but simply an adroit describer of people as the ordinary man sees and judges them. Add to this a clear head, a love of the stage, and a fair talent for fiction, all highly cultivated by hard and honorable work as a writer of effective stage plays for the modern commercial theatre; and you have him on his real level. On that level he is entitled to all the praise *The Second Mrs Tanqueray* has won him; and I very heartily regret that the glamor which Mrs Patrick Campbell[9] cast round the play has forced me to examine pretensions which Mr Pinero himself never put forward rather than to acknowledge the merits with which his work is so concisely packed.

9   Mrs Patrick Campbell (1865–1940) was a leading actress of the period. She made her mark in Pinero's *The Second Mrs Tanqueray* and, on the heels of that success, *The Notorious Mrs Ebbsmith* (1895). In 1914, she rather improbably starred at forty-nine years of age as Eliza Doolittle (who is described as 'perhaps eighteen, perhaps twenty, hardly older') in the successful London première of Shaw's *Pygmalion*.

APPENDIX II

*I have translated the following excerpt from Louis Forestier's critical edition
of Guy de Maupassant's Yvette[10] (Paris: Gallimard, 1997), pp. 113–20. The
night before, Yvette, on a walk in the rain, spies her prostitute mother through
the lighted window making love to one of her clients. Unaware of her mother's
profession, this scene shocks Yvette's romantic and naïve nature, causing her
to cry out in the night. The next day, Yvette awakes in her suite of the country
manor in which they are vacationing:*

The sun had risen. The servants were about the house. The chambermaid
brought chocolate. Yvette placed the platter on the table and said:

— Tell my mother that I'm not well, that I'm going to stay in bed until
those men leave, that I couldn't sleep last night, and that I ask that no one
bothers me, because I want to try to get some rest.

The servant looked surprised at the carpet where the dress lay soaked
and fallen like a rag.

— Did Miss go out? she asked.

— Yes, I went for a walk in the rain to cool myself off.

The maid picked up the dirty skirts, stockings, ankle boots; then on one
arm she carried, with disgusted precautions, those clothes that were soaked
like drowned rags.

And Yvette waited, knowing well that her mother would come.

The marquise entered, having jumped from her bed at the first words
from the chambermaid, as she harboured a doubt since she heard from
the shadow the cry 'Maman.'

— What's the matter? she asked.

Yvette, watching her, stammered:

— I . . . I . . .

Then, taken by a sudden and terrible feeling, she began to choke.

The marquise, shocked, asked again:

— What's the matter?

10   Guy de Maupassant (1850–93) was a French writer and master of the short story who
     apprenticed under Gustave Flaubert (1821–80). He published *Yvette* in 1884. His best
     known story is 'Boule de Suif', which features a prostitute and reveals the hypocrisy in
     much of contemporary middle-class morality.

Forgetting all of her plans and prepared sentences, the young girl hid her face in her hands and spluttered:

— Oh! maman, oh! maman!

Madame Obardi remained standing before the bed, too emotional to understand, but guessing almost everything with that subtle instinct from which she derived her strength.

As Yvette could not speak, choked by her tears, her mother, becoming irritated and fearing a horrible explanation, demanded sharply:

— Tell me, what's the matter with you?

Yvette could barely speak:

— Oh, last night . . . I saw . . . your window.

The marquise, very pale, uttered:

— Yes, well?

Her daughter continued, still sobbing:

— Oh! maman, oh! maman!

Madame Obardi, in whom fear and embarrassment became anger, raised her shoulders and turned to go.

— I really believe you're crazy. Tell them to come and get me when you're finished.

But suddenly the young girl took her hands from her face that was streaming with tears.

— No! . . . Listen . . . I have to speak with you . . . Listen . . . You have to promise me . . . We're going to go away together, just the two of us, far away, to live in the country like a couple of peasants: and no one will know what's become of us! What do you say, maman, please, I beg you, don't you want to go?

Stunned, the marquise remained in the middle of the room. She had the blood of the common people in her veins, irascible blood. Then she was shamed, a sense of a mother's modesty mixed with a vague feeling of fear and the exasperation of a passionate woman for whom love is threatened. She trembled, ready to ask for forgiveness or to wreak some form of violence.

— I don't understand, she said.

Yvette repeated:

— I saw you . . . maman . . . last night . . . It's not necessary . . . if you only knew . . . we're going to go away together . . . I'll love you even when you forget . . .

Madame Obardi spoke with a trembling voice:

— Listen, my daughter, there are some things you still don't under-stand. And well . . . don't forget . . . don't forget . . . that I forbid you . . . to ever speak to me . . . about . . . about . . . about these things.

But the young girl, abruptly taking the role of the saviour that she had imposed upon herself, said:

— No, maman, I'm no longer a child, and I have the right to know. And, well, I know that we host some disreputable people, thrill seekers. I also know that we're not respected because of that. I know still more. And, well, no more, do you hear? I don't want it any more. We're going to leave; you'll sell your jewels; we'll travel if we have to, and we'll live like honest women, somewhere, far away. And if I can get married, even better.

Her mother glared at her, irritated. She responded:

— You're crazy. You're going to do me the favour of getting up and having breakfast with everyone.

— No, maman. There's someone I don't want to see again, you understand? I want him to leave, or else I'll leave. You choose between him and me.

She was sitting on her bed, and she raised her voice, speaking as one speaks on stage, finally entering into the drama of which she had always dreamed, almost forgetting her troubles while remembering only her goal.

Astounded, the marquise repeated once again:

— You're crazy . . ., finding nothing else to say.

Yvette continued with theatrical energy:

— No, maman, that man will leave the house, or I'll be the one to go, because I won't waver.

— And where will you go? . . . What will you do? . . .

— I don't know, anywhere . . . I want us to be honest women.

That repeated phrase 'honest women' aroused the marquise to a fury and she screamed:

— Shut up! I won't allow you to speak to me like that. I'm worth as much as anyone else, do you understand? I'm a courtesan. That's true. And I'm proud of it; honest women don't consider me.

Yvette, aghast, watched her; she stammered:

— Oh, maman!

But the marquise, becoming excited:

— Yes, I'm a courtesan. And what of it? If I weren't a courtesan, you'd be a cook, just like I used to be, and you'd make only thirty sous a day,[11] and you'd do the dishes, and your mistress would send you to the butcher's, do you understand, and she would kick you out the door if you were lazy, whereas you laze about all day because I'm a courtesan. There you have it. When you're nothing but a maid, a poor girl with fifty francs in your

11 *Sous* is a colloquial way of referring to money, like *bucks* or *quid* for dollars or pounds. Here it refers to the currency of French francs. A *sou* was a French coin in medieval times whose value was a twentieth of a franc, or five centimes.

pockets, you have to know how to get yourself out of the situation if you don't want to starve to death; and there's not but two ways for you, there's only two, do you hear, when you're a servant! You can't make a fortune in that job or with that budget. You have nothing but your body, nothing but your body.

She struck her chest, like a confessing penitent, and red, exalted, advancing towards the bed:

— Too bad, when you're a pretty girl, you have to live by that, or else suffer the misery all of your life . . . all of your life . . . no choice.

Then abruptly returning to her idea:

— That's what honest women are deprived of. They're the tramps, do you hear, because they're obliged to do nothing. They have money, enough to live on and amuse themselves, and they take men because they're vicious. They're the ones who are the tramps.

She was standing near Yvette who, overwhelmed and wanting to scream 'help,' to save herself, was crying aloud like a beaten child.

The marquise quieted, watched her daughter, and seeing her distraught with despair, felt herself struck with pain, with remorse, with tenderness, with pity, and dropping on the bed while opening her arms, she too began to sob, and she stammered:

— My poor girl, my poor girl, if you only knew how you hurt me.

And they cried together for some time.

Then the marquise, in whom sadness didn't take hold for long, slowly got up. And she said in a lowered voice:

— Come, dearie, what do you expect? That's just the way it is. We can't change anything. You simply have to take life as it is.

Yvette continued to cry. The blow was too brutal and too unexpected for her to have reflected and collected herself.

Her mother persisted:

— Come, get up and eat so no one will notice.

The young girl shook her head, unable to speak; finally, she broke through her sobs, speaking with a slow voice:

— No, maman, you know what I told you, and I won't change my mind. I won't come out of my room until they've left. I never, never want to see those people again. If they return, I . . . I . . . you'll never see me again.

The marquise had wiped her eyes and, tired from her emotions, she whispered:

— Come, think about it, be reasonable.

Then, after a minute of silence:

— Yes, perhaps it would be better if you were to rest this morning. I'll come to see you this afternoon.

And having kissed her daughter on her forehead, she left to dress, already calmed.

Yvette, as soon as her mother had departed, rose, and ran to lock the door to be alone, all alone, and then she began to think.

The chambermaid knocked around eleven o'clock and asked her through the door:

— Madame the marquise would like to know if Miss needs anything, and what she would like for her lunch.

Yvette responded:

— I'm not hungry. I only wish that no one would bother me.

And she remained in bed as though she were very ill.

Around three o'clock, there was another knock. She asked:

— Who's there?

It was the voice of her mother.

— It's me, dearie, I've come to see how you're doing.

She hesitated. What would she do? She opened the door, then got back into bed.

The marquise approached, and speaking in a tender voice as though to a convalescent:

— Well, are you feeling better? You wouldn't like to eat an egg?

— No, thank you, nothing at all.

Madame Obardi sat close to the bed. They remained silent; then, finally, as her daughter was unmoved, her hands inert on the covers:

— Aren't you going to get up?

Yvette responded:

— Yes, soon.

Then, in a grave and slow tone of voice:

— I've thought a lot, maman, and this is . . . this is my resolution. The past is the past, we won't speak of it any more. But the future will be different . . . or, well . . . or well I know what I'll have to do. Now, I don't want to speak of it any more.

The marquise, who thought she had finished all explanation, felt increasingly impatient. This was too much. The idiot should have known a long time ago. But she didn't say anything, instead repeating:

— Are you getting up?

— Yes, I'm ready.

Her mother acted as her chambermaid, brought her her stockings, her corset, her skirts; then she kissed her.

— Would you care to go for a walk before dinner?

— Yes, maman.

And they went for a walk along the water, hardly even speaking apart from mundane subjects.

APPENDIX III

William Acton (1813–75) was an English doctor who wrote a number of medical treatises on sexual organs and reproduction, but he is perhaps best known today as the author of his more sociological tract on prostitution, published in 1857. The following passages are taken from the second edition, which was published in 1870 and reissued in 1972 by Frank Cass and Company, London.

1

*Estimates of the number of prostitutes
in nineteenth-century London*

The number of prostitutes in London has been variously estimated, according to the opportunities, credulity, or religious fervour of observers, and the width of interpretation they have put upon the word. To attempt to reconcile or construct tables upon the estimates I have met with would be a hopeless task. I can merely give a few of the more moderate that have been handed down by my predecessors. Mr Colquhoun, a magistrate at the Thames Police Court, rated them at 50,000 some sixty years ago. The Bishop of Exeter spoke of them as reaching 80,000; Mr Talbot, secretary of a society for the protection of young females, made the same estimate. The returns on the constabulary force presented to Parliament in 1839, furnished an estimate of 6,371 – viz. 3,732 'known to the police as kept by the proprietors of brothels', and 2,639 as resident in lodgings of their own, and dependent on prostitution alone for a livelihood. It was estimated by the Home authorities in 1841, that the corresponding total was 9,409 – which, I need hardly point out, does not include the vast numbers who regularly or occasionally abandon themselves, but in a less open manner.

(p. 3)

2

*Recounting a run-in one of his friends had with a young woman,
Acton describes the conditions of brothel workers in London*

In the year 1858 his sympathy and curiosity were awakened by the behaviour of a very handsome girl, who, seemingly against her will, was very urgently forced upon his notice by a brothel-keeper, who was hawking her about the streets. Acquiescing in the offer of her company and paying the demands of the house, he put some searching questions to the girl. She at first half confessed slight indisposition, but on his avowing himself a medical man, and showing clearly enough that his curiosity like his gift was dictated by mere charity, she submitted to a superficial examination. No more was required to prove that she was a mass of syphilis.

The rouged and whitewashed creatures, with painted lips and eyebrows, and false hair, accustomed to haunt Langham Place, portions of the New Road, the Quadrant, the Peristyle of the Haymarket Theatre, the City Road, and the purlieus of the Lyceum, were the most prominent gangs of this description in London.[12] They were watched by persons of their own sex, employed purposely to prevent their abstraction of lodging-house finery, and clandestine traffic with men. These wretched women, virtually slaves, though nominally free, with bodies and time no longer their own, were restricted, for the convenience of the real proprietors, to certain parades or beats, and from year's end to year's end might be observed on the same side of one particular street, and within a few hundred yards or less of one particular spot. If their solicitations proved unsuccessful, their exertions were stimulated by the proprietor in person, who would sally forth from her den to aid the canvass, to admonish and to swear; and sometimes by the sentinel in charge, who assumed for the time being these functions of authority.

Women under like sad conditions may still be observed in some of the principal streets of London, but I am happy to say a great improvement has taken place in this respect during the last twelve years.[13] There still exist establishments in which the women live with their landlady, by whom they are provided with food, dress, and lodging, all which are charged to the women at an exorbitant price, and the landlady usually contrives to keep them in her debt; they have, however, the right of receiving and retaining

---

12   The depiction of theatres as haunts where clients actively sought prostitutes is prevalent in studies of prostitution. The theatre also features prominently in fictional prostitute narratives.

13   The twelve years mentioned here refers to the time that had elapsed between the writing of the two editions.

their own money, and the privilege of accepting or declining, at their own discretion, the attentions offered by their visitors.   (p. 10)

3
Brothels were also referred to as dress houses.
Acton further describes London brothel-keepers

The keepers of the old dress houses were mostly females of extreme avarice, and often ferocious manners – the former sharpened by the unprincipled atmosphere in which they live, and the latter by the necessity of preserving discipline among their tenants and dependents. They were ordinarily persons who had been bred to the business from youth, as relatives or old servants of their predecessors. Such an establishment was considered to be too lucrative to permit the idea of its dispersion upon the death or retirement of a proprietor; and as a matter of fact, the lease, goodwill, and stock-in-trade of a brothel were, in such an event, disposed of like those of any other lodging-house. Women who had been themselves kept or frequented by men of property were sometimes able to found or purchase one or more of them. A large share of their tenants' earnings passed through their hands, and a liberal portion always remained there. They were highly paid for liquors and eatables they procured on account of male visitors; and several instances are well authenticated of their having left ample means behind them, or having retired wealthy into private life.
(p. 13)

4
Acton details some of the more expensive brothels
and the patronage that they received

The establishments of certain procuresses (Latin, *proxenetoe*; French, *proxénète*: brokers, go-betweens, match-makers), vulgarly called 'introducing houses,' which resemble, to some extent, the *maisons à parties*[14] kept for a similar purpose by somewhat used-up *lorettes*[15] of the first water in Paris, are worth notice as the leading centres of the more select circles of prostitution here. Unobtrusive, and dependent upon great

---

14   *Maisons à parties*, literally translated as party houses, were private residences where men of wealth were invited to meet and engage with prostitutes.

15   *Lorettes* were prostitutes named after the parish of Notre-Dame-de-Lorette in the ninth arrondissement of Paris, just below Montmartre, where they tended to congregate.

exterior decency for a good connexion, they concern us as little from a sanitary as from a police point of view, but are not without an influence upon the morals of the highest society. Their existence depends upon the co-operation and discretion of various subordinate accomplices, and on the patronage of some of the many wealthy, indolent, sensual men of London, who will pay any premium for assurance against social discredit and sanitary damage. Disease is therefore rarely traceable to such a source, and notoriety and scandal almost as seldom; although impolitic economy on the gentleman's part, or indiscreet bearing towards any of the characters among whom he cannot be a hero, will induce them occasionally to hunt him and his follies into daylight, as a warning to others, not against the lusts of the flesh, but against sentiments which horse-leeches might consider illiberal. He usually obtains for his money security, comfort, and a superior class of prostitute, who is, according to his knowledge of the world or desires, presented to him as maid, wife, or widow – British, or imported direct from foreign parts. The female obtains fairly liberal terms, either directly from the paramour, or from the *entrepreneuse* (who, of course, takes good care of herself), the company of gentlemen, and when this is an object with her, unquestionable privacy. A number of the first-class prostitutes have relations with these houses, and are sent for as occasion and demand may arise. I have heard of one establishment at which no female is welcome who has not some particular accomplishment, as music or singing. (p. 14)

5

In the first edition, Acton detailed how prostitution
was treated by authorities in several continental countries.
The cities from which he took his sources included Brussels
and Vienna, two places in which Mrs Warren has brothels.
In the second edition, he added some sections describing
the life of prostitutes to complement his statistics.
The following is taken from the section on Paris,
but it could very well describe Kitty's establishments

The *dames de maison*[16] are of course a vicious and, as a general rule, ferocious mercenary band, tyrannising over the unfortunate helots who form their stock-in-trade, and abjectly crouching before the inspector, the surgeon, and the *mouchard*.[17] The possession of a house of this kind is the

16 A *dame de maison* is a female brothel manager, or procuress.
17 A *mouchard* is an informer or a snitch, one who reports activities to the authorities.

highest aspiration of the prostitute. Such a woman sometimes succeeds in attaining to this pernicious eminence, but it is more frequently in the hands of families in whom houses and goodwill descend as heritable property. The recent editors of Parent's[18] work instance that as much as £2,400 has been given for such an establishment, and £8 has been offered as fine to avoid suspension for three days of one of the lowest. Large as these sums may seem, especially when reduced into francs, they will by no means surprise persons cognizant of the property amassed by those who minister, for ready money only, to the lower gratifications of even our more thrifty countrymen.

The gains of the mistresses of these houses in the better part of Paris are enormous. A medical friend told me that he once, while attending a woman of this class, said he supposed she gained a great deal? – 'Yes, my income is considerable,' she replied, 'more than the pay of a French maréchal!'[19]

I have above alluded to the external signs by which these houses may be recognised; they are not unfrequently pointed out to the stranger by the *laquais de place*,[20] who think that all foreigners are anxious to see them. And certainly the visitor discovers on entering them scenes of sensual extravagance, to which his eyes are unaccustomed in England. Here vice finds a retreat of voluptuous splendour, to which in soberer climes she is a stranger. The visitor is received by a curtain being drawn aside, a door is revealed to him, containing a circular piece of glass about the size of a crown piece,[21] through which he can reconnoitre at his ease a small, but well-lighted and elegantly-furnished, drawing-room, occupied by the women of the establishment. They are usually to be seen seated on sofa chairs, elegantly attired in different-coloured silks, with low bodies, and having their hair dressed in the extreme of fashion; the whole group being arranged artistically, as in a *tableau vivant*,[22] and the individuals who comprise it representing the poses of different celebrated statues, selected apparently with the object of showing off to the best advantage the peculiar attractions of the different women. From the room of observation the

---

18   The reference is to Alexandre Parent-Duchâtelet's *De la prostitution dans la ville de Paris*, which was published posthumously in 1836, the same year that he died.

19   'Some of these mistresses are said to gain as much as from £20 to £30 a day, and if, as is often the case, the same individual owns two or three houses, she may retire on a fortune in about five years.' (Acton's note.)

20   A *lacquais de place* is a doorman who attracts business and often serves as a bouncer.

21   The crown was a large coin worth five shillings. It had been phased out even before British currency was decimalised in 1971.

22   A *tableau vivant*, which directly translated means a living picture, is an orchestrated arrangement of people in a theatrical manner.

visitor can, if he pleases, select his victim, in the same way as a traveller in Galway, on his arrival at a certain hotel, can choose from a number of fish swimming about in the tank the particular salmon on which he would prefer to dine. If this somewhat cold-blooded process of selection is distasteful to him, and he desires to become acquainted with the women in a less summary manner – or if the object of his visit is merely amusement, or the satisfaction of curiosity, without any ulterior aim, he can enter the room, and enjoy the society of its occupants, and will find that the terms of the invitation addressed by the old women at the street door to passers-by are strictly carried out – 'Si vous montez voir les jolies filles cela vous engagé [sic] a [sic] rien,'[23] all that is expected from him being to stand a reasonable amount of champagne, or other refreshment, and to make himself generally agreeable. It is almost unnecessary to add that to indulge such curiosity is an act of extreme rashness, for in such places all that is possible is done to rob vice of its hideousness, and the visitor is surrounded by an atmosphere of luxury, and by all accessories calculated to captivate the senses and arouse desire.   (pp. 108–9)

6

*Acton defines prostitution. Here he begins to take on
a more puritanical and accusatory tone*

Every unchaste woman is not a prostitute. By unchastity a woman becomes liable to lose character, position, and the means of living; and when these are lost is too often reduced to prostitution for support, which, therefore, may be described as the trade adopted by all women who have abandoned or are precluded from an honest course of life, or who lack the power or the inclination to obtain a livelihood from other sources. What is a prostitute? She is a woman who gives for money that which she ought to give only for love; who ministers to passion and lust alone, to the exclusion and extinction of all the higher qualities, and nobler sources of enjoyment which combine with desire, to produce the happiness derived from the intercourse of the sexes. She is a woman with half the woman gone, and that half containing all that elevates her nature, leaving her a mere instrument of impurity; degraded and fallen she extracts from the sin of others the means of living, corrupt and dependent on corruption, and therefore interested directly in the increase of immorality – a social pest, carrying contamination and foulness to every quarter to which she has access, who –

23   It should read *Si vous montez voir les jolies filles, cela vous engage à rien.* This translates
     as 'It'll cost you nothing to come in and see the girls.'

> 'like a disease,
> Creeps, no precaution used, among the crowd,
> Makes wicked lightnings of her eyes,'
> ——————————— 'and stirs the pulse,
> With devil's leaps, and poisons half the young.'[24]

Such women, ministers of evil passions, not only gratify desire, but also arouse it. Compelled by necessity to seek for customers, they throng our streets and public places, and suggest evil thoughts and desires which might otherwise remain undeveloped. Confirmed profligates will seek out the means of gratifying their desires; the young from a craving to discover unknown mysteries may approach the haunts of sin, but thousands would remain uncontaminated if temptation did not seek them out. Prostitutes have the power of soliciting and tempting. Gunpowder remains harmless till the spark falls upon it; the match, until struck, retains the hidden fire, so lust remains dormant till called into being by an exciting cause. (p. 166)

7
Acton considers the causes of prostitution

We have seen that many women stray from the paths of virtue, and ultimately swell the ranks of prostitution through being by their position peculiarly exposed to temptation. The women to whom this remark applies are chiefly actresses, milliners, shop girls, domestic servants, and women employed in factories or working in agricultural gangs. Of these many, no doubt, fall through vanity and idleness, love of dress, love of excitement, love of drink, but by far the larger proportion are driven to evil courses by cruel biting poverty. It is a shameful fact, but no less true, that the lowness of the wages paid to workwomen in various trades is a fruitful source of prostitution; unable to obtain by their labour the means of procuring the bare necessities of life, they gain, by surrendering their bodies to evil uses, food to sustain and clothes to cover them. Many thousand young women

24 These lines are misquoted from 'Guinevere', by English Poet Laureate Lord Alfred Tennyson (1809–92). King Arthur, after he has discovered Guinevere's affair with Lancelot, says: 'I hold that man the worst of public foes / Who either for his own or children's sake, / To save his blood from scandal, lets the wife / Whom he knows false, abide and rule the house: / For being thro' his cowardice allow'd / Her station, taken everywhere for pure, / She like a new disease, unknown to men, / Creeps, no precaution used, among the crowd, / Makes wicked lightnings of her eyes, and saps / The fealty of our friends, and stirs the pulse / With devil's leaps, and poisons half the young.' The implication here appears to be that, like Guinevere, prostitutes lead to the corruption and downfall of society.

in the metropolis are unable by drudgery that lasts from early morning till late into the night to earn more than from 3s. to 5s. weekly.[25] Many have to eke out their living as best they may on a miserable pittance for less than the least of the sums above-mentioned. What wonder if, urged on by want and toil, encouraged by evil advisers, and exposed to selfish tempters, a large proportion of these poor girls fall from the path of virtue? Is it not a great wonder that any of them are found abiding in it? Instances innumerable might be adduced in support of this statement. I have said enough to acquaint the reader with the miserable condition of these children of want; it is not my purpose to pain and horrify or to distract the attention from the main purpose of my book; those who desire a narrative of facts fully supporting this statement, I would refer to Mr Mayhew's work on *London Labour and London Poor*.[26] Misplaced love, then, inordinate vanity, and sheer destitution are the causes that lead to woman's fall and that help to fill the ranks of prostitution.   (pp. 180–1)

8

Acton cites inadequate living conditions as also being particularly noxious and contributing to prostitution. He describes cramped, low lodging-houses and their effects on the inhabitants' morality

In these detestable haunts of vice men, women, and children are received indiscriminately, and pass the night huddled together, without distinction of age or sex, not merely in one common room, but often one common bed; even if privacy is desired, it is impossible of attainment; no accommodation is made for decency, and the practices of the inmates are on a par with the accommodation. It is fearful to contemplate human beings so utterly abandoned, reduced below the level of the brute creation. By constant practice, vice has become a second nature; with such associates, children of tender years soon become old in vice. This is no fancy sketch, or highly-coloured picture. In this manner thousands pass from childhood to youth, from youth to age, with every good feeling trampled out and every evil instinct cherished and matured; trained to no useful art, and yet dependent for a living on their own exertions, what wonder if all the males are thieves and all the females prostitutes.   (pp. 182–3)

25 3s. to 5s. means three to five shillings. The shilling, five pence in 'new money', was phased out following decimalisation in 1971. Under the previous monetary system, twelve pence made a shilling and twenty shillings a pound.

26 *London Labour and the London Poor* (1851), a massive multi-volume study of work and poverty among London's underclasses, was written by Henry Mayhew (1812–87), a journalist and crusader for social reform.

APPENDIX IV

MRS WARREN'S PROFESSION was written in 1894[27] to draw attention to the truth that prostitution is caused, not by female depravity and male licentiousness, but simply by underpaying, undervaluing, and overworking women so shamefully that the poorest of them are forced to resort to prostitution to keep body and soul together. Indeed all attractive unpropertied women lose money by being infallibly virtuous or contracting marriages that are not more or less venal. If on the large social scale we get what we call vice instead of what we call virtue it is simply because we are paying more for it. No normal woman would be a professional prostitute if she could better herself by being respectable, nor marry for money if she could afford to marry for love.

Also I desired to expose the fact that prostitution is not only carried on without organization by individual enterprise in the lodgings of solitary women, each her own mistress as well as every customer's mistress, but organized and exploited as a big international commerce for the profit of capitalists like any other commerce, and very lucrative to great city estates, including Church estates, through the rents of the houses in which it is practised.

I could not have done anything more injurious to my prospects at the outset of my career. My play was immediately stigmatized by the Lord Chamberlain, who by Act of Parliament has despotic and even supermonarchical power over our theatres,[28] as 'immoral and otherwise improper for the stage'. Its performance was prohibited, I myself being branded by implication, to my great damage, as an unscrupulous and blackguardly author. True, I have lived this defamation down, and am apparently none the worse. True too that the stage under the censorship became so licentious after the war that the ban on a comparatively prudish play like mine became ridiculous and had to be lifted. Also I admit that my career as a revolutionary critic of our most respected social institutions kept me so continually in hot water that the addition of another jugful of boiling fluid by the Lord Chamberlain troubled me too little to entitle me to

27 The play was actually written in 1893. See Introduction, pp. xvi–xvii.
28 The Lord Chamberlain's powers as censor of British theatres were created under the Licensing Act of 1737 and consolidated by the Theatres Act of 1843.

personal commiseration, especially as the play greatly strengthened my repute among serious readers. Besides, in 1894 the ordinary commercial theatres would have nothing to say to me, Lord Chamberlain or no Lord Chamberlain. None the less the injury done me, now admittedly indefensible, was real and considerable, and the injury to society much greater; for when the White Slave Traffic, as Mrs Warren's profession came to be called, was dealt with legislatively, all that Parliament did was to enact that prostitutes' male bullies and parasites should be flogged, leaving Mrs Warren in complete command of the situation, and its true nature more effectually masked than ever. It was the fault of the Censorship that our legislators and journalists were not better instructed.

In 1902 the Stage Society,[29] technically a club giving private performances for the entertainment of its own members, and therefore exempt from the Lord Chamberlain's jurisdiction, resolved to perform the play. None of the public theatres dared brave his displeasure (he has absolute power to close them if they offend him) by harboring the performance; but another club which had a little stage, and which rather courted a pleasantly scandalous reputation, opened its doors for one night and one afternoon. Some idea of the resultant sensation may be gathered from the following polemic, which appeared as a preface to a special edition of the play, and was headed

The Author's Apology

Mrs Warren's Profession has been performed at last, after a delay of only eight years; and I have once more shared with Ibsen the triumphant amusement of startling all but the strongest-headed of the London theatre critics clean out of the practice of their profession. No author who has ever known the exultation of sending the Press into an hysterical tumult of protest, of moral panic, of involuntary and frantic confession of sin, of a horror of conscience in which the power of distinguishing between the work of art on the stage and the real life of the spectator is confused and overwhelmed, will ever care for the stereotyped compliments which every successful farce or melodrama elicits from the newspapers. Give me that critic who rushed from my play to declare furiously that Sir George Crofts ought to be kicked. What a triumph for the actor, thus to reduce a jaded London journalist to the condition of the simple sailor in the Wapping

---

29 The Incorporated Stage Society was founded in 1899 to support the New Drama. Lacking its own theatre, it rented spaces to stage plays that would not have been performed by the commercial companies. It especially made a name for itself in producing plays that had been banned by the Lord Chamberlain for private members-only performances.

gallery,[30] who shouts execrations at Iago and warnings to Othello not to believe him! But dearer still than such simplicity is that sense of the sudden earthquake shock to the foundations of morality which sends a pallid crowd of critics into the street shrieking that the pillars of society are cracking and the ruin of the State at hand. Even the Ibsen champions of ten years ago remonstrate with me just as the veterans of those brave days remonstrated with them. Mr Grein,[31] the hardy iconoclast who first launched my plays on the stage alongside *Ghosts* and *The Wild Duck*, exclaims that I have shattered his ideals. Actually his ideals! What would Dr Relling[32] say? And Mr William Archer[33] himself disowns me because I 'cannot touch pitch without wallowing in it'. Truly my play must be more needed than I knew; and yet I thought I knew how little the others know.

Do not suppose, however, that the consternation of the Press reflects any consternation among the general public. Anybody can upset the theatre critics, in a turn of the wrist, by substituting for the romantic commonplaces of the stage the moral commonplaces of the pulpit, the platform, or the library. Play *Mrs Warren's Profession* to an audience of clerical members of the Christian Social Union[34] and of women well experienced in Rescue, Temperance, and Girls' Club work, and no moral panic will arise: every man and woman present will know that as long as poverty makes virtue hideous and the spare pocket-money of rich bachelordom makes vice dazzling, their daily hand-to-hand fight against prostitution with prayer and persuasion, shelters and scanty alms, will be a losing one. There was a time when they were able to urge that though 'the white-lead factory where Anne Jane was poisoned' may be a far more terrible place than Mrs Warren's house, yet hell is still more dreadful. Nowadays they no longer believe in hell; and the girls among whom they are working know that they do not believe in it, and would laugh at them if they did. So well have the rescuers learnt that Mrs Warren's defence of herself and indictment of society is the thing that most needs saying, that those who know me personally reproach me, not for writing this play, but

---

30   Wapping is an eastern district of London, situated on the northern bank of the River Thames. In the nineteenth century, the London Docks were built there. It was an impoverished area at the time that Shaw wrote the preface. The brothel of Bertolt Brecht's *The Threepenny Opera* (1928) is in Wapping.

31   J.T. Grein (1862–1935) was the founder of the Independent Theatre in 1891. His review of the 1902 production of *Mrs Warren's Profession* is in Appendix VI, pp. 152–5.

32   Dr Relling is a character in Ibsen's *The Wild Duck* (1885) who maintains the idealist illusions of the Ekdal family.

33   William Archer (1856–1924), a prominent theatre critic and one of Ibsen's earliest translators, was a good friend of Shaw's.

34   The Christian Social Union was an organisation founded within the Church of England to examine and remedy social conditions in the country.

for wasting my energies on 'pleasant plays' for the amusement of frivolous people, when I can build up such excellent stage sermons on their own work. *Mrs Warren's Profession* is the one play of mine which I could submit to a censorship without doubt of the result; only, it must not be the censorship of the minor theatre critic, nor of an innocent court official like the Lord Chamberlain's Examiner, much less of people who consciously profit by Mrs Warren's profession, or who personally make use of it, or who hold the widely whispered view that it is an indispensable safety-valve for the protection of domestic virtue, or, above all, who are smitten with a sentimental affection for our fallen sister, and would 'take her up tenderly, lift her with care, fashioned so slenderly, young, and *so* fair.' Nor am I prepared to accept the verdict of the medical gentlemen who would compulsorily examine and register Mrs Warren, whilst leaving Mrs Warren's patrons, especially her military patrons, free to destroy her health and anybody else's without fear of reprisals. But I should be quite content to have my play judged by, say, a joint committee of the Central Vigilance Society[35] and the Salvation Army.[36] And the sterner moralists the members of the committee were, the better.

Some of the journalists I have shocked reason so unripely that they will gather nothing from this but a confused notion that I am accusing the National Vigilance Association and the Salvation Army of complicity in my own scandalous immorality. It will seem to them that people who would stand this play would stand anything. They are quite mistaken. Such an audience as I have described would be revolted by many of our fashionable plays. They would leave the theatre convinced that the Plymouth Brother[37] who still regards the playhouse as one of the gates of hell is perhaps the safest adviser on the subject of which he knows so little. If I do not draw the same conclusion, it is not because I am one of those who claim that art is exempt from moral obligations, and deny that the writing or performance of a play is a moral act, to be treated on exactly the same footing as theft or murder if it produces equally mischievous consequences. I am convinced that fine art is the subtlest, the most seductive,

---

35   The Central Vigilance Society was one of many English groups, among them the Society for Suppression of Vice and the National Vigilance Association, active in campaigns against allegedly obscene literature.

36   The Salvation Army was (and remains) a Protestant Christian organisation founded in London's East End in 1878 by William and Catherine Booth to minister to the material and spiritual needs of impoverished people. The title character of Shaw's *Major Barbara* (1905) is a member of the Salvation Army.

37   The Plymouth Brethren, founded in Dublin in the 1820s but named for the city in which it held its first English assembly in 1831, is a non-denominational, evangelical Christian movement.

the most effective instrument of moral propaganda in the world, excepting only the example of personal conduct; and I waive even this exception in favor of the art of the stage, because it works by exhibiting examples of personal conduct made intelligible and moving to crowds of unobservant unreflecting people to whom real life means nothing. I have pointed out again and again that the influence of the theatre in England is growing so great that private conduct, religion, law, science, politics, and morals are becoming more and more theatrical, whilst the theatre itself remains impervious to common sense, religion, science, politics, and morals. That is why I fight the theatre, not with pamphlets and sermons and treatises, but with plays; and so effective do I find the dramatic method that I have no doubt I shall at last persuade even London to take its conscience and its brains with it when it goes to the theatre, instead of leaving them at home with its prayer-book as it does at present. Consequently, I am the last man to deny that if the net effect of performing *Mrs Warren's Profession* were an increase in the number of persons entering that profession or employing it, its performance might well be made an indictable offence.

Now let us consider how such recruiting can be encouraged by the theatre. Nothing is easier. Let the Lord Chamberlain's Examiner of Plays, backed by the Press, make an unwritten but perfectly well understood regulation that members of Mrs Warren's profession shall be tolerated on the stage only when they are beautiful, exquisitely dressed, and sumptuously lodged and fed; also that they shall, at the end of the play, die of consumption to the sympathetic tears of the whole audience, or step into the next room to commit suicide, or at least be turned out by their protectors and passed on to be 'redeemed' by old and faithful lovers who have adored them in spite of all their levities.[38] Naturally the poorer girls in the gallery will believe in the beauty, in the exquisite dresses, and the luxurious living, and will see that there is no real necessity for the consumption, the suicide, or the ejectment: mere pious forms, all of them, to save the Censor's face. Even if these purely official catastrophes carried any conviction, the majority of English girls remain so poor, so dependent, so well aware that the drudgeries of such honest work as is within their reach are likely enough to lead them eventually to lung disease, premature death, and domestic desertion or brutality, that they would still see reason to prefer the primrose path to the stony way of virtue, since both, vice at worst and virtue at best, lead to the same end in poverty and overwork. It is true that the Elementary School mistress will tell you that only girls of a certain kind will reason in this way. But alas! that certain kind turns out on inquiry to

38 These describe the plots of Dumas, *fils' La Dame aux Camélias*, Pinero's *The Second Mrs Tanqueray*, and Dion Boucicault's *Formosa* (1869), respectively.

be simply the pretty, dainty kind: that is, the only kind that gets the chance of acting on such reasoning. Read the first report of the Commission on the Housing of the Working Classes [Bluebook C 4402, 1889]; read the Report on Home Industries (sacred word, Home!) issued by the Women's Industrial Council [*Home Industries of Women in London,* 1897]; and ask yourself whether, if the lot in life therein described were your lot in life, you would not rather be a jewelled Vamp. If you can go deep enough into things to be able to say no, how many ignorant half-starved girls will believe you are speaking sincerely? To them the lot of the stage courtesan is heavenly in comparison with their own. Yet the Lord Chamberlain's Examiner, being an officer of the Royal Household, places the King in the position of saying to the dramatist 'Thus, and thus only, shall you present Mrs Warren's profession on the stage, or you shall starve. Witness Shaw, who told the untempting truth about it, and whom We, by the Grace of God, accordingly disallow and suppress, and do what in Us lies to silence.' Fortunately, Shaw cannot be silenced. 'The harlot's cry from street to street'[39] is louder than the voices of all the kings. I am not dependent on the theatre, and cannot be starved into making my play a standing advertisement of the attractive side of Mrs Warren's business.

Here I must guard myself against a misunderstanding. It is not the fault of their authors that the long string of wanton's tragedies, from *Antony and Cleopatra* to *Iris,*[40] are snares to poor girls, and are objected to on account by many earnest men and women who consider *Mrs Warren's Profession* an excellent sermon. Pinero is in no way bound to suppress the fact that his Iris is a person to be envied by millions of better women. If he made his play false to life by inventing fictitious disadvantages for her, he would be acting as unscrupulously as any tract-writer. If society chooses to provide for its Irises better than for its working women, it must not expect honest playwrights to manufacture spurious evidence to save its credit. The mischief lies in the deliberate suppression of the other side of the case: the refusal to allow Mrs Warren to expose the drudgery and repulsiveness of plying for hire among coarse tedious drunkards. All that, says the Examiner in effect, is horrifying, loathsome. Precisely: what does he expect it to be? would he have us represent it as beautiful and gratifying? His answer to this question amounts, I fear, to a blunt Yes; for it seems impossible to root out of an Englishman's mind the notion that vice is delightful, and that abstention from it is privation. At all events, as long as the tempting side of it is kept towards the public, and softened by plenty of sentiment and sympathy, it is welcomed by our Censor, whereas the

39   See the note on the title page.
40   These are plays by Shakespeare and Pinero. *Iris* was first performed in 1901.

slightest attempt to place it in the light of the policeman's lantern or the Salvation Army shelter is checkmated at once as not merely disgusting, but, if you please, unnecessary.

Everybody will, I hope, admit that this state of things is intolerable; that the subject of Mrs Warren's profession must be either tapu[41] altogether, or else exhibited with the warning side as freely displayed as the tempting side. But many persons will vote for a complete tapu, and an impartial clean sweep from the boards of Mrs Warren and Gretchen[42] and the rest: in short, for banishing the sexual instincts from the stage altogether. Those who think this impossible can hardly have considered the number and importance of the subjects which are actually banished from the stage. Many plays, among them *Lear, Hamlet, Macbeth, Coriolanus, Julius Caesar*,[43] have no sex complications: the thread of their action can be followed by children who could not understand a single scene of *Mrs Warren's Profession* or *Iris*. None of our plays rouse the sympathy of the audience by an exhibition of the pains of maternity, as Chinese plays constantly do. Each nation has its particular set of tapus in addition to the common human stock; and though each of these tapus limits the scope of the dramatist, it does not make drama impossible. If the Examiner were to refuse to license plays with female characters in them, he would only be doing to the stage what our tribal customs already do to the pulpit and the bar. I have myself written a rather entertaining play with only one woman in it, and she quite heartwhole; and I could just as easily write a play without a woman in it at all. I will even go as far as to promise the Examiner my support if he will introduce this limitation for part of the year, say during Lent,[44] so as to make a close season for that dullest of stock dramatic subjects, adultery, and force our managers and authors to find out what all great dramatists find out spontaneously: to wit, that people who sacrifice every other consideration to love are as hopelessly unheroic on the stage as lunatics or dipsomaniacs. Hector and Hamlet are the world's heroes; not Paris and Antony.[45]

But though I do not question the possibility of a drama in which love should be as effectively ignored as cholera is at present, there is not the slightest chance of that way out of the difficulty being taken by the Examiner. If he attempted it there would be a revolt in which he would be

41 *Tapu* and *tabu* are the original Polynesian forms of 'taboo' that were common in Shaw's time.

42 Gretchen is the title character's love interest in Goethe's *Faust* (1808).

43 All works by Shakespeare. *Lear* should read as *King Lear*.

44 Lent is the Christian period of fasting and prayer between Ash Wednesday and Easter.

45 Paris absconded with Helen, the Queen of Sparta, thus instigating the Trojan War. Hector, his older brother, was considered a courageous and noble warrior.

swept away, in spite of my singlehanded efforts to defend him. A complete tapu is politically impossible. A complete toleration is equally impossible to the Examiner, because his occupation would be gone if there were no tapu to enforce. He is therefore compelled to maintain the present compromise of a partial tapu, applied, to the best of his judgment, with a careful respect to persons and to public opinion. And a very sensible English solution of the difficulty, too, most readers will say. I should not dispute it if dramatic poets really were what English public opinion generally assumes them to be during their lifetime: that is, a licentiously irregular group to be kept in order in a rough and ready way by a magistrate who will stand no nonsense from them. But I cannot admit that the class represented by Eschylus, Sophocles, Aristophanes, Euripides,[46] Shakespear, Goethe,[47] Ibsen, and Tolstoy, not to mention our own contemporary playwrights, is as much in place in the Examiner's office as a pickpocket is in Bow Street.[48] Further, it is not true that the Censorship, though it certainly suppresses Ibsen and Tolstoy, and would suppress Shakespear but for the absurd rule that a play once licensed is always licensed (so that Wycherly[49] is permitted and Shelley[50] prohibited), also suppresses unscrupulous playwrights. I challenge the Examiner to mention any extremity of sexual misconduct which any manager in his senses would risk presenting on the London stage that has not been presented under his licence and that of his predecessor. The compromise, in fact, works out in practice in favor of loose plays as against earnest ones.

To carry conviction on this point, I will take the extreme course of narrating the plots of two plays witnessed within the last ten years by myself at London West End theatres,[51] one licensed under Queen Victoria, the other under her successor.[52] Both plots conform to the strictest rules of the period when *La Dame aux Camellias* [*sic*] was still a forbidden play, and when *The Second Mrs Tanqueray* would have been tolerated only on

---

46   Aeschylus (525/4–456/5 BC), Sophocles (496–406 BC), Aristophanes (450–388 BC), and Euripides (484–406 BC) were major Greek playwrights. While Aristophanes was a comedic writer, the others were tragedians.

47   Johann Wolfgang von Goethe (1749–1832) is considered by many to be the greatest German writer of the modern era.

48   Bow Street was a magistrates' court in the street of that name in Covent Garden, a place for hearing cases pertaining to minor offences. It remained in use until 2006.

49   William Wycherley (1641–1716) was a Restoration writer of satirical plays.

50   Percy Bysshe Shelley (1792–1822) was a Romantic writer. His play *The Cenci* (1819) was banned in England until 1922.

51   London's West End theatre district is the most important concentration of large commercial theatres in the United Kingdom. It is only rivalled in reputation by New York's Broadway theatre district.

52   Queen Victoria (1819–1901) and her son, King Edward VII (1841–1910).

condition that she carefully explained to the audience that when she met Captain Ardale she sinned 'but in intention'.

Play number one. A prince is compelled by his parents to marry the daughter of a neighboring king, but loves another maiden. The scene represents a hall in the king's palace at night. The wedding has taken place that day; and the closed door of the nuptial chamber is in view of the audience. Inside, the princess awaits her bridegroom. A duenna is in attendance. The bridegroom enters. His sole desire is to escape from a marriage which is hateful to him. A means occurs to him. He will assault the duenna, and be ignominiously expelled from the palace by his indignant father-in-law. To his horror, when he proceeds to carry out this stratagem, the duenna, far from raising an alarm, is flattered, delighted, and compliant. The assaulter becomes the assaulted. He flings her angrily to the ground, where she remains placidly. He flies. The father enters; dismisses the duenna; and listens at the keyhole of his daughter's nuptial chamber, uttering various pleasantries, and declaring, with a shiver, that a sound of kissing, which he supposes to proceed from within, makes him feel young again.

Story number two. A German officer finds himself in an inn with a French lady who has wounded his national vanity. He resolves to humble her by committing a rape upon her. He announces his purpose. She remonstrates, implores, flies to the doors and finds them locked, calls for help and finds none at hand, runs screaming from side to side, and, after a harrowing scene, is overpowered and faints. Nothing further being possible on the stage without actual felony, the officer then relents and leaves her. When she recovers, she believes that he has carried out his threat; and during the rest of the play she is represented as vainly vowing vengeance upon him, whilst she is really falling in love with him under the influence of his imaginary crime against her. Finally she consents to marry him; and the curtain falls on their happiness.

This story was certified by the Examiner, acting for the Lord Chamberlain, as void in its general tendency of 'anything immoral or otherwise improper for the stage.' But let nobody conclude therefore that the Examiner is a monster, whose policy it is to deprave the theatre. As a matter of fact, both the above stories are strictly in order from the official point of view. The incidents of sex which they contain, though carried in both to the extreme point at which another step would be dealt with, not by the Examiner, but by the police, do not involve adultery, nor any allusion to Mrs Warren's profession, nor to the fact that the children of any polyandrous group will, when they grow up, inevitably be confronted, as those of Mrs Warren's group are in my play, with the insoluble problem of their own possible consanguinity. In short, by depending wholly on the coarse humors and the physical fascination of sex, they comply with all the formulable requirements of the Censorship, whereas plays in which these humors and fascinations are discarded, and the social problems created by sex seriously faced and dealt with, inevitably ignore the official formula and are suppressed. If the old rule against the exhibition of illicit sex relations on the stage were revived, and the subject absolutely barred, the only result would be that *Antony and Cleopatra*, *Othello* (because of the Bianca episode), *Troilus and Cressida*, *Henry IV*, *Measure for Measure*, *Timon of Athens*, *La Dame aux Camellias*, *The Profligate*, *The Second Mrs Tanqueray*, *The Notorious Mrs Ebbsmith*, *The Gay Lord Quex*, *Mrs Dane's Defence*, and *Iris*[53] would be swept from the stage, and placed under the same ban as Tolstoy's *Dominion of Darkness*[54] and *Mrs Warren's Profession*, whilst such plays as the two described above would have a monopoly of the theatre as far as sexual interest is concerned.

What is more, the repulsiveness of the worst of the certified plays would protect Censorship against effective exposure and criticism. Not long ago an American Review of high standing asked me for an article on the Censorship of the English Stage. I replied that such an article would involve passages too disagreeable for publication in a magazine for general family reading. The editor persisted nevertheless; but not until he had declared his readiness to face this, and had pledged himself to insert the article unaltered (the particularity of the pledge extending even to a specification of the exact number of words in the article) did I consent to the proposal. What was the result? The editor, confronted with the two stories given above, threw his pledge to the winds, and, instead of returning the article, printed it with the illustrative examples omitted, and nothing left but the argument from political principle against the Censorship.[55] In doing this he fired my broadside after withdrawing the cannon balls; for neither the Censor nor any other Englishman, except perhaps a few veterans of the dwindling old guard of Benthamism,[56] cares a dump about political principle. The ordinary Briton thinks that if every other Briton is not under

---

53 *Antony and Cleopatra, Othello, Troilus and Cressida, Henry IV, Measure for Measure*, and *Timon of Athens* are plays by Shakespeare; *The Profligate* (1889), *The Second Mrs Tanqueray, The Notorious Mrs Ebbsmith, The Gay Lord Quex* (1899), and *Iris* are plays by Pinero; and *Mrs Dane's Defence* (1900) is a play by Henry Arthur Jones (1851–1929).

54 Tolstoy's play, more commonly translated as *Power of Darkness* (1886), was banned in both Britain and his native Russia.

55 Shaw refers to his article 'The Censorship of the Stage in England' that appeared in the *North American Review*, August 1899. It is repeated, with the censored passages indicated, in *The Drama Observed*, ed. Bernard F. Dukore (University Park, PA: Pennsylvania State University Press, 1993), pp. 1065–77.

56 Jeremy Bentham (1748–1832) was a pre-eminent philosopher and social reformer, driven by a stern regard for ethics.

some form of tutelage, the more childish the better, he will abuse his freedom viciously. As far as its principle is concerned, the Censorship is the most popular institution in England; and the playwright who criticizes it is slighted as a blackguard agitating for impunity. Consequently nothing can really shake the confidence of the public in the Lord Chamberlain's department except a remorseless and unbowdlerized narration of the licentious fictions which slip through its net, and are hallmarked by it with the approval of the royal household. But as such stories cannot be made public without great difficulty, owing to the obligation an editor is under not to deal unexpectedly with matters that are not *virginibus puerisque*,[57] the chances are heavily in favor of the Censor escaping all remonstrance. With the exception of such comments as I was able to make in my own critical articles in *The World* and *The Saturday Review*[58] when the pieces I have described were first produced, and a few ignorant protests by churchmen against much better plays which they confessed they had not seen nor read, nothing has been said in the press that could seriously disturb the easygoing notion that the stage would be much worse than it admittedly is but for the vigilance of the Examiner. The truth is, that no manager would dare produce on his own responsibility the pieces he can now get royal certificates for at two guineas per piece.

I hasten to add that I believe these evils to be inherent in the nature of all censorship, and not merely a consequence of the form the institution takes in London. No doubt there is a staggering absurdity in appointing an ordinary clerk to see that the leaders of European literature do not corrupt the morals of the nation, and to restrain Sir Henry Irving[59] from presuming to impersonate Samson or David on the stage,[60] though any other sort of artist may daub these scriptural figures on a signboard or carve them on a tombstone without hindrance. If the General Medical Council, the Royal College of Physicians, the Royal Academy of Arts, the Incorporated Law Society, and Convocation[61] were abolished, and their

---

57   *Virginibus puerisque* is Latin, meaning 'for girls and boys.'

58   Shaw wrote art and music criticism for *The World* in the late 1880s and early 1890s and theatre criticism for *The Saturday Review* from 1895 to 1898.

59   Sir Henry Irving (1838–1905) was the most popular actor-manager of London's West End throughout the late nineteenth century. He was the first actor to be knighted (1895) for services to the stage.

60   This reference to the biblical characters Samson and David alludes to the Lord Chamberlain's tendency to discourage representations of religious figures on stage.

61   The General Medical Council was created by the Medical Act of 1858 to control who was admitted to practise medicine in Britain; the Royal College of Physicians, which established a system that examined medical practitioners, was founded in 1518; the Royal Academy of Arts, the principal society for artists in London, was founded in 1768; the Law Society, a voluntary group incorporated by Parliament, sets and enforces standards

functions handed over to the Examiner, the Concert of Europe[62] would presumably certify England as mad. Yet, though neither medicine nor painting nor law nor the Church moulds the character of the nation as potently as the theatre does, nothing can come on the stage unless its dimensions admit of its first passing through the Examiner's mind! Pray do not think that I question his honesty. I am quite sure that he sincerely thinks me a blackguard, and my play a grossly improper one, because, like Tolstoy's *Dominion of Darkness*, it produces, as they are both meant to produce, a very strong and very painful impression of evil. I do not doubt for a moment that the rapine play which I have described, and which he licensed, was quite incapable in manuscript of producing any particular effect on his mind at all, and that when he was once satisfied that the ill-conducted hero was a German and not an English officer, he passed the play without studying its moral tendencies. Even if he had undertaken that study, there is no more reason to suppose that he is a competent moralist than there is to suppose that I am a competent mathematician. But truly it does not matter whether he is a moralist or not. Let nobody dream for a moment that what is wrong with the Censorship is the shortcoming of the gentleman who happens at any moment to be acting as Censor. Replace him tomorrow by an Academy of Letters and an Academy of Dramatic Poetry, and the new filter will still exclude original and epoch-making work, whilst passing conventional, old-fashioned, and vulgar work. The conclave which compiles the expurgatory index of the Roman Catholic Church[63] is the most august, ancient, learned, famous, and authoritative censorship in Europe. Is it more enlightened, more liberal, more tolerant than the comparatively unqualified office of the Lord Chamberlain? On the contrary, it has reduced itself to a degree of absurdity which makes Catholic university a contradiction in terms. All censorships exist to prevent anyone from challenging current conceptions and existing institutions. All progress is initiated by challenging current conceptions, and executed by supplanting existing institutions. Consequently the first condition of progress is the removal of censorships. There is the whole case against censorships in a nutshell.

for solicitors; the Convocation of the English Clergy is a synod, or a governing body, of the Church of England whose origins can be traced back to the seventh century.

62   The Concert of Europe was a federation of countries founded after the Napoleonic Wars in 1815 to maintain the balance of power on the Continent. It weakened in the second half of the nineteenth century due to conflicts between signatories. The outbreak of World War One in 1914 completed its slow demise.

63   The *Index Librorum Prohibitorum*, or list of prohibited books, was established by the Catholic Church in 1559 and remained in effect until it was abolished in 1966. It contained many of the greatest works ever produced in science, philosophy, and literature.

It will be asked whether theatrical managers are to be allowed to produce what they like, without regard to the public interest. But that is not the alternative. The managers of our London music halls are not subject to any censorship.[64] They produce their entertainments on their own responsibility, and have no two-guinea certificates to plead if their houses are conducted viciously. They know that if they lose their character, the County Council will simply refuse to renew their licence at the end of the year; and nothing in the history of popular art is more amazing than the improvement in music halls that this simple arrangement has produced within a few years. Place the theatres on the same footing, and we shall promptly have a similar revolution: a whole class of frankly blackguardly plays, in which unscrupulous low comedians attract crowds to gaze at bevies of girls who have nothing to exhibit but their prettiness, will vanish like the obscene songs which were supposed to enliven the squalid dullness, incredible to the younger generation, of the music halls fifteen years ago. On the other hand, plays which treat sex questions as problems for thought instead of as aphrodisiacs will be freely performed. Gentlemen of the Examiner's way of thinking will have plenty of opportunity of protesting against them in Council; but the result will be that the Examiner will find his natural level; Ibsen and Tolstoy theirs; so no harm will be done.

This question of the Censorship reminds me that I have to apologize to those who went to the recent performance of *Mrs Warren's Profession* expecting to find it what I have just called an aphrodisiac. That was not my fault: it was the Examiner's. After the specimens I have given of the tolerance of his department, it was natural enough for thoughtless people to infer that a play which overstepped his indulgence must be a very exciting play indeed. Accordingly, I find one critic so explicit as to the nature of his disappointment as to say candidly that 'such airy talk as there is upon the matter is utterly unworthy of acceptance as being a representation of what people with blood in them think or do on such occasions'.[65] Thus am I crushed between the upper millstone of the Examiner, who thinks me a libertine, and the nether popular critic, who thinks me a prude. Critics of all grades and ages, middle-aged fathers of families no less than ardent young enthusiasts, are equally indignant with me. They revile me as lacking in passion, in feeling, in manhood. Some of them even sum the matter up by denying me any dramatic power: a melancholy betrayal of what dramatic power has come to mean on our stage under the Censorship! Can I be expected to refrain from laughing at the spectacle

---

64 Only theatres fell under the Lord Chamberlain's jurisdiction.
65 This is a passage from a review of the Stage Society's production that appeared in the *Morning Leader* on 7 January 1902.

of a number of respectable gentlemen lamenting because a playwright lures them to the theatre by a promise to excite their senses in a very special and sensational manner, and then, having successfully trapped them in exceptional numbers, proceeds to ignore their senses and ruthlessly improve their minds? But I protest again that the lure was not mine. The play had been in print for four years; and I have spared no pains to make known that my plays are built to induce, not voluptuous reverie but intellectual interest, not romantic rhapsody but humane concern. Accordingly, I do not find those critics who are gifted with intellectual appetite and political conscience complaining of want of dramatic power. Rather do they protest, not altogether unjustly, against a few relapses into staginess and caricature which betray the young playwright and the old playgoer in this early work of mine. As to the voluptuaries, I can assure them that the playwright, whether he be myself or another, will always disappoint them. The drama can do little to delight the senses: all the apparent instances to the contrary are instances of the personal fascination of the performers. The drama of pure feeling is no longer in the hands of the playwright: it has been conquered by the musician, after whose enchantments all the verbal arts seem cold and tame. *Romeo and Juliet* with the loveliest Juliet is dry, tedious, and rhetorical in comparison with Wagner's *Tristan*, even though Isolde be both fourteen stone and forty,[66] as she often is in Germany. Indeed, it needed no Wagner to convince the public of this. The voluptuous sentimentality of Gounod's *Faust* and Bizet's *Carmen*[67] has captured the common playgoer; and there is, flatly, no future now for any drama without music except the drama of thought. The attempt to produce a genus of opera without music (and this absurdity is what our fashionable theatres have been driving at for a long time past without knowing it) is far less hopeful than my own determination to accept problem as the normal material of the drama.

That this determination will throw me into a long conflict with our theatre critics, and with the few playgoers who go to the theatre as often as the critics, I well know; but I am too well equipped for the strife to be deterred by it, or to bear malice towards the losing side. In trying to produce the sensuous effects of opera, the fashionable drama has become

---

66 *Tristan und Isolde*, which was written between 1857 and 1859 and premièred in Munich in 1865, is an opera by German composer Wilhelm Richard Wagner (1813–83). In his first article in *The Saturday Review*, on 5 January 1895, Shaw claimed that *Tristan und Isolde* was 'the greatest work of its kind' in the nineteenth century.

67 *Faust* (1859) is an opera by French composer Charles Gounod (1818–93). *Carmen* (1875), which remains a popular opera, was composed by Georges Bizet (1838–75), who as a child studied under Gounod.

so flaccid in its sentimentality, and the intellect of its frequenters so atrophied by disuse, that the reintroduction of problem, with its remorseless logic and iron framework of fact, inevitably produces at first an overwhelming impression of coldness and inhuman rationalism. But this will soon pass away. When the intellectual muscle and moral nerve of the critics has been developed in the struggle with modern problem plays, the pettish luxuriousness of the clever ones, and the sulky sense of disadvantaged weakness in the sentimental ones, will clear away; and it will be seen that only in the problem play is there any real drama, because drama is no mere setting up of the camera to nature: it is the presentation in parable of the conflict between Man's will and his environment: in a word, of problem. The vapidness of such drama as the pseudo-operatic plays contain lies in the fact that in them animal passion, sentimentally diluted, is shewn in conflict, not with real circumstances, but with a set of conventions and assumptions half of which do not exist off the stage, whilst the other half can either be evaded by a pretence of compliance or defied with complete impunity by any reasonably strong-minded person. Nobody can feel that such conventions are really compulsory; and consequently nobody can believe in the stage pathos that accepts them as an inexorable fate, or in the reality of the figures who indulge in such pathos. Sitting at such plays we do not believe: we make-believe. And the habit of make-believe becomes at last so rooted, that criticism of the theatre insensibly ceases to be criticism at all, and becomes more and more a chronicle of the fashionable enterprises of the only realities left on the stage: that is, the performers in their own persons. In this phase the playwright who attempts to revive genuine drama produces the disagreeable impression of the pedant who attempts to start a serious discussion at a fashionable at-home. Later on, when he has driven the tea services out and made the people who had come to use the theatre as a drawing-room understand that it is they and not the dramatists who are the intruders, he has to face the accusation that his plays ignore human feeling, an illusion produced by that very resistance of fact and law to human feeling which creates drama. It is the *deus ex machina*[68] who, by suspending that resistance, makes the fall of the curtain an immediate necessity, since drama ends exactly where resistance ends. Yet the introduction of this resistance produces so strong an impression of heartlessness nowadays that a distinguished critic has summed up the impression made on him by *Mrs Warren's Profession*, by declaring that 'the difference between the spirit of Tolstoy and the spirit of Mr Shaw is the difference between the spirit of

---

68   A *deus ex machina*, Latin for 'God from the machine', is an improbable plot device that
     resolves a difficult problem or situation.

Christ and the spirit of Euclid'.[69] But the epigram would be as good if Tolstoy's name were put in place of mine and D'Annunzio's[70] in place of Tolstoy's. At the same time I accept the enormous compliment to my reasoning powers with sincere complacency; and I promise my flatterer that when he is sufficiently accustomed to and therefore undazzled by problem on the stage to be able to attend to the familiar factor of humanity in it as well as to the unfamiliar one of a real environment, he will both see and feel that *Mrs Warren's Profession* is no mere theorem, but a play of instincts and temperaments in conflict with each other and with a flinty social problem that never yields an inch to mere sentiment.

I go further than this. I declare that the real secret of the cynicism and inhumanity of which shallower critics accuse me is the unexpectedness with which my characters behave like human beings, instead of conforming to the romantic logic of the stage. The axioms and postulates of that dreary mimanthropometry[71] are so well known that it is almost impossible for its slaves to write tolerable last acts to their plays, so conventionally do their conclusions follow from their premises. Because I have thrown this logic ruthlessly overboard, I am accused of ignoring, not stage logic, but, of all things, human feeling. People with completely theatrified imaginations tell me that no girl would treat her mother as Vivie Warren does, meaning that no stage heroine would in a popular sentimental play. They say this just as they might say that no two straight lines would enclose a space. They do not see how completely inverted their vision has become even when I throw its preposterousness in their faces, as I repeatedly do in this very play. Praed, the sentimental artist (fool that I was not to make him a theatre critic instead of an architect!) burlesques them by expecting all through the piece that the feelings of the others will be logically deducible from their family relationships and from his 'conventionally unconventional' social code. The sarcasm is lost on the critics: they, saturated with the same logic, only think him the sole sensible person on the stage. Thus it comes about that the more completely the dramatist is emancipated from the illusion that men and women are primarily reasonable beings, and the more powerfully he insists on the ruthless indifference of their great dramatic antagonist, the external world,

69   Euclid was an important mathematician in Ancient Greece whose work still forms the basis of the field.

70   Gabriele D'Annunzio (1863–1938) was, in addition to being a political leader and military hero, the pre-eminent Italian writer of the late nineteenth and early twentieth centuries.

71   This appears to be a term that Shaw created. Anthropometry is the measurement of human bodies to establish their average dimensions at specific ages and in different races and classes.

to their whims and emotions, the surer he is to be denounced as blind to the very distinction on which his whole work is built. Far from ignoring idiosyncrasy, will, passion, impulse, whim, as factors in human action, I have placed them so nakedly on the stage that the elderly citizen, accustomed to see them clothed with the veil of manufactured logic about duty, and to disguise even his own impulses from himself in this way, finds the picture as unnatural as Carlyle's suggested painting of parliament sitting without its clothes.[72]

I now come to those critics who, intellectually baffled by the problem in *Mrs Warren's Profession*, have made a virtue of running away from it on the gentlemanly ground that the theatre is frequented by women as well as by men, and that such problems should not be discussed or even mentioned in the presence of women. With that sort of chivalry I cannot argue: I simply affirm that *Mrs Warren's Profession* is a play for women; that it was written for women; that it has been performed and produced mainly through the determination of women that it should be performed and produced; that the enthusiasm of women made its first performance excitingly successful; and that not one of these women had any inducement to support it except their belief in the timeliness and the power of the lesson the play teaches. Those who were 'surprised to see ladies present' were men; and when they proceeded to explain that the journals they represented could not possibly demoralize the public by describing such a play, their editors cruelly devoted the space saved by their delicacy to reporting at unusual length an exceptionally abominable police case.

My old Independent Theatre manager, Mr Grein, besides that reproach to me for shattering his ideals, complains that Mrs Warren is not wicked enough, and names several romancers who would have clothed her black soul with all the terrors of tragedy. I have no doubt they would; but that is just what I did not want to do. Nothing would please our sanctimonious British public more than to throw the whole guilt of Mrs Warren's profession on Mrs Warren herself. Now the whole aim of my play is to throw that guilt on the British public itself. Mr Grein may remember that when he produced my first play, *Widowers' Houses*, exactly the same misunderstanding arose. When the virtuous young gentleman rose up in wrath against the slum landlord, the slum landlord very effectually shewed

---

72 Thomas Carlyle (1795–1881) was a Scottish writer whose works influenced the development of Socialism. He also edited *The Letters and Speeches of Oliver Cromwell* in two volumes (New York: Harper, 1851). The image Shaw alludes to probably comes from Oliver Cromwell's speech on 11 April 1657 in which he says that he will never deny proposals made by Parliament 'if they come in the bare and naked authority of such an Assembly' (Volume II, p. 290).

him that slums are the product, not of individual Harpagons,[73] but of the indifference of virtuous young gentlemen to the condition of the city they live in, provided they live at the west end of it on money earned by somebody else's labor. The notion that prostitution is created by the wickedness of Mrs Warren is as silly as the notion – prevalent, nevertheless, to some extent in Temperance circles – that drunkenness is created by the wickedness of the publican. Mrs Warren is not a whit a worse woman than the reputable daughter who cannot endure her. Her indifference to the ultimate social consequences of her means of making money, and her discovery of that means by the ordinary method of taking the line of least resistance to getting it, are too common in English society to call for any special remark. Her vitality, her thrift, her energy, her outspokenness, her wise care of her daughter, and the managing capacity which has enabled her and her sister to climb from the fried fish shop down by the Mint to the establishments of which she boasts, are all high English social virtues. Her defence of herself is so overwhelming that it provokes the *St James's Gazette* to declare that 'the tendency of the play is wholly evil' because 'it contains one of the boldest and most specious defences of an immoral life for poor women that has ever been penned'. Happily the *St James's Gazette* here speaks in its haste. Mrs Warren's defence of herself is not only bold and specious, but valid and unanswerable. But it is no defence at all of the vice which she organizes. It is no defence of an immoral life to say that the alternative offered by society collectively to poor women is a miserable life, starved, overworked, fetid, ailing, ugly. Though it is quite natural and *right* for Mrs Warren to choose what is, according to her lights, the least immoral alternative, it is none the less infamous of society to offer such alternatives. For the alternatives offered are not morality and immorality, but two sorts of immorality. The man who cannot see that starvation, overwork, dirt, and disease are as anti-social as prostitution – that they are the vices and crimes of a nation, and not merely its misfortunes – is (to put it as politely as possible) a hopelessly Private Person.[74]

The notion that Mrs Warren must be a fiend is only an example of the violence and passion which the slightest reference to sex rouses in undisciplined minds, and which makes it seem natural to our lawgivers to punish silly and negligible indecencies with a ferocity unknown in dealing with, for example, ruinous financial swindling. Had my play been entitled *Mr Warren's Profession*, and Mr Warren been a bookmaker, nobody would have expected me to make him a villain as well. Yet gambling is a vice, and

73 Harpagon is a miserly moneylender in *L'Avare* (1668), a satirical comedy by the French playwright Molière (1622–73).
74 An idiot formerly meant a private, or selfish, person.

bookmaking an institution, for which there is absolutely nothing to be said. The moral and economic evil done by trying to get other people's money without working for it (and this is the essence of gambling) is not only enormous but uncompensated. There are no two sides to the question of gambling, no circumstances which force us to tolerate it lest its suppression lead to worse things, no consensus of opinion among responsible classes, such as magistrates and military commanders, that it is a necessity, no Athenian records of gambling made splendid by the talents of its professors, no contention that instead of violating morals it only violates a legal institution which is in many respects oppressive and unnatural, no possible plea that the instinct on which it is founded is a vital one. Prostitution can confuse the issue with all these excuses: gambling has none of them. Consequently, if Mrs Warren must needs be a demon, a bookmaker must be a cacodemon.[75] Well, does anybody who knows the sporting world really believe that bookmakers are worse than their neighbors? On the contrary, they have to be a good deal better; for in that world nearly everybody whose social rank does not exclude such an occupation would be a bookmaker if he could; but the strength of character required for handling large sums of money and for strict settlements and unflinching payment of losses is so rare that successful bookmakers are rare too. It may seem that at least public spirit cannot be one of a bookmaker's virtues; but I can testify from personal experience that excellent public work is done with money subscribed by bookmakers. It is true that there are abysses in bookmaking: for example, welshing.[76] Mr Grein hints that there are abysses in Mrs Warren's profession also. So there are in every profession: the error lies in supposing that every member of them sounds these depths. I sit on a public body which prosecutes Mrs Warren zealously;[77] and I can assure Mr Grein that she is often leniently dealt with because she has conducted her business 'respectably' and held herself above its vilest branches. The degrees in infamy are as numerous and as scrupulously observed as the degrees in the peerage: the moralist's notion that there are depths at which the moral atmosphere ceases is as delusive as the rich man's notion that there are no social jealousies or snobberies among the very poor. No: had I drawn Mrs Warren as a fiend in human form, the very people who now rebuke me for flattering her would probably be the first to deride me for deducing character logically from occupation instead of observing it accurately in society.

One critic is so enslaved by this sort of logic that he calls my portraiture of the Reverend Samuel Gardner an attack on religion. According to this

---

75 A cacodemon is an evil spirit.
76 To welsh, or welch, is to not pay one's gambling debts.
77 Shaw was a councillor for the Metropolitan Borough of St Pancras from 1897 to 1903.

view Subaltern Iago is an attack on the army, Sir John Falstaff an attack on knighthood, and King Claudius an attack on royalty.[78] Here again the clamor for naturalness and human feeling, raised by so many critics when they are confronted by the real thing on the stage, is really a clamor for the most mechanical and superficial sort of logic. The dramatic reason for making the clergyman what Mrs Warren calls 'an old stick-in-the-mud,' whose son, in spite of much capacity and charm, is a cynically worthless member of society, is to set up a mordant contrast between him and the woman of infamous profession, with her well brought-up, straightforward, hardworking daughter. The critics who have missed the contrast have doubtless observed often enough that many clergymen are in the Church through no genuine calling, but simply because, in circles which can command preferment, it is the refuge of the fool of the family; and that clergymen's sons are often conspicuous reactionists against the restraints imposed on them in childhood by their father's profession. These critics must know, too, from history if not from experience, that women as unscrupulous as Mrs Warren have distinguished themselves as administrators and rulers, both commercially and politically. But both observation and knowledge are left behind when journalists go to the theatre. Once in their stalls, they assume that it is 'natural' for clergymen to be saintly, for soldiers to be heroic, for lawyers to be hard-hearted, for sailors to be simple and generous, for doctors to perform miracles with little bottles, and for Mrs Warren to be a beast and a demon. All this is not only not natural, but not dramatic. A man's profession only enters into the drama of his life when it comes into conflict with his nature. The result of this conflict is tragic in Mrs Warren's case, and comic in the clergyman's case (at least we are savage enough to laugh at it); but in both cases it is illogical, and in both cases natural. I repeat, the critics who accuse me of sacrificing nature to logic are so sophisticated by their profession that to them logic is nature, and nature absurdity.

Many friendly critics are too little skilled in social questions and moral discussions to be able to conceive that respectable gentlemen like themselves, who would instantly call the police to remove Mrs Warren if she ventured to canvass them personally, could possibly be in any way responsible for her proceedings. They remonstrate sincerely, asking me what good such painful exposures can possibly do. They might as well ask what good Lord Shaftesbury did by devoting his life to the exposure of evils (by no means yet remedied) compared to which the worst things

---

78   These are characters in Shakespeare's *Othello* (Iago), *Henry IV* and *The Merry Wives of Windsor* (Falstaff), and *Hamlet* (Claudius).

brought into view or even into surmise in this play are trifles.[79] The good of mentioning them is that you make people so extremely uncomfortable about them that they finally stop blaming 'human nature' for them, and begin to support measures for their reform. Can anything be more absurd than the copy of *The Echo* which contains a notice of the performance of my play? It is edited by a gentleman who, having devoted his life to work of the Shaftesbury type, exposes social evils and clamors for their reform in every column except one; and that one is occupied by the declaration of the paper's kindly theatre critic, that the performance left him 'wondering what useful purpose the play was intended to serve'.[80] The balance has to be redressed by the more fashionable papers, which usually combine capable art criticism with West-End solecism on politics and sociology. It is very noteworthy, however, on comparing the press explosion produced by *Mrs Warren's Profession* in 1902 with that produced by *Widowers' Houses* about ten years earlier, that whereas in 1892 the facts were frantically denied and the persons of the drama flouted as monsters of wickedness, in 1902 the facts are admitted, and the characters recognized, though it is suggested that this is exactly why no gentleman should mention them in public. Only one writer has ventured to imply this time that the poverty mentioned by Mrs Warren has since been quietly relieved, and need not have been dragged back to the footlights. I compliment him on his splendid mendacity, in which he is unsupported, save by a little plea in a theatrical paper which is innocent enough to think that ten guineas[81] a year with board and lodging is an impossibly low wage for a barmaid. It goes on to cite Mr Charles Booth[82] as having testified that there are many laborers' wives who are happy and contented on eighteen shillings a week. But I can go further than that myself. I have seen an Oxford agricultural laborer's wife looking cheerful on eight shillings a week; but that does not console me for the fact that agriculture in England is a ruined industry. If poverty does not matter as long as it is contented, then crime does not matter as long as it is unscrupulous. The truth is that it is only then that it

---

79 Anthony Ashley-Cooper (1801–85), the 7th Earl of Shaftesbury, was an English politician responsible for promoting legislation that reformed factory labour and eased the lives of the working classes in the nineteenth century. He was also acknowledged as the head of the evangelical movement within the Church of England.

80 At this time, S.K. Ratcliffe, a reform-minded journalist, was the editor of *The Echo*.

81 A guinea was a coin worth twenty-one shillings, or the equivalent of one pound five pence. It was no longer issued after 1813.

82 Charles Booth (1840–1916) was an English shipowner and philanthropist who documented the lives of the London working classes. His seventeen-volume study *Life and Labour of the London People* (1889–91, 1892–7, 1902) contributed to the awareness of social problems and the development of a scientific method of statistical measurement.

does matter most desperately. Many persons are more comfortable when they are dirty than when they are clean; but that does not recommend dirt as a national policy.

In 1905 Arnold Daly produced *Mrs Warren's Profession* in New York. The press of that city instantly raised a cry that such persons as Mrs Warren are 'ordure' and should not be mentioned in the presence of decent people. This hideous repudiation of humanity and social conscience so took possession of the New York journalists that the few among them who kept their feet morally and intellectually could do nothing to check the epidemic of foul language, gross suggestion, and raving obscenity of word and thought that broke out. The writers abandoned all self-restraint under the impression that they were upholding virtue instead of outraging it. They infected each other with their hysteria until they were for all practical purposes indecently mad. They finally forced the police to arrest Daly and his company, and led the magistrate to express his loathing of the duty thus forced upon him of reading an unmentionable and abominable play. Of course the convulsion soon exhausted itself. The magistrate, naturally somewhat impatient when he found that what he had to read was a strenuously ethical play forming part of a book which had been in circulation unchallenged for eight years, and had been received without protest by the whole London and New York Press, gave the journalists a piece of his mind as to their moral taste in plays. By consent, he passed the case on to a higher court, which declared that the play was not immoral; acquitted Daly; and made an end of the attempt to use the law to declare living women to be 'ordure', and thus enforce silence as to the far-reaching fact that you cannot cheapen women in the market for industrial purposes without cheapening them for other purposes as well. I hope *Mrs Warren's Profession* will be played everywhere, in season and out of season, until Mrs Warren has bitten that fact into the public conscience, and shamed the newspapers which support a tariff to keep up the price of every American commodity except American manhood and womanhood.

Unfortunately, Daly had already suffered the usual fate of those who direct public attention to the profits of the sweater or the pleasures of the voluptuary. He was morally lynched side by side with me. Months elapsed before the decision of the courts vindicated him; and even then, since his vindication implied the condemnation of the Press, which was by that time sober again, and ashamed of its orgy, his triumph received a rather sulky and grudging publicity. In the meantime he had hardly been able to approach an American city, including even those cities which had heaped applause on him as the defender of hearth and home when he produced *Candida*, without having to face articles discussing whether mothers could allow their daughters to attend such plays as *You Never Can Tell*, written by the infamous author of *Mrs Warren's Profession*, and acted by the monster who produced it. What made this harder to bear was that though no fact is better established in theatrical business than the financial disastrousness of moral discredit, the journalists who had done all the mischief kept paying vice the homage of assuming that it is enormously popular and lucrative, and that Daly and I, being exploiters of vice, must therefore be making colossal fortunes out of the abuse heaped on us, and had in fact provoked it and welcomed it with that express object. Ignorance of real life could hardly go further.

I was deeply disgusted by this unsavory mobbing. And I have certain sensitive places in my soul: I do not like that word 'ordure'. Apply it to my work, and I can afford to smile, since the world, on the whole, will smile with me. But to apply it to the woman in the street, whose spirit is of one substance with your own and her body no less holy: to look your women folk in the face afterwards and not go out and hang yourself: that is not on the list of pardonable sins.

Shortly after these events a leading New York newspaper, which was among the most abusively clamorous for the suppression of *Mrs Warren's Profession*, was fined heavily for deriving part of its revenue from advertisements of Mrs Warren's houses.[83]

Many people have been puzzled by the fact that whilst stage entertainments which are frankly meant to act on the spectators as aphrodisiacs are everywhere tolerated, plays which have an almost horrifying contrary effect are fiercely attacked by persons and papers notoriously indifferent to public morals on all other occasions. The explanation is very simple. The profits of Mrs Warren's profession are shared not only by Mrs Warren and Sir George Crofts, but by the landlords of their houses, the newspapers which advertize them, the restaurants which cater for them, and, in short, all the trades to which they are good customers, not to mention the public officials and representatives whom they silence by complicity, corruption, or blackmail. Add to these the employers who profit by cheap female labor, and the shareholders whose dividends depend on it (you find such people everywhere, even on the judicial bench and in the highest places in Church and State) and you get a large and powerful class with a strong pecuniary incentive to protect Mrs Warren's profession, and a correspondingly strong

---

83 The newspaper in question is the *New York Herald*, which was fined $5,000 for allowing prostitutes to openly advertise in its personal columns. See George E. Wellwarth, '*Mrs Warren* Comes to America, or the Blue-Noses, the Politicians and the Procurers', *The Shaw Review* 2.8 (May 1959), 8–16. See also the review that appeared in the *New York Herald* in Appendix VI, pp. 158–61.

incentive to conceal, from their own consciences no less than from the world, the real sources of their gain. These are the people who declare that it is feminine vice and not poverty that drives women to the streets, as if vicious women with independent incomes ever went there. These are the people who, indulgent or indifferent to aphrodisiac plays, raise the moral hue and cry against performances of *Mrs Warren's Profession*, and drag actresses to the police court to be insulted, bullied, and threatened for fulfilling their engagements. For please observe that the judicial decision in New York State in favor of the play did not end the matter. In Kansas City, for instance, the municipality, finding itself restrained by the courts from preventing the performance, fell back on a local bye-law against indecency. It summoned the actress who impersonated Mrs Warren to the police court, and offered her and her colleagues the alternative of leaving the city or being prosecuted under this bye-law.[84]

Now nothing is more possible than that the city councillors who suddenly displayed such concern for the morals of the theatre were either Mrs Warren's landlords, or employers of women at starvation wages, or restaurant keepers, or newspaper proprietors, or in some other more or less direct way sharers of the profits of her trade. No doubt it is equally possible that they were simply stupid men who thought that indecency consists, not in evil, but in mentioning it. I have, however, been myself a member of a municipal council, and have not found municipal councillors quite so simple and inexperienced as this. At all events I do not propose to give the Kansas councillors the benefit of the doubt. I therefore advise the public at large, which will finally decide the matter, to keep a vigilant eye on gentlemen who will stand anything at the theatre except a performance of *Mrs Warren's Profession*, and who assert in the same breath that (*a*) the play is too loathsome to be bearable by civilized people, and (*b*) that unless its performance is prohibited the whole town will throng to see it. They may be merely excited and foolish; but I am bound to warn the public that it is equally likely that they may be collected and knavish.

At all events, to prohibit the play is to protect the evil which the play exposes; and in view of that fact, I see no reason for assuming that the pro-hibitionists are disinterested moralists, and that the author, the managers, and the performers, who depend for their livelihood on their personal reputations and not on rents, advertisements, or dividends, are grossly inferior to them in moral sense and public responsibility.

---

84 Mary Shaw, no relation to the playwright, starred as Kitty in the New Haven and New York productions in 1905. She revived her role in 1907 and took the play on tour across America. She recounted these experiences in 'My Immoral Play: The Story of the First American Production of *Mrs Warren's Profession*', *McClure's Magazine* 38 (April 1912), 684–94.

It is true that in *Mrs Warren's Profession*, Society, and not any individual, is the villain of the piece; but it does not follow that the people who take offence at it are all champions of society. Their credentials cannot be too carefully examined.

PICCARD'S COTTAGE, *January 1902*

P.S. (1930) On reading the above after a lapse of 28 years, with the ban on *Mrs Warren* withdrawn and forgotten, I should have discarded it as an overdone fuss about nothing that now matters were it not for a recent incident. Before describing this I must explain that with the invention of the cinematograph a new censorship has come into existence, created, not this time by Act of Parliament, but by the film manufacturers to provide themselves with the certificates of propriety which have proved so useful to the theatre managers.[85] This private censorship has acquired public power through its acceptance by the local authorities, without whose licence the films cannot be exhibited in place of public entertainment.

A lady who has devoted herself to the charitable work of relieving the homeless and penniless people who are to be found every night in London on the Thames Embankment had to deal largely with working men who had come to London from the country under the mistaken impression that there is always employment there for everybody, and with young women, also from the provinces, who had been lured to London by offers of situations which were really traps set for them by the agents of the White Slave traffic. The lady rightly concluded that much the best instrument for warning the men, and making known to the women the addresses of the organization for befriending unprotected girl travellers, is the cinema. She caused a film to be made for this purpose.[86] The Film Censor immediately banned the part of the film which gave the addresses to the girls and shewed them the risks they ran. The lady appealed to me to help her to protest. After convincing myself by witnessing a private exhibition of the film that it was quite innocent I wrote to the Censor, begging him to examine the film personally, and remedy what seemed to be a rule-of-thumb mistake by his examiners. He not only confirmed their veto, but left uncontradicted a report in all the papers that he had given as his reason that the lady had paraded the allurements of vice, and that such parades could not be tolerated by him. The sole allurements were the smart motor car in which the heroine of the film was kidnapped, and the fashionable clothes of the two very repulsive agents who drugged her in it. In every

---

85   The British Board of Film Censors was founded in 1912. In 1984 its name was changed to the British Board of Film Classification.

86   The film was Betty Baxter's *Night Patrol* (1930).

other respect her experiences were as disagreeable as the sternest moralist could desire.

I then made a tour of the picture houses to see what the Film Censor considers allowable. Of the films duly licensed by him two were so nakedly pornographic that their exhibition could hardly have been risked without the Censor's certificate of purity. One of them presented the allurements of a supposedly French brothel so shamelessly that I rose and fled in disgust long before the end, though I am as hardened to vulgar salacity in the theatre as a surgeon is to a dissecting room.

The only logical conclusion apparent is that the White Slave traffickers are in complete control of our picture theatres, and can close them to our Rescue workers as effectively as they can reserve them for advertisements of their own trade. I spare the Film Censor that conclusion. The conclusion I press upon him and on the public is my old one of twenty-eight years ago: that all the evil effects of such corrupt control are inevitably produced gratuitously by Censors with the best intentions.[87]

POSTSCRIPT 1933. In spite of the suppression of my play for so many years by the censorship the subject broke out into a campaign for the abolition of the White Slave Traffic which still occupies the League of Nations at Geneva. But my demonstration that the root of the evil is economic was ruthlessly ignored by the profiteering Press (that is, by the entire Press); and when at last parliament proceeded to legislate, its contribution to the question was to ordain that Mrs Warren's male competitors should be flogged instead of fined. This had the double effect of stimulating the perverted sexuality which delights in flogging, and driving the traffic into female hands, leaving Mrs Warren triumphant.

The ban on performances of the play has long since been withdrawn; and when it is performed the critics hasten to declare that the scandal of underpaid virtue and overpaid vice is a thing of the past. Yet when the war created an urgent demand for women's labor in 1914 the Government proceeded to employ women for twelve hours a day at a wage of five ha'pence an hour. It is amazing how the grossest abuses thrive on their reputation for being old unhappy far-off things in an age of imaginary progress.

---

87   Shaw alerted the press to the fate of Betty Baxter's film with a letter to *The Times* on 17 February 1930. The resultant publicity caused some politicians to inquire into the institution, but nothing of substance was done to change the censorship.

APPENDIX V

CENSORS' REPORTS ON
MRS WARREN'S PROFESSION

Under the Theatres Act of 1843, in order to perform a play in a theatre for the general public, managers had to submit the playscript and have it approved for licence. Plays were read by an Examiner, or a Reader of Plays, who wrote a report assessing the play's suitability. If a play was considered questionable or unacceptable, the Lord Chamberlain, after 1910, could consult an Advisory Board for further advice in the matter. Plays could be deemed acceptable, acceptable if they were revised according to the Lord Chamberlain's requests, or unacceptable, in which case the play was refused a licence. The following reports are located in the British Library's collection of the Lord Chamberlain's correspondence, file LCP CORR 1924/5632.

1
George Street,[88] 5 October 1916, in response to the request made by George S. King of the Repertory Theatre, Plymouth

I do not think this play should have a licence for general performance. My opinion is based not on the dialogue or incidents – given the theme – but simply on the theme itself, which is the question of the advantages and disadvantages of prostitution as a profession for women, as compared with other professions, and which involves the presentment of a brothel-keeper as the chief character. Such a discussion and such a character are not fitted for casual audiences of various ages. I agree with Sir W. Raleigh[89] that the author is entirely in earnest, and no doubt the theme is important and can be rightly discussed in the press. But the theatre is not the place, except before an audience well knowing what it is to expect and of a special kind, as is the Stage Society.

---

88 George Street was a playwright. He served as a Reader of Plays from 1913 to his death in 1936.
89 Sir Walter Raleigh (1861–1922) was Chair of English Literature at Oxford University and a member of the Advisory Board for the Lord Chamberlain.

2
Ernest Bendall,[90] 18 October 1917, in response to Edwin T. Heys'
request to perform the play in an unnamed West End theatre

I have re-read this play, which is accurately classified by its author as an 'unpleasant' one: and I find no reason for changing my former opinion that its subject unfits it for our stage. That subject is prostitution; and although it is treated without indecency or impropriety I still feel that its discussion before a general theatrical audience is undesirable.

Its almost negligible story is that of a worthy but rather priggish Newnham girl who, after taking high mathematical honours, discovers to her horror that the money which has been paid for her education has been earned by her mother as a keeper of fashionable brothels on the Continent for her moneyed partner Sir George Crofts.

This bold bad man, of no recognizable type, has it seems put £40,000 into the 'business', and now wants to marry his brothel-keeper's daughter. When the girl, who has another lover, rejects in disgust the preposterous villain, he tells her that her successful rival – the son of a clergyman with a dissolute past – is her own half-brother.

The moral, such as it is, of the disagreeable drama, with its un-lifelike characterization, is enforced mainly by dull long-winded arguments between mother and daughter over what may be called the social economics of prostitution, which the mother defends, pp.194–7, as a means of livelihood preferable to that of less well-paid labour.

It is, I understand, now contended that as 'propaganda' *Mrs Warren's Profession* may, like *Damaged Goods*,[91] serve a useful didactic purpose. This may be so; but I cannot myself regard the work of Bernard Shaw as on all fours with [that] of Brieux, nor can I imagine any preventive or curative result likely to be effected by this particularly nasty medicine. The dose is accordingly NOT Recommended for Licence.

---

90 Ernest Bendall was a drama critic. He served as a Reader of Plays from 1911 until his death in 1920.
91 *Damaged Goods* is the English translation of *Les Avariés* (1905), a didactic play about syphilis by French playwright Eugène Brieux (1858–1932). It had been banned from English stages, but it was licensed in early 1917 to spread awareness about venereal disease, especially among soldiers.

3
George Street, 2 July 1921, in response to the request
made by Bache Matthews of the Birmingham Repertory Theatre

This play has been refused a licence more than once. The refusal was entirely justified at the time, but for reasons to be stated later I think on the whole a licence may now be granted. I give a brief account of the play according to custom, though it is no doubt well known by the Lord Chamberlain and the Board. Mrs Warren is a woman who was a prostitute in her youth and is now proprietor of brothels in continental cities. She has a daughter, Vivie, who has been brought up away from her and is [a] highly educated and very practical modern young woman. Vivie is staying in a country cottage, where she and a boy, Frank, son of the Rector, Mr Gardner, indulge in innocent love-making. Mrs Warren arrives at the cottage with Sir George Crofts, a partner in her business and her old lover. Mr Gardner turns out to be also an old lover. In Act II Vivie learns from her mother the outline of her past, with elaborate and more or less plausible excuses for it – the great *scène à faire*[92] of the play. She does not know of the business still going on and is told of that in the third Act by Crofts, furious at her rejection of his matrimonial advances. He also alleges that Vivie is Frank's half sister, which according to both her mother and Frank's father is false. Vivie rushes away to London and joins a friend in business as an actuary. In the last Act she and Frank part and she refuses, in another strong scene, to have anything more to do with her mother. This is of course only an outline of the facts of the play without going into its philosophy. As a study of life it has always seemed a poor thing to me.

The chief reasons for its rejection have been the nature of Mrs Warren's business and the suggestion of incest. The latter seems unimportant to me; the possibility of it is denied by those who should know in the play and in any case it does not happen. My reasons for reconsidering the refusal are: (1) the play has been performed more than once by private societies in England and publicly in other countries. It has been freely circulated in book form. It has been extensively discussed for years. It is in fact very well known to a large public. Therefore it is in a way futile to prohibit its public performance; (2) the far greater liberty in the case of serious plays now enjoyed by the stage might cover the presentment of such a character as Mrs Warren, done seriously and in good faith. An audience will no longer be shocked as it would have been; (3) a considerable number of people regard it as a valuable play on the side of morality. It may be difficult to

---

92 A *scène à faire* is the most important scene in a play.

follow this argument, but the fact remains. Certainly the play is deeply serious in intention; (4) beyond the frankness necessary to state the theme there is no offence in the play.

If there should be any inconsistency in granting a licence I share it, since I agreed with my colleague in not recommending a licence some years ago. After very careful consideration I have changed my mind. The Lord Chamberlain will no doubt have other advice. So far as I am concerned the play is, though quite without enthusiasm,

Recommended for Licence.

4

George Street was unaware that the recommendation he made on 2 July 1921 had been rejected by Lord Sandhurst.[93] His third report, on 15 August 1924, was drafted in response to Charles Macdona's request to perform the play at the Regent Theatre, London

I last reported on this Play in favour of its being licensed, when it was sent in for the last time while Lord Sandhurst was Lord Chamberlain. That report was mislaid, or perhaps destroyed because he turned the play down without referring it again to the Board. It was sent in again in the Duke of Atholl's period of office.[94] He expressed himself in favour of a licence in conversation with me but subsequently decided against it.

It is hardly necessary to write another elaborate report as the Play is so familiar.

I think a Licence should be granted, because the Play contains nothing indecent and the frankness with which its painful subject is discussed no longer shocks an adult audience. Times have changed very much indeed in this respect since the Play was first refused a Licence. The Play has been performed all over Europe and America and has been produced many times by private societies in England, and in book form is familiar to everyone interested in the stage or contemporary literature. It seems to me, therefore, to be a little absurd still to refuse a Licence for public performance unless on the strongest grounds and these, as I have explained, I think do not exist. It is an 'unpleasant' Play to be sure, as Mr Shaw calls it, and in my opinion a crude and poor one, greatly inferior to his best work, but I do not think its unpleasantness goes beyond the limits to which we are now accustomed.

---

93   William Mansfield (1855–1921), Lord Sandhurst, was the Lord Chamberlain from 1912 to 1921.

94   John Stewart-Murray (1871–1942), the Duke of Atholl, was the Lord Chamberlain from 1921 to 1922.

5

Lord Cromer,[95] the Lord Chamberlain, 17 August 1924,
in response to Street's report

I fully appreciate and respect the motives which prompted my predecessors in the Office of the Lord Chamberlain to refuse a Licence for this Play.

Times have however greatly changed since 1898 when this Play was first stopped by Mr Redford.[96] Since then, as Mr Street points out, the Play has been frequently produced by private societies in England, where it can be procured and read throughout the country in book form.

In my opinion the facts of this Play having been performed all over Europe & America, or its suppression being harmful to Censorship may be left out of account as being beside the point.

The point really is that in these days the mentality of the average adult audience would neither be shocked [n]or harmed by the presentation of this subject on the stage merely because it is unpleasant. This may be regrettable, but I think it is the case.

It would therefore be absurd to go on refusing a Licence to this Play, ignoring the march of time and the change it brings about in public opinion over facing such questions openly.

I do not propose to refer this Play to the Advisory Board any further. I gather the majority would now doubtless be disposed to support Mr Street's opinion. Even if they did not, I have no wish to involve any of them in the responsibility of licensing this Play which must necessarily rest with me.

After the most careful consideration I am therefore prepared, though reluctantly, to license this Play, subject to some fictitious name being substituted for that of the Duke of Beaufort[97] which appears twice in Act II, p.180.

95 Rowland Thomas Baring (1877–1953), the Earl of Cromer, was the Lord Chamberlain from 1922 to 1938.

96 George Redford was the Reader of Plays from 1895 to 1911, when he was pushed out of the job for having brought too much unwanted attention to the censorship as a result of his questionable decisions.

97 Shaw deleted the reference to Beaufort in simply revising it to read 'the Duke' (II.120–1). He maintained this nondescript change in all later editions.

APPENDIX VI

St James's Gazette,
7 January 1902

Yesterday afternoon the protracted efforts of the Committee of the Stage Society were at length crowned with success, and a performance was duly given of *Mrs Warren's Profession*, by Mr George Bernard Shaw, at the theatre of the New Lyric Club. Everything that could possibly have happened to prevent the performance seems to have occurred. The Censor of Plays had long since refused to license the play. Manager after Manager had refused the Society the use of his theatre for its production. Notices of the date of the performance were sent out and cancelled in a lavish manner. There were difficulties about the cast. Even at the very last moment the time of the production had to be changed from the evening to the afternoon to the great inconvenience of the audience. And all for what? In order that a play might be performed which deals with an unmentionable subject in a manner that even the least squeamish might find revoltingly offensive. Mr Shaw, in one of his usual speeches after the fall of the curtain, congratulated the Society on having found a cast to interpret his play so admirably, and to overcome successfully the thousand and one obstacles which had arisen to its production. But this was doubtless Mr Shaw's humour. Had he been serious (and had he not been the author of the play) he might more fitly have condoled with the Society on having found a committee who recklessly sacrificed the convenience of members in order to carry through a performance which was very generally regretted and on having found a cast who were willing to expend really admirable acting on this dingy drama. The play is in its parts undeniably clever. But as Mr Shaw himself acknowledged in his speech, it is not the treatment but the subject which carries *Mrs Warren's Profession* successfully through the ordeal of even a private performance. For if you take a sufficiently disgusting theme it is comparatively easy to interest an audience so long as you select that carefully.

Get together a few hundred 'advanced' people in a London playhouse and write a drama about incest, contagious disease, vice or crime of a startling character, and your audience will listen attentively enough. They may be disgusted. They may wish they had not come, and determine not to come again. But they will give you a hearing. And if your handling of the theme is at all able they will even get a certain not very wholesome pleasure out of your work. But it is important to realise what is the cause of such success as plays like *Mrs Warren* contain. Some of Mr Shaw's audience yesterday probably went away under the impression that they had been interested in the play in spite of its subject. That is a delusion. The play interested because the subject is a tremendous one. Grossly unsuitable for stage treatment before a mixed audience, grossly unsuitable for tricking out in Mr Shaw's verbal humours with his pert youngsters and comic clergymen, it remains a theme of painful and absorbing interest, and, granted that you can find an audience willing to listen to it at all, their attention cannot help being riveted by it. That the tendency of the play is wholly evil we are convinced. The second act contains one of the boldest and most specious defences of an immoral life for poor women that has ever been written. But what a waste of a quite appreciable talent! What a theme for the stage! We need not explain the plot at length here. The cast was extraordinarily competent, and did everything that earnestness and talent could do to make it successful. Miss Fanny Brough, though physically quite unsuited to the part of Mrs Warren, played it with great tact and skill. Miss Madge McIntosh, who took the difficult and not very sympathetic role of her daughter, acted with insight and judgment, and showed herself to be a comedy actress of the very first rank. Mr Granville Barker, as the insufferable Frank, displayed all that marked ability as a character actor which members of the Stage Society have come to expect from him. Mr Charles Goodhart played the vulgar and brutal Crofts to the life, and Mr Cosmo Stuart, though he rather burlesqued the part, got much humour out of the Rev. Samuel Gardner. The excellent acting secured toleration for the performance, but it is to be hoped that the Stage Society, which has been responsible for several really interesting and valuable productions in the two years of its existence, intends to eschew dramatic garbage in the future.

J.T. Grein, *The Sunday Special*,
12 January 1902

It was an exceedingly uncomfortable afternoon, for there was a majority of women to listen to that which could only be understood by a minority of men. Nor was the play fit for women's ears. By all means let us initiate our daughters before they cross the threshold of womanhood into those duties and functions of life which are vital in matrimony and maternity. But there is a boundary line, and its transgression means peril – the peril of destroying ideals. I go further. Even men need not know all the ugliness that vegetates below the surface of everyday life. To some male minds too much knowledge of the seamy side is poisonous, for it leads to pessimism, that pioneer of insanity and suicide. And, sure, as I feel that most of the women and a good many of the men who were present at the production of *Mrs Warren's Profession* by the Stage Society did not at first know, and finally merely guessed, what was the woman's trade, I cannot withhold the opinion that the representation was unnecessary and painful. It is mainly for these reasons that, in spite of my great admiration for Bernard Shaw, the play was not brought out by the late Independent Theatre. As a 'straight talk to men only' it is not sufficiently true to life and useful to be productive of an educational effect. As a drama it is unsatisfactory because the characters have no inner life, but merely echo certain views of the author. As literature, however, the merits of *Mrs Warren's Profession* are considerable, and its true place is in the study.

Mrs Warren's Profession is a 'problem play' in the fullest sense of the word. Mr Shaw will probably deny it, and claim that it is ordinary actable drama, but the text will give evidence in my favour. We hear Mr Shaw all the time, and whatever vitality the characters possess is not their own, but Mr Shaw's. They own also much of his contradictory elements – his depth of observation and thought, and his extraordinary 'cussedness'. Here, as in most of G.B.S.'s work, the sublime is constantly spoilt by the ridiculous. It is the author's manner, and his way to express his contempt for the public. But that is a mere side issue. The main point is whether the problem is worth discussing and whether it has been dealt with in an adequate, convincing manner. I say no on both counts. The problem is neither vital nor important. It has none of the *raison d'être* of *Le fils de Coralie* by Delpit,[98] of *La Dame aux Camélias*, and of *Ghosts*. The case of Mrs Warren has been invented with such ingenuity and surrounded by such impossibilities that it produces revolt instead of reasoning. For Mr Shaw has made the great mistake of tainting all the male characters with a streak of a demoralised tar brush; he has created a cold-blooded, almost sexless daughter as the sympathetic element; and he has built the unspeakable Mrs Warren of such motley material that in our own mind pity and disgust for the woman are constantly at loggerheads. If the theme was worth treating at all the human conflict was the tragedy of the daughter through the infamy of the mother. Instead of that we get long arguments – spiced with

---

98   *Le fils de Coralie* (1879) was written by Albert Delpit (1849–93). Delpit was at one time a secretary for Alexandre Dumas, *père*.

platform oratory and invective – between a mother really utterly degraded, but here and there whitewashed with sentimental effusions, and a daughter so un-English in her knowledge of the world, so cold of heart, and 'beyond human power' in reasoning, that we end by hating both: the one who deserves it, as well as the other who is a victim of circumstances. Thus there are false notes all the time and apart from a passing interest in a few scenes, saved by the author's cleverness, the play causes only pain and wonderment, while it should have shaken our soul to its innermost chords.

It is not so easy to explain this singular effect, or, rather, it would be easy if it did behove to touch this work – in a newspaper – with kid-gloved fingers. Mr Shaw in his attempt to portray a woman of Mrs Warren's type either lacked the courage to play *misère-ouverte*,[99] or, what is more likely, he had not sufficient knowledge of the monstrosity of such beings. His Mrs Warren is a black soul with spots of human feelings dotted on in whitish chalk. But the real Mrs Warren is the most abject creature in all humanity. I cannot say more. I can but refer Mr Shaw to Parent-Duchatel [*sic*], to Yves Guyot, to Dr. Commange, to Leo Taxil's 'Corruption fin de siècle'[100] – to a whole library on the colossal subject of human debasement. If Mr Shaw had fully known the nature of Mrs Warren's profession he would have left the play unwritten or produced a tragedy of unsurpassable heart-rending power. Now he has merely philandered around a dangerous subject; he has treated it in earnest, half in that peculiar jesting manner which is all his own. He has given free reins to his brain and silenced his heart. He has therefore produced a play of a needlessly 'unpleasant' understructure to no useful end. A play that interests in part, repels in others; a drama that plays fast and loose with our emotions, and will in some way awaken our curiosity which would have best been left in a slumber.

It is the fashion in some quarters to express condolences with the actors when a play is of an outspoken, unpleasant nature. I see no reason for such

---

99 A *misère-ouverte* is a bid in cards in which the caller deliberately takes no tricks, often lacking any trump, and plays the hand openly, with his or her cards face-up on the table.

100 Alexandre Parent-Duchâtelet (1790–1836), a famous French doctor and promoter of social hygiene, advocated the need to create a better sewage system to improve public health and published the important *De la Prostitution dans la ville de Paris* (1836), one of the first sociological works on the profession. Yves Guyot (1843–1928), a French journalist and politician, was also the author of *La Prostitution* (1882), which condemned the French regulation of prostitution as state-sanctioning of a social evil that must be eradicated. I have not been able to trace the reference to a Dr Commange. There is nothing by him in the catalogues of either the Bibliothèque Nationale de France or the British Library. Léo Taxil (1854–1907) was a fervent anti-clerical author. His *La Corruption fin-de-siècle* (1890) was written very much along the same lines of Guyot's *La Prostitution*.

uncalled-for patronage. Condolence is in its right place when talent is wasted on futility; but when actors of their own accord choose to appear in works of uncompromising candour, they should be criticised in the ordinary way, and not humiliated by doubtful apologies. Artists like Miss Fanny Brough, Miss Madge McIntosh, like Mr Granville Barker and their companions, know full well what they do when they appear in plays like *Mrs Warren's Profession*; they are aware also that writers like Mr Shaw have no ulterior motives when they deal with strong subjects, and that they afford great chances of distinction to the actor.

The performances of *Mrs Warren's Profession* proved no exception to the rule. In spite of the disadvantage of a cramped stage and impracticable scenery in the theatre of the Lyric Club, the setting reached the highest mark. Miss Fanny Brough, a woman of more brain and heart than half a dozen of our more or less leading ladies *en bloc*, achieved that which had long been predicted by her admirers. She proved that she is not only a splendid comedienne, but that she is endowed with the profounder gifts which characterise tragic actresses. Whatever vitality the character of Mrs Warren now and again seemed to achieve, whatever feeling of sympathy there was aroused in the spectator, sprung from Miss Brough's magnificent impersonation. She had to play upon the entire clavier[101] of emotions, and in that exceedingly difficult concerto there was not a wavering note let alone an inharmonious chord. The younger actress Miss McIntosh was also fully equal to her task. She did her best to minimise the frigid side of the daughter's strange character, and to kindle every little spark of womanhood into flame. Her performance betrayed great study and a carefully planned conception of a part which in less capable hands would seriously try the patience and the sense of humour of the audience.

But the play was admirably cast from first to last, Mr Charles Goodhart and Mr Julius Knight, Mr Granville Barker and Mr Cosmo Stuart, they all worked with an ardour unwonted in any theatre except where 'art for art's sake'[102] is the motto.

---

101 A clavier is the keyboard of a musical instrument.
102 This is a popular slogan of the time, translated from the French '*l'art pour l'art*'. It refers to the belief that art needs no justification to exist, and that it should neither serve politics nor be didactic.

The New York Times,
31 October 1905

Arnold Daly has made a serious mistake. *Mrs Warren's Profession,* whatever its merits or demerits as a play for the closet, or as an exposition of the author's views upon a sociological question, has absolutely no place in a theatre before a mixed assemblage such as witnessed it at the Garrick last night. The post-mortem and the clinic undoubtedly have their place as utilities of scientific investigation. But they would lose their value if permitted to become subjects of general and morbid curiosity.

Mrs Warren's Profession, as an acted play, bears about the same relation to the drama that the post-mortem bears to the science of which it is a part. Mr Shaw takes a subject, decayed and reeking, and analyzes it for the edification of those whose unhealthy tastes find satisfaction in morbific suggestion.

As a play to be read by a limited number of persons capable of understanding its significance, of estimating Mr Shaw and his themes at their full value, and of discounting them through their personal knowledge of him and their general knowledge of the life he seeks to portray, it undoubtedly has a place. But as a play to be acted before a miscellaneous assemblage, it cannot be accepted.

If there had been any doubt upon that subject it was dispelled after seeing the performance last night. *Mrs Warren's Profession* is not only of vicious tendency in its exposition, but it is also depressingly stupid. And those who would be likely to condone the first fault will find it extremely difficult to forgive the latter. Lines that impressed one in the reading as examples of Mr Shaw's brilliant capacity for argumentation, when delivered by the actors became simply long, dry, tedious shallows of nugatory talk. The fact that the dialogue had been pruned to some extent was hardly apparent in the actual effect of the representation. The whole thesis involving Mr Shaw's value as a moralist, of *Mrs Warren's Profession* as a moral treatise, becomes ridiculous in the consideration of it as acted drama.

As it stood revealed last night, it was neither drama nor moral. It failed to qualify as the one primarily by reason that in its writing no attempt has been made to mould it to any sort of form suggestive of a play to be acted, beyond the fact that it is divided into scenes and its dialogue is framed in the familiar manner of the theatrical manuscript. It failed to qualify as the other by reason of the fact, first, that its lesson, if any, is not conveyed in such a way that it is readily received by an audience; second, by reason of the fact that the audience which had assembled to see it was not prepared to recognize or accept any lesson.

In these matters there is always this element of the audience to be taken into consideration, and here it is that Mr Shaw in his larger way, and Mr Daly in his lesser one, have failed to take account of the conditions that exist, that up to the present have always existed, and will probably continue to exist. The persons in the Garrick Theatre last night represented an average theatre assemblage. There was so far as could be determined no preponderance of any one class such as might have been expected under the circumstances.

It was, on the other hand, an audience of average intelligence and of average quality. But when it laughed – and the laughs were few enough – one had the uncomfortable feeling that it was a moment that might better justify tears, and when it applauded one knew that the sentiment would have been more properly met with silence or some show of disapprobation.

While we do not admit that Mr Shaw's works are as inscrutable or triple-plated with meanings as some of his critics would have us believe, and while there is every reason for attributing much credit to his magnificent powers of mentality, and while we feel that tragic seriousness, not willful flippancy, may be the motive for his work, we must exclude Mrs Warren from our theatre – reject her, as a moral derelict. She is of no use to us as a lesson or a study.

When she becomes a subject for laughter and amusement, as occurred last night, she is something more than useless – she is vicious. She may serve a purpose when we are free to ponder over her under our own vine and fig tree, without the uncomfortable conviction that others, not, perhaps, so earnest as we, are gaining a certain amount of unholy enjoyment from the utter profundity of the horror.

In the acting of the chief rôle there was exactly the overemphasis of its more repugnant features that might have been expected. Mary Shaw, an artist of broad experience and undoubted ability, has been successful in the theatre exactly in proportion to her knowledge of theatrical needs. In playing such a rôle as Mrs Warren she approaches it primarily from the point of view of the actress who knows when and how to get her effects. As a result we find Mrs Warren depicted from the very outset in the broadest tints.

Miss Shaw lays on her colors too heavily, and the result is that, while giving us a portrait of a person who undoubtedly has existed and does exist, she fails to impress us as reproducing the particular type that Mr Shaw has in mind. Mrs Warren's exact status would have been at once patent to her daughter and to every one else had she been the sort of person shown to us by Mary Shaw.

Viewed merely as an exhibition of theatrical characterization, however, Miss Shaw's performance justifies a share of appreciative comment. She reflected to an astonishingly offensive, natural degree the abandoned creatures after whom she has evidently modeled her study. It is not the creature of the text, but it is true to the type it seeks to reproduce, so true in fact that it contributes to the generally revolting picture another and a nauseating quality. But, though it was for the most part highly colorful acting, it was acting of a most uneven character. As an artistic achievement it did not approximate her performance in *Ghosts*.

Mr Daly's fault in the exploitation of *Mrs Warren*, however misguided it may have proved itself to be, can in no wise be laid at the door of personal vanity as regards the hope of distinguishing himself in the rôle of Frank Gardner, for it is a part about which he can have had no beforehand delusions. He is perhaps the more to be pitied – that his aim in producing it was so single. There are only two possible exculpating reasons for the acting presentation of the play – a blind, unreasoning desire to revolutionize the moral state-of-being, or else a wholly unnatural and somewhat disgraceful attempt to win much tainted notoriety. Personally we believe Mr Daly has simply made the error of attaching to this work of Mr Shaw's an artistically dramatic value which it does not possess.

Of the actors in the cast, Chrystal Herne, though temperamentally opposed to the rôle of Vivie, and generally unable to realize it, had occasional impressive moments, and the others acted as well as could be expected under the circumstances.

New York Herald,
31 October 1905

'The lid' was lifted by Mr Arnold Daly and 'the limit' of stage indecency reached last night in the Garrick Theatre in the performance of one of Mr George Bernard Shaw's 'unpleasant comedies' called *Mrs Warren's Profession*.

'The limit of indecency' may seem pretty strong words, but they are justified by the fact that the play is morally rotten. It makes no difference that some of the lines may have been omitted and others toned down; there was superabundance of foulness left. The whole story of the play, the atmosphere surrounding it, the incidents, the personalities of the characters are wholly immoral and degenerate. The only way successfully to expurgate *Mrs Warren's Profession* is to cut the whole play out. You cannot have a clean pig stye. The play is an insult to decency because –

It defends immorality.

It glorifies debauchery.

It besmirches the sacredness of a clergyman's calling.

It pictures children and parents living in calm observance of most unholy relations.

And, worst of all, it countenances the most revolting form of degeneracy, by flippantly discussing the marriage of brother and sister, father and daughter, and makes the one supposedly moral character of the play, a young girl, declare that choice of shame, instead of poverty, is eminently right.

These things cannot be denied. They are the main factors of the story. Without them there would be no play. It is vileness and degeneracy brazenly considered. If New York's sense of shame is not aroused to hot indignation at this theatrical insult, it is in a sad plight.

This is an outline, or, rather, a suggestion of the story that Mr Arnold Daly saw fit to enact in the Garrick Theatre last night before a morbidly curious audience that packed the theatre to suffocation, and doubtless will continue to do so as long as the play is permitted to be given.

Mrs Warren, a child of the slums, has become a courtesan and is the mistress of several disreputable houses in Brussels, Berlin, Vienna and Budapest. Her profession has brought her wealth. She has a daughter, Vivian, educated in England in ignorance of her mother's real character, and who has achieved fame in college as a mathematician. This clever young daughter of a vile mother is in love with and is beloved by Frank, the flippant, good-for-nothing son of a prominent clergyman.

The mother goes to England to visit Vivian, and with her are two men, Praed, a mooning artist, with weak morals, and Crofts, a dissolute baronet with no morals whatever. Crofts is the business partner of Mrs Warren in her 'profession'. He is the capitalist who put up the money for her to start with.

Crofts would like to marry Vivian, but is in doubt about her parentage. He is not sure but that she is his own daughter. Nevertheless, he presses his suit through three acts. Possibly it is Praed, thinks Crofts, but Praed is quite sure that he (Praed) is not her father. They discuss the matter at length. As Crofts says, 'It's very awkward to be uncertain about it'; that is, it is an awkward thing to marry your own child.

Then it develops that the clergyman was a former intimate of Mrs Warren, and Crofts asserts that he must be Vivian's father. When the girl rejects his suit in favor of Frank he blocks the match by telling the young couple they are brother and sister, Frank's father, the clergyman, having been the girl's parent.

Mrs Warren tells her daughter all the revolting details of her life of shame, and glories in it, as it saved her and 'Liz', her sister, the drudgery of menial labor.

You may think that the pure and clever daughter is shocked, but forgives and tries to reclaim her mother. Not a bit of it. Her views coincide with those of her shameless parent, and Vivian admits that in the circumstances she herself would have considered licentiousness and sin quite the better choice. She almost envies the career of her aunt, who became rich through the ill-gotten gains of the 'profession' of shame and is posing now as the social leader in a cathedral town and the chaperon of young girls.

The clergyman, who, mind you, is not made by Mr Shaw a deposed or unfrocked clergyman, but the spiritual and religious head of a large and prominent church, confesses himself to be a debauche[103] and a rake[104] – a subject which father and son familiarly discuss and laugh over. The clergyman sits up all night with Crofts and becomes bestially intoxicated; then he starts in to write his sermon for the following day.

Frank, in love with Vivian, makes advances to Vivian's mother, whom he knows to be a lewd woman, and suggests they go to the Continent together. And so on through the revolting story until Vivian goes away to London to earn her own living and the other characters sink into obscurity in the old moral degradation.

Does not this literary muck leave a bad taste in the mouth? Does it not insult the moral intelligence of New York theatre-goers and outrage the decency of the New York stage?

There was not one redeeming feature about it last night, not one ray of sunshine, of cleanliness, to lighten up the moral darkness of situation and dialogue; not the semblance of a moral lesson pointed. As Letchmere says of his family in *Letty*,[105] 'We are rotten to the core,' and the same might be said of the characters in *Mrs Warren's Profession*.

The play was well acted from a technical standpoint by Mr Daly as Frank, Miss Shaw as Mrs Warren, and others of the cast; but while that is ordinarily cause for praise in a performance, it constituted an added sin to last night's production, for the better it was acted the more the impurity and degeneracy of the characters, the situations and the lines were made apparent. There were a few slight excisions made in the play as written, but what was left filled the house with the ill odor of evil suggestion, where it was not blatantly immoral.

The audience was not that of a New York premiere, those who are prominent at first night performances being notable by their absence.

How did the audience take it? The orchestra circle was mostly a study in repose, and only occasionally did the auditors in that part of the house respond to the inspiring influence of the ticket speculator claque which brought up the rear.

103 A debauchee or debauché is one who indulges excessively in sex, drugs, and/or alcohol.
104 A rake is a wealthy person of promiscuous and immoral habits.
105 *Letty* is a play by Arthur Wing Pinero, produced in 1903.

Some of the women of the lower house chuckled audibly, and many sat as though lost in thought.

For the most part, however, the patrons of the Garrick last night heard the recital of unpleasant things with equanimity. It was only when Mrs Warren kicked the chairs about or grew melodramatic that the spectators sat up and began to feel more at home in this wilderness of talk which was so overgrown with moral ailanthus.[106]

The men who had read the book for psychological and sociological reasons did not applaud, but merely looked like the figures of their grandsires cut in alabaster.

Birmingham Gazette,
28 July 1925

Even the magic words: 'Bernard Shaw's hitherto banned play' did not succeed in quite filling the Prince of Wales Theatre, Birmingham, last night, for the first public performance in England of *Mrs Warren's Profession.* This was regrettable, for the Macdona Players gave the best performance of their visit so far in one of the finest plays in the Shavian catalogue.

One is at a complete loss to understand why *Mrs Warren's Profession* was ever banned. It is, perhaps, the most truly moral play ever produced on the English stage, not excepting miracle plays, morality plays, or religious propaganda plays. A vicarage soirée, with an up-lift address from the rector, would be an orgy of licentiousness compared with this play. There is no suggestion that the profession of Mrs Warren is a desirable career, or that to live life fully and to live it whole one should necessary [sic] be immoral. The play amounts to a scathing exposure of the society that tolerates Mrs Warren's profession and fattens on it. And the play was censored, since when hundreds of little comedies calculated to lead one to believe that the fast life was the merry one, and that there was a sort of riotous joy and merit in immorality, have been passed as a matter of course.

One has said that this was the best performance of the Macdona Players' visit. It was also the best Shaw production one has seen for a long time. The passion, the ruthlessness, and the quiet strength of Valerie Richard's Vivie had genius in it. Oliver Johnston (formerly of the Birmingham Repertory Company), as Praed, the man who is too kindly ever to be perfectly honest about life and to strip himself of illusion, was admirable,

106 Ailanthus is a flowering plant native to eastern and southern Asia and northern Australia. It has invaded and taken over some North American ecosystems to the detriment of the local plant culture.

and excellently skilled, too, were the performances of Charles Sewell and George E. Bancroft. Florence Jackson's Mrs Warren was an almost ideal piece of acting, her only fault being a tendency at times to over-emphasise the vulgarity of the part – a theatricality a little too reminiscent of her role in *Pygmalion*.[107]

Mrs Warren's Profession will be played again to-night.

---

107   *Pygmalion* (1913) is another of Shaw's major plays.

APPENDIX VII

ACT I, 252

*After 'the sort of perfectly splendid modern young lady I am',
MS continues as follows.*

VIVIE

Have one of my cigars.

PRAED (in anguish)

Miss Warren!

VIVIE

Whats the matter?

PRAED

Nothing – I dont smoke.

VIVIE (withdrawing the case)

Oh! Well, you dont mind my smoking, do you?

PRAED

No, of course not. But – but – er – I know its [*sic*] quite out of date, but if you wouldnt mind not smoking a cigar all at once.

VIVIE

All at once!

PRAED

I mean, if you would begin with a cigarette, just to break me in.

VIVIE (laughing)

Well, I'll let you off altogether: I wont smoke at all. (putting up case) There!

PRAED

Oh no, no, no, no, by no means, *really*. I dont want to deprive you –

VIVIE

Never mind. I can do without anything when I want to (She turns her chair round & settles herself for further chat with him). And now, since you have made my acquaintance pretty thoroughly, tell me how you think I shall get on with my mother.

ACT I, 312–13

*Struck out in MS. This passage provides some insight
into Praed's past and further develops the theme of
generational conflict.*

VIVIE

Besides – I think you said you hated authority, didnt you?

PRAED

Yes, I am a born Anarchist.

VIVIE

Well, my mother doesnt realize that I am a grown woman, and that my
way in life is going to be my own way & not hers. I suppose there came
a time in your life when you had to open your father's eyes on that
subject.

PRAED

But mine was a specially hard case. He wanted me to go into the church.
You'll admit that that was impossible.

VIVIE

Anyhow, there came a day when you had to make him understand that
you too were no longer father and son, monarch and subject, but more
man & man, equal and independent.

PRAED (excited)

Quite true, quite true. I let him thwart me for five years, like a softy as
I was, but I astonished him at last I did, by God: yes. He respected me
ever after.

VIVIE

Well, I am going to astonish my mother now.

PRAED

But remember, pray – there is a difference. Your mother is a woman
and she is very sensitive. You may hurt her more than you know.

VIVIE

Very likely, since you wont tell me why she cannot bear to have her life
talked about. And I shall use that disadvantage if necessary.

ACT II, 434–40

*The stage directions are not in MS. Instead, there is an exchange
between the Reverend Samuel and Mrs Warren before
the others enter that Shaw struck out. Here Kitty lies
about Vivie's age to toy with the Reverend Samuel.*

REV. S (quietly)

Let me seize the opportunity before the others come. We are agreed,
I hope, that anything between Frank & Miss Warren is out of the
question.

MRS WARREN

Quite.

REV. S

I was sure you would say so. Ah – er – how old is Miss Warren, pray.

MRS WARREN

You'll not tell Crofts? Honor bright!

REV. S

Certainly not.

MRS WARREN

She's twenty-three last March.

REV. S (appalled)

Twenty-three last March!

MRS WARREN

Twenty-three last March. Go home and figure that out, Sam; and then
consider whether you hadn't better talk seriously to Master Frank.

ACT II, 674–725

MS is more condensed and describes Lizzie as a half-sister.

MRS WARREN

Oh, it is easy to talk, very easy, isnt it? Here, would you like to know
what my circumstances were? I started life as a barmaid at Waterloo
Station. Fourteen hours a day serving drinks & washing tumblers for
four shillings a week and my board. One of my half sisters worked in a
factory until she died of lead poisoning. She only expected to get her
hands a little paralyzed; but she died. Another half sister was always
held up to us as a model because she married a laborer in the Deptford
victualling yard and left his room and children neat and tidy on

eighteen shillings a week – until he took to drink. Another half sister was pretty & ladylike, not like the rest – more like me. She knew how to take care of herself, did Liz. I was at a church school where she'd been; and I know the ministers thought I'd follow her example; for the clergyman was always warning me that Lizzie's money & clothes & good times wouldnt last. He believed she would end by jumping off Waterloo Bridge. Poor fool: that was all he knew about it. But I was a good deal more afraid of the factory & the lead poisoning than of the river; and so would you have been in my place. That clergyman got me a place as a scullery maid in a temperance restaurant where they sent out for anything you liked. Then I was waitress; and then I went to the Waterloo bar. That was considered a great promotion for me. One cold, wretched night, when I could hardly keep myself awake with fatigue, who should come up for a half of Scotch but Lizzie, in a long fur cloak, plump and comfortable, with a lot of sovereigns in her purse.

ACT III, 72–3

MS adds these lines after striking out the following.
In revisions, the Reverend Samuel's invitation is offered earlier.

REV. S

Er, in case I shouldnt happen to be at home, you know, would you – er – would you mind suggesting to your mother that she might perhaps ask Miss Warren over – just for a cup of tea.

FRANK

Including her mother?

REV. S

Er – what do you think? I suppose it would be a slight to leave her out.

FRANK

Well, if you dont mind, I'd rather leave it to you, governor. You see, you know so much more about Mrs Warren than I do.

REV. S

I dare you not to speak in that way, sir. It is disrespectful. Theyll think it very strange if we do not ask them over this afternoon.

FRANK

So my mother thought, I fancy, when she found that she must go to town by the 11:13 train.

REV. S

But she did not object to Sir George Crofts.

FRANK

My dear governor, Crofts is a <u>man</u>, not a woman. The two cases are perfectly different. Otherwise my mother wouldnt have married you.

ACT III, 147–8

*After 'What . . . mother?' MS adds the following lines
before Shaw struck them out. In revisions, Praed does not
interfere in the Reverend Samuel's affairs.*

REV. S

I think they must be coming here.

FRANK

Very likely: Praed tells me you pressed Crofts last night to bring them here. He could do no less than take you at your word.

REV. S

But I didnt – I – I dont recollect saying anything of the sort. Are you quite sure, Mr Praed?

PRAED

I assure you you did, Mr Gardner.

REV. S

Dear me, one's instinctive hospitality makes one forget. Er – Frank. (Praed turns away) They may suppose my story. What am I to do?

ACT III, 616–47

*After the stage direction 'He takes aim . . . round against her breast',
MS has a different ending for the act, discussing Vivie's outlook
on sex and sexuality much more directly: she will refuse sex
in the future because her mother's trade has tainted the notion
of it for her. She is more subdued in this earlier version,
not inviting Frank to fire the rifle and raising the barrel
away from her breast herself.*

VIVIE (pushing the barrel gently up)

Yes, dear, without hesitation if it were necessary. But I forgive him now. Listen to me dear. (she puts the rifle against the stone seat & draws him beside her on it) Oh Frank, I'm so glad.

FRANK

Indeed?

VIVIE

All this morning a great cloud of horror has been gathering over me like a storm after the moonlight last night. From moment to moment it has been growing on me that I must get away from it all – away from the sentimental tie I formed under the spell of that ghastly moonlight, away from the very air breathed by my mother and that man, away from the world they are part of. I thought of killing myself –

FRANK

My dear Viv, what about Frank?

VIVIE

Frank was the most unbearable thought of all, for I know that he would press on me the sort of relation that my mother's life had tainted for ever for me. I felt that I would rather die than let him touch me with that in his mind. Never that for me – never while I live. I shrank from you more than from him when you came to rescue me; and then – oh my darling little boy, then the blackest cloud vanished. Our affection is innocent: we are brother and sister, the babes in the wood really and truly. (leaning against him) Oh, now it is I who am ready to get covered up with leaves.

FRANK

The wise little girl with her silly little boy.

VIVIE (almost sobbing)

The dear little boy with the dowdy little girl. (quite sobbing)

FRANK (smothering the sobs)

Sh–sh–sh– little boy wants to see his darling little girl quite happy in her play. (lifts her face & presses his lips on hers)

ACT IV

Shaw struck out the beginning of the third act in MS.
What he had begun would eventually become the fourth act,
although in this version Vivie is more violent and Praed, as opposed
to preparing to leave, has improbably already returned from Italy.

Saturday afternoon in October.
Room in a flat in Stone Buildings, Chancery Lane, finished partly as office partly as sitting room. Cheerful curtains, everything new. Looking glass on mantelpiece over gas stove. Easy chair at fire. Frank seated in it, reading newspaper. His hat and stick are on the table. He throws the paper aside, gets up impatiently, and goes to writing table, humming a tune. Turns over the papers – finds nothing interesting. Opens a drawer,

glances in & shuts it, then another, then another, in which he finds a hand mirror. Looks at himself in it; then goes to the mantelpiece & starts with his back to it, looking at the back of his head. Tries his hat on the same way. Hears someone outside & rushes to the drawer; puts back the mirror; & just gets into the chair again with the paper when Vivie enters.

VIVIE

Frank!

FRANK

Been waiting for you ever such a time. The youth who works your typewriter kept me company for a while, but eventually went off to play football. So you permit the staff to exercise itself when it pleases?

VIVIE

It's Saturday – half holiday for the staff. You have not been waiting for hours, because I have been only out twenty-five minutes for lunch.

FRANK

Well, come off for a walk. Let's go to Richmond or somewhere & come back in time for some theatre. You require fresh air. Never mind the expense: I have gold – see! (shows handful of sovereigns)

VIVIE

How did that come?

FRANK

Gambling, Vivvums, gambling. Poker.

VIVIE

Hm! Well, you can spend it on someone else: I shall be at work here until late at night: I take my holiday tomorrow.

FRANK (remonstrably)

Oh, Vivvums!

VIVIE

When did you come up from Haslemere?

FRANK

Yesterday. Couldnt stand it without you: even the inexhaustible topic of my reverend parents' imbecility began to pall. I think it's ever so nasty of you not to come & make an afternoon of it with me after so long a separation. I've a lot of things to say to you.

VIVIE

Can you say them in the course of the next twenty minutes, while I am digesting my lunch?

FRANK

Not possibly.

VIVIE

You will have to go then, in any case. I shall have something to say to you, too, perhaps, Frank.

FRANK (suddenly changing to a shrewder, less trifling tone)

Viv: I'll tell you what you are going to say to me.

VIVIE

What?

FRANK

That it is all up between us.

VIVIE

How did you know that?

FRANK

My dear Viv, I am not a fool in the ordinary sense of being different in perception. I am only a fool in the Scriptural sense – the man who does all the things that the wise man declared to be folly, after trying them himself on the largest possible scale. I have a fine ear, Viv; and that ear detects a change in your voice which means that I am no longer Vivvums's little boy. Dont be alarmed: I shall never call you Vivvums again – at least until you are tired of your new little boy, whoever he may be.

VIVIE

It's not a new little boy, Frank; but you're right.

FRANK

Must be a new little boy. Always happens that way – no other way, in fact.

VIVIE

None that you know of, fortunately for you.

FRANK

Except getting religion & sending all the little boys to the right about.

VIVIE

That's more like it, Frank.

FRANK

Eh! Whew. Come, my dear Viv, this is ever so impossible. But still, ever such a relief to your little boy's mind. If that's all, I can wait until the fit is over: a healthy girl like my Vivvums will throw off the attack soon.

VIVIE

Take care, Frank. Take care! You are on the brink of – (knock without) Go and open the door, and bring whoever it is in here.

FRANK

It's the milkman, no doubt. However, I'll bring him in to afternoon tea. (Exit. Vivie passes her hand over her face with a gesture of desperation)

FRANK (without)

Why, it's Praed. How are you, old man. Come in (Enters with Praed)

PRAED

How do you do, Miss Warren (Vivie takes his hand) I am just back from Italy.

VIVIE

Why?

PRAED

Because it is the place to saturate you with beauty and romance. (Vivie shrinks) I am saturated with it. I am indignant with myself for having let you persuade me that you were indifferent to them.

FRANK

It is too true, Praddy. Viv is a little Philistine. She is indifferent to my romance, and insensible to my beauty.

VIVIE

Mr Praed: once for all, there is no beauty & no more romance in life for me.

PRAED

You would not say that in Venice: you would cry with such pure delight in living in such a beautiful world. I cried – at fifty. Why on the way home, even after parting from Italy, I was charmed – I confess it – with the gaiety, the vivacity, the happy airs of Brussels – (Vivie half shrinks, half shudders) What's the matter?

FRANK

Hello, Viv! (they hurry up anxiously to her)

VIVIE (with a look of deep reproach at Praed)

Can you find no better example of beauty & romance than that to talk to me about?

PRAED (puzzled)

Of course, it's very different to Verona. I dont suggest for a moment that –

VIVIE

I expect you will find that the beauty & romance come to much the same thing in both places.

PRAED

My dear Miss Warren, how bitter you have become. You used to be indifferent to Art. Now you seem positively to hate it.

FRANK

She thinks it sinful. She has had ever such a serious call.

VIVIE (sharply)

Hold your tongue, Frank. Dont be silly.

FRANK (calmly to Praed)

Do you call this good manners, Praed?

PRAED (rising)

I feel sure we have disturbed you at work. Shall I take him away[?]

FRANK

I have an express contract for twenty minutes. However (rising), as the atmosphere seems stormy, I am content to defer the engagement.

VIVIE

Sit down: I am not ready to go back to work yet. (they sit) You both think I have an attack of nerves. Not a bit of it. But there are two subjects that I want dropped, if you dont mind. One of them (to Frank) is the subject of love in any shape or form whatsoever; and the other (meaningly to Praed) is the romance & beauty of life, especially as exemplified by the gaiety of Brussels. You are welcome to any illusions you may have left on these subjects: I have none. Please dont think that I have been crossed in love, Frank. It's very clever of you; but it's not within miles of the truth. If we three are to remain friends, I must be treated as a woman of business, permanently single (this to Frank) and (to Praed) permanently unromantic.

PRAED

But how difficult that is, Miss Warren. There are only two gospels in the world nowadays – the Gospel of Art, Beauty & Romance and the Gospel of Getting On in the world. I must not talk Art with you; and though I know you are a great devotee of the Gospel of Getting On, we must not talk about that before Frank, who is determined not to get on.

FRANK

Oh, dont mind me. Give me some improving advice by all means. It does me ever so much good. Have another try to make a successful man of me, Viv. Come: lets have it all – energy, thrift, foresight, self respect, character – dont you hate people who have no character, Viv?

VIVIE (shuddering)

Oh, stop, stop; let us have no more of that horrible cant. Mr Praed, if there are really only those two gospels in the world, then I think the sooner we shoot ourselves the better; for both are contaminated to the very core.

FRANK

There is a dash of poetry about you today, Viv, which has hitherto been lacking. If you will be good enough to produce the pistols, you and Praed can begin. I should like to see how it looks before venturing.

PRAED

My dear Frank, arent you a little unsympathetic?

VIVIE

No, it's good for me. It keeps me from being sentimental.

FRANK

Checks your strong natural propensity that way, doesnt it?

VIVIE (almost hysterically)

Oh yes, go on, rub it in. I was sentimental for one minute in my life – beautifully sentimental – in the moonlight – and now I have to extricate myself from the consequences of that moment of folly. (P & F look at one another) Yes, in that moment [I] formed a tie that I must break, and I dont know how to do it except by brute force. If that hideous blunder cant be remedied, I'll kill myself.

FRANK

I say, Viv: take care. If you've any secret, dont give it away in a tantrum.

PRAED

Quite right, Frank, quite right.

VIVIE (turning to Praed)

Oh you know; and he had better sooner as later. I want to consult someone – nobody has a right to act alone in such emergencies. There is no use in consulting women: even when they know the right advice they are afraid to give it. I know Frank better than any other man: I trust you more.

PRAED

But on what are we to advise you[?]